A SHORT HISTORY OF

GREENVILLE

A SHORT HISTORY OF

GREENVILLE

JUDITH T. BAINBRIDGE

THE UNIVERSITY OF
SOUTH CAROLINA PRESS

© 2024 University of South Carolina

Published by the University of South Carolina Press
Columbia, South Carolina 29208

uscpress.com

Printed in the United States of America

Library of Congress Cataloging-in-Publication Data
can be found at https://lccn.loc.gov/2023058475

ISBN: 978-1-64336-467-4 (paperback)
ISBN: 978-1-64336-468-1 (ebook)

FOR BOB

CONTENTS

Chapter 1

THE WILD WEST,
1766–83

At the beginning of the eighteenth century, the seven hundred ninety-five square miles of modern Greenville County were part of the vast Carolina Frontier. "Tygers" (panthers), bears, and wildcats prowled its swamps and wooded thickets. Bordered on the north by the ancient Blue Ridge Mountains, formed perhaps three hundred fifty million years ago, and watered by the Saluda, Reedy, and Enoree Rivers and hundreds of creeks, it was hunting grounds for the Cherokees. These Native Americans hunted here but lived in permanent villages—the "Lower Towns" of Keowee, Seneca, and Estatoe—further west. They camped along the falls of the Reedy River and near Cedar Mountain in the summer, leaving behind thousands of white flint arrowheads.

Although the Cherokee, a member of the Iroquoian language group, had lived here for centuries, in more recent times, their dominion had been challenged by the Catawbas, a member of the Siouan language family, who had moved into the area around modern-day Rock Hill in the 1650s. Soon afterward, following a battle at Nations Ford near Charlotte, the two tribes agreed that the region between the Saluda and the Enoree would be shared hunting ground.

These foothills were fine for hunting. The climate was mild and game abundant. Despite the majestic chestnut, hickory, and sycamore trees, deer and bears could be seen from a great distance, because little undergrowth impeded the view. Following animal tracks, the Cherokees carved out paths along high dry ridges

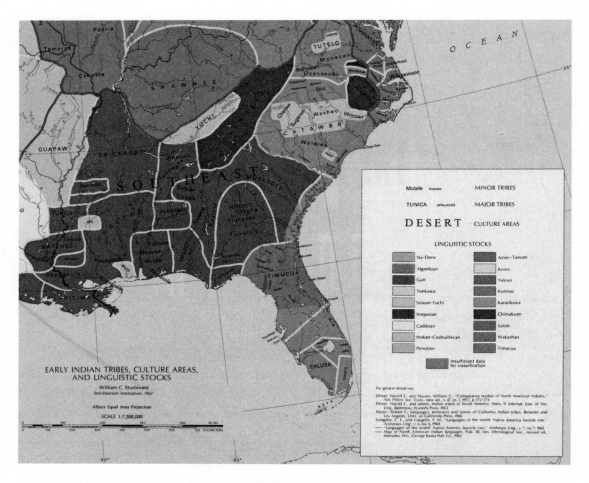

Map of Native American linguistic and cultural areas. William C. Sturtevant, Smithsonian Institution. Library of Congress Geography and Map Division.

that led to salt licks and springs where game abounded. Those Indian trails would become pioneers' "waggon roads," later the routes of trains and, often, modern highways. (Augusta Road is an example.)

In the 1700s, white men from the coast, trading for furs and skins, brought whisky, guns, and smallpox. Whole Indian villages were decimated by disease. By 1764, according to one British visitor to Keowee, there were only twenty-seven hundred fifty warriors and perhaps thirteen thousand five hundred Cherokees in the Upcountry. Fifty years earlier, there had been about seven thousand warriors. Elk, buffalo, and bison disappeared at about the same time, driven away by the encroachment of white settlers to the south and east, while deer and bear moved deeper into the mountains.

The British government needed the tribe as allies against the threatening French and Spanish. In 1735, five Cherokee chiefs visited London and gave their allegiance to the British Crown. That friendship was strategically important during England's interminable Seven Years War with France, fought on this continent as the French and Indian War. In 1763, when the war ended, King George III signed a proclamation limiting white settlement to east of the crest of the Appalachians. The colony's governors attempted to enforce boundary treaties forbidding white settlement and thus maintaining peaceful relations with the Indians. Settlers, however, looked covetously at the fertile land on the frontier and began plantations near (and sometimes beyond) the legal limits.

Those limits were contentious. Surveys and meetings attempted to establish the boundaries of Indian Territory as well as the border between North and South Carolina. In 1766, a gathering of Cherokee leaders and government representatives at DeWitt's Corners near modern-day Due West established the boundaries of the Indian Territory (and the southern boundary of the future county), with the Reedy River above modern-day Travelers Rest becoming the line between the two states.

At about that time, though, the first semilegal white settler, Richard Pearis, had settled by the falls of the Reedy River. Born in Ireland in 1725 to a family who later emigrated to the Shenandoah Valley of Virginia, Pearis had become an experienced Indian agent by 1754 when he began traveling into South Carolina. Over the years, he traded with and gained the trust of the Cherokees. While his family remained at home in Virginia, he became intimate with the daughter of a local Cherokee chief who bore him a son whom he named George.

Because of that relationship and his friendship with the Cherokees, on July 29, 1769, "fourteen chiefs and Seventy other Indians" ceded to Pearis twelve square miles of land between the Reedy and the Saluda Rivers. Sometime in 1770, he arrived with his wife, three children, and three wagons loaded with his household goods and with guns to trade with the Indians for more land. Authorities in Charleston were not pleased; Pearis (or Paris or Parris, depending on the speller) was not a model citizen. In fact, Alexander Watts, a Cherokee interpreter, warned the royal governor about Pearis, saying "I take him to be a very dangerous Fellow."

Friends of that "dangerous fellow" from Virginia joined him. They included Jacob Hite, who had collaborated with him in the Indian trade, and Baylis Earle, who purchased five hundred acres of his land. Tradition, not deeds, says that other families—the Austins at Gilder Creek, the Dills in the north, for example—moved into the Indian Territory at about the same time. When colonial authorities refused to recognize Pearis's original deed and his sales of tracts within it, he and his son George solved the problem neatly. They convinced Cherokee chiefs to convey (the same) twelve square miles plus fifty-seven thousand additional acres to George, as the grandson of a chief. The young man then swore allegiance to King George and, after reserving fifty thousand acres for himself, promptly (and now lawfully) conveyed the remainder to his father.

By 1773, then, Pearis could legally claim his "Great Plains Plantation." His twelve enslaved people cleared a hundred acres near the falls of the Reedy River and planted fields of grain and orchards. Pearis built a grist mill at the shoals (tradition says, at the future location of the Gower and Cox Carriage Factory on the north side of the river), a trading post at the shallow ford at Main Street, and a substantial home on the hill to the east at the modern intersection of East Court and Spring Streets. The location was convenient. "Pearis's waggon road," the old Indian path to Keowee, passed nearby. The falls of the Reedy powered the grist mill. A bubbling spring was near their home.

However, while Pearis was prospering from his trade with the Cherokees and his dubious land dealings, colonial politics were becoming contentious. British officials, feeling intense financial pressure because of the war with the French, attempted to pass some of its costs along to the colonies, which, members of Parliament argued, had derived benefit from the war and thus should be taxed to help pay its costs. Colonists immediately opposed the new taxes on imported goods like stamps and tea, arguing "No taxation without representation." The British, who for many years had been more concerned about continental affairs than about their American colonies and had, as a result, pursued a policy of benign neglect, began to flex their muscles.

At the same time, settlers on the South Carolina Upcountry frontier were contending for power and recognition, not with a parliament three thousand miles away but with the General Assembly in Charles Town. The Lowcountry merchants and rich plantation owners who controlled it denied both representation and courts to the fast-growing back country. By the middle of the 1770s, uneasy allegiances had formed along the frontier, with Loyalists to the Crown on one side and Patriots on the other. In the Ninety Six District, just south of Greenville, Loyalists (Tories) predominated.

The Cherokees, whose boundaries were secured, supposedly, by the Crown, faced constant pressures from whites. Both sides wooed their support in the looming struggle. As an experienced Indian trader, Pearis was the natural go-between. Initially allied with the Patriots, when he was denied the position of Indian Commissioner by the colonial government, he switched his allegiance to the Loyalists and brought the Cherokees with him. In 1775 and 1776, he incited Cherokee (and Loyalist) raids on local Patriots, with his trading post on the Reedy River as the staging point.

By midsummer 1775, the South Carolina backcountry was caught up in the struggle, as brothers, families, and neighbors fought each other. Patriots, determined to break the Loyalist domination in Ninety Six, launched a campaign in December. They captured Pearis and several other officers, and on December 22, 1775, during a raging snowstorm, a patriot troop under Colonel William Thompson was ordered to attack Tories who had fled into Indian Territory with guns and ammunition for the Cherokees.

Marching through the night, they found the enemy camped at a "Brake of Canes" on the Reedy River seven miles southwest of Simpsonville. Loyalists under Patrick Cunningham were still asleep when Thompson's Patriot force attacked at dawn. The Tories, totally surprised, fled for their lives; Cunningham, without his

Battle of Great Cane Break Historical Marker, near Simpsonville, Greenville County. Photograph by Brian Scott, hmdb.org.

breeches, jumped on his horse, shouted that every man should fend for himself, and dashed away. The Battle of the Great Canebrake was a Patriot victory. Only one man was wounded, and five or six Loyalists were killed and one hundred thirty Loyalists were captured. The culmination of the "Snow Campaign" fifteen inches fell in three days) broke Loyalist control in the Ninety Six District and diverted wagonloads of arms from the Indians.

The Cherokees, encouraged by Pearis and other Loyalists, launched a series of attacks on Patriot families along the frontier in the summer

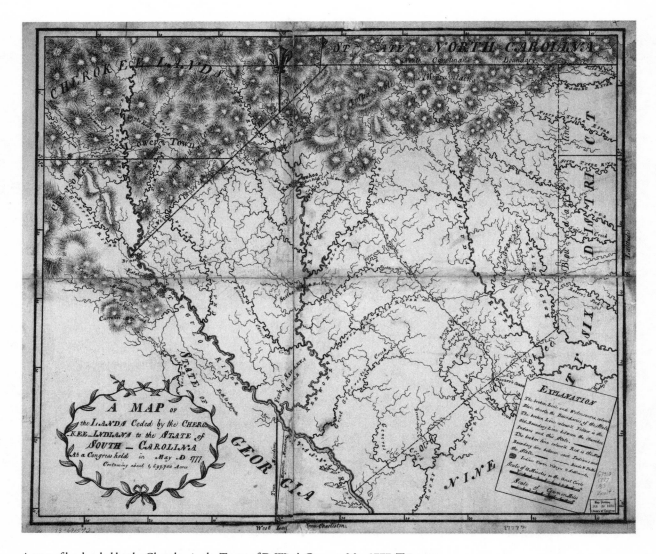

A map of land ceded by the Cherokee in the Treaty of DeWitt's Corners, May 1777. This treaty ended the Second Cherokee War (1776–1777), which was part of the larger global conflict that included the American Revolution. As a result of the treaty, the Lower Cherokee surrendered almost all of their remaining landholdings in South Carolina except for a narrow strip of land located on the western border. The lands ceded under the terms of the treaty totaled nearly 1.7 million acres and included most of what are today Anderson, Greenville, Oconee, and Pickens Counties.

of 1776. They massacred five members of the Hampton family and Jacob Hite and his family and forced others to flee to forts for protection. As a result, Patriots under John Thomas, after a skirmish on the east side of Paris Mountain, were ordered to burn Indian villages to the ground and, because it was the meeting place for the attackers, to destroy Pearis's plantation, grist mill, and trading post. They captured his enslaved people, confiscated the goods at his trading post, and later sold them at auction. The Patriot government of the state claimed his ten thousand acres. Their scorched-earth policy was successful; by August 1776, the Cherokees had agreed to negotiate with South Carolina's Patriot-controlled government.

In May 1777, eight Cherokee chiefs met with South Carolina and Georgia officials at DeWitt's Corners. They acknowledged defeat, agreed to retreat further into the mountains, and ceded the lands previously reserved for their use to the government of South Carolina. The hundreds of square miles between the Enoree and the Saluda would be open to settlement if the Patriot cause was successful.

That outcome seemed unlikely. In the North, British troops and Hessian mercenaries generally won battles but never managed a total victory. Stalemated in New York and New England, in 1779, they decided to attack the South. After capturing General Benjamin Lincoln's Patriot force and occupying Charlestown in May

1780, British regulars and Loyalist militia alike sought military control by establishing fortified garrisons throughout the colony, including one at Ninety Six. Ragtag Patriot forces, hungry and unpaid, fought back from swamps and ambushes while Loyalists conducted a reign of terror on the frontier to destroy patriot resistance.

During 1780 and 1781, Upcountry settlers were at the mercy of Loyalists and "plundering renegades," often deserters from either side who had little regard for human life. Stories of villains and heroes from those difficult years were repeated around Greenville hearths for generations.

They told of "Bloody Bill" Bates, who terrorized the northern frontier, torturing and killing former neighbors, and who, years later, was lynched by a survivor of his atrocities and buried on the site of Greenville's modern-day City Hall. They shuddered at the tales of "Bloody Bill" Cunningham, who pillaged and looted to the south, spreading a reign of terror behind him. They remembered the deeds of Jane Thomas, whose husband, the commander of the "Spartan Regiment," was imprisoned at the fort at Ninety Six. She fled through the night to warn her son, who had taken over his father's command, of a British attack. And of Dicey Langston, a sixteen-year-old who lived near Laurens, who risked her life in another night flight to warn her brother and his Patriot troop of an attack by Cunningham's "Bloody

Portrait of General Nathanael Greene (1742–1786). National Portrait Gallery, Smithsonian Institution.

Scouts." Because Dicey Langston Springfield (she later married a young Patriot and bore him twenty-one children) lived near Travelers Rest after the Revolution, she became a Greenville heroine.

After a series of defeats culminating in the Patriot loss of Camden, Commander-in-Chief George Washington sent General Nathanael Greene to South Carolina. Greene, a Rhode Island Quaker and a seasoned tactician, was able to draw British regulars west from their coastal supply lines. Thanks to Patriot victories led by Daniel Morgan at Kings Mountain near Charlotte in October 1780 and at Cowpens in Spartanburg County in January 1781, the Patriot cause had a glimmer of hope. Greene kept retreating through North Carolina, followed by Cornwallis and his army, until they finally met the British at Guilford Courthouse in August 1781. Cornwallis won—barely—but it was a pyrrhic victory. He returned with a decimated army to the coast and then marched to Yorktown in Virginia.

After the American victory there in October, hostilities were over, but the British continued to occupy Charleston until December 14, 1782, when they finally left the city. Richard Pearis went with them. After his capture and brief imprisonment, he had joined the Loyalist forces in South Carolina and then commanded a Tory troop in Florida. With his home, trading post, and mill destroyed, he demanded restitution from the state government, which allowed him £700 sterling for his losses. With other Loyalists, he settled in the Bahamas after the war; sought more restitution for his losses, this time from the British government; and lived to a prosperous old age on the island of Aruba. His only legacy to Greenville was his name—misspelled—on Paris Mountain.

Chapter 2

BECOMING GREENVILLE,
1783–1815

When the British finally left Charleston, the new state of South Carolina faced a financial crisis. It owed money to men who had fought for the Patriot cause or had provided supplies. The government had one major resource: land in the former Indian Territory. Land grants of six hundred forty acres would recompense former soldiers, and sales would provide funds to cover other debts.

Sales began on May 4, 1784. The best land, generally along streams, went fast and early—on that first day, 97,036 acres were spoken for. Within six months, the first conveyance book was full, recording more than a thousand sales to future settlers and current speculators. Slightly over six thousand acres went to Revolutionary War veterans.

In 1785, the old Ninety Six Judicial District was separated into six new counties—Abbeville, Edgefield, Laurens, Newberry, Spartanburg, and Union. The former Indian Territory between the Saluda and the Enoree was divided, with the land northeast of Pearis's wagon road going to "Spartanburgh County," and the land southwest of it annexed to Laurens County. The division was created to provide settlers with access to courts on the frontier. Most complained, however, that those courts were inconveniently distant.

As a result, on March 22, 1786, the General Assembly agreed that "a county shall be established in the new ceded lands, by the name of Greeneville." Its boundaries would be the Saluda River to the west, the old Indian boundary to the south, the Spartanburg County line to the east, and the North Carolina border to the north.

The source of the name? Three theories have been proposed. In his *Statistics of South Carolina*, Robert Mills speculated that the name derived from the county's "remarkably verdant appearance." A. S. Salley, longtime head of the South Carolina Department of Archives and History, proposed Isaac Green, who had a mill on the Reedy, as the namesake. James Richardson, in his 1930 *History of Greenville County*, agreed with Mills and effectively demolished the argument for Isaac Green, pointing out that he had only lived in the area for six months before it was named.

The third choice was articulated by politician John C. Calhoun, who, speaking in Greenville in October 1826, raised his glass in a toast to "the village of Greenville, picturesque and lovely in its situation, may it so prosper as to be worthy of the memory of him whose illustrious name it wears."

That "illustrious name" was Nathanael Greene's, and Calhoun was surely correct. In 1780, after General Horatio Gates was ignominiously defeated at the Battle of Camden, General George Washington sent General Nathanael Greene to rally dispirited Patriot forces. It was he whose long campaign of attrition hurt the British forces before the final defeat at Yorktown.

Greene was, indeed, illustrious; he was, in fact, so great a hero that, after the war, he had

been granted large plantations by both Georgia and South Carolina. Like Greene's, the county's name was originally spelled with a middle "e" ("Greeneville"), a usage that continued for at least a decade. Furthermore, between 1784 and 1801, the Assembly consistently named new counties for patriots: Henry Laurens, Thomas Sumter, Peter Horry, Andrew Pickens, and Francis Marion were all honored.

The legislature also appointed seven local judges, all large landowners. They first met in 1786 in the parlor of John Ford's plantation on Golden Grove Creek near the Saluda River. When they erected a separate building on Ford's property, it became Greenville's first courthouse. However, disgruntled citizens in the isolated northern part of the new county complained that the Golden Grove location was still too far away, and they argued the courthouse should be built in a "more suitable and convenient place." Initially the state's General Assembly ignored their grumbling, but after several years of petitions (and probably some trading of political favors), the legislators finally agreed to relocate the courthouse to the geographical center of the county. Landowners Elias Earle and Lemuel Alston both offered sites; the legislators chose Alston's property near the falls of the Reedy River.

Alston, a North Carolinian who may have been trained as a lawyer, had assembled about eleven thousand acres of land and had built his home, "Prospect Hill," on its highest point. Called by one visitor "without exception the most beautiful that I have seen [in the Upstate]," its grounds stretched from the Reedy River to Buncombe Road. The "mansion" was built of clapboard over logs and stood above a tall brick basement, where the kitchen was located. A flight of stone steps led to a veranda that extended across the front of the home. On the first floor there was a square reception hall, a dining room, and a drawing (or "keeping") room with windows offering mountain views to the west. First-floor wings provided space for two bedrooms. A winding staircase led to the second floor, four additional bedrooms, and a balcony. It was a big house; for the time and place, it was a mansion. Alston entertained some visitors as paying guests, including South Carolina Governor Joseph Allston (a distant relative) and his wife, Theodosia, the daughter of Vice President Aaron Burr.

Alston was one of Greenville's earliest politicians. As a candidate for the US House of Representatives in 1806, he campaigned vigorously throughout Greenville and Pickens Districts, speaking at churches and militia musters, buying drinks for potential voters (and probably kissing babies); he was easily elected to the first of two terms. Partisan opponents suggested that his political ambitions led him to purchase a large Bible that he prominently displayed in his drawing room.

In 1795, the village of Greenville Courthouse was created with a one-story log courthouse facing the river in the middle of Main Street. A court square was laid out around it, and a two-story log jail was erected a block to the east. In 1797, Alston laid out a plat for a subdivision he called "Pleasantburg," which showed the square configuration with both courthouse and "gaol." He designed a settlement with fifty-two lots on eight square blocks bordering Richard Pearis's wagon road, which he labeled "the Street from the river to the Avenue." He also laid out three "cross streets," modern-day Broad and Court Streets, as well as the "Avenue" (McBee Avenue), lined with sycamore trees leading to his Prospect Hill home.

In 1805, a visitor described the village as "quite pretty and rural: the streets are covered with green grass and handsome trees growing here and there." There were, he said, six homes, two or three shops, and several log buildings. The courthouse had been replaced with a two-story shingled building; the jail was a handsome three-story building heated with fireplaces.

Pleasantburg should have been a success. It had law and order, a high traffic count (after the Buncombe Road was completed, drovers led thousands of pigs, cattle, and wild turkeys from the mountains down the wagon road during the late summer and fall), plenty of water from springs, waterpower from the Reedy, cheap land, a mild climate, and an appealing name.

Yet it did not flourish. Alston sold the first two lots in "Greenville C.H. [courthouse] Village of Pleasantburg" to Isaac Wickliffe on April 22, 1797, for $100. More than a year passed before the next sale: six lots (the whole block where City Hall now stands) to John McBeth for $600. As A.V. Huff pointed out in his county history, Greenvillians were primarily farmers who saw little reason to live in the town, and, certainly, there wasn't much to attract new residents. Sales were slow: eight lots in 1799, eight more in 1800, one in 1801, one in 1804, and one in 1807. Only twenty-six of the fifty-two platted lots were sold. Alston was certainly not getting rich on real estate deals.

Furthermore, his chosen name was not catching on. Pleasant the burg may have been, but the village, as the initial transaction indicated, already had a name: Greenville Courthouse. No Pleasantburg deeds are recorded after 1807. In 1831, when the village was chartered by the General Assembly, it was officially named Greenville, although it was commonly and consistently referred to as Greenville Courthouse until after the Civil War.

Although the new Greeneville County's soil wasn't particularly good, there was lots of it—seven hundred fifty square miles—and it was well watered and new to planting. Corn and wheat flourished here, but markets, especially those in Charleston and Augusta, were distant; without access to them, farmers couldn't

prosper and, more important, Charleston merchants did not benefit. As a result, in 1794, the state senate appointed Greenville Senator John Ford, Joshua Saxon of Pendleton, and local landowner Elias Earle to study the possibility of a "waggon road over the Western Mountains." A year later, legislators approved building a road across the mountains by way of the Saluda Gap to newly formed Buncombe County in North Carolina. The road would eventually reach Knoxville. The governor explained that the rationale for its building was to "open communications between Charleston and the Inhabitants of the Southwest Territory of the United States."

Legislators allocated $2,000 for construction, ordering that the road be wide enough for four horses to pull a wagon with a load weighing a ton. Elias Earle and his nephew, John William Gowen, took two years to build the road. In November 1797, commissioners reported to the General Assembly that it had been completed from Greenville to the west and that a wagon with a one-ton weight had driven over it.

Although the Buncombe Road was designed for wagons, its most frequent early travelers were the animals who came in droves from the mountains of North Carolina and Tennessee. They were on their way to Augusta and, if they hadn't been sold in the meantime, eventually to Charleston. The animals and their drovers forded the Reedy River at its shallowest point—the new village's main street—and then followed the well-worn red clay path to "Guster," one hundred twelve miles away. They stopped every evening at "stands" or inns spaced about every five miles along the Buncombe and Augusta Roads, sometimes sharing space with wealthy stagecoach passengers. The McCullough House near Princeton, built in about 1812, still stands, as does the Rock House, erected in 1820, on the Buncombe Road.

As a courthouse town, Greenville was the seat of law and judgments. Some legal fragments of from the 1790s still exist: a single summons, a witness's deposition, a true bill of indictment. Some of these fragile documents show outcomes, with court costs listed on an outside fold, including mileage (forty miles for serving a warrant, $2.14), attorneys' fees, ranging from $4.40 to $14.40, and case continuations for $1.00. Other cases are more thoroughly described, like the $3,000 slander suit brought by James Harrison against John Hawkins, charging Hawkins with saying that Harrison had stolen $5 from his breeches during a muster. It includes a one-thousand-word plea by his attorney arguing (with more than two hundred eighty uses of the word "aforesaid") that Harrison is "a good, true, and honest man." A note by Clerk of Court George Washington Earle on the cover indicates that Hawkins was found "not guilty with accord and satisfaction and did drink grogg together."

In 1800, the South Carolina legislature divided the state into judicial districts. As a result, the former "county" designation changed to "district" until a new constitution was approved in 1868. The only lawyer in the village was Waddy Thompson. He was elected to the General Assembly in 1796, but after serving two terms in Columbia, he resigned when his fellow legislators elected him solicitor of the Chancery Court for the Western District of South Carolina (a part-time job) in 1799. In the next few years, he was involved in nearly every case that was heard locally, either as prosecutor, for which he earned a pound per trial (pounds and shillings remained the local currency until about 1815), or as defense lawyer, which was a far more remunerative position, with fees from four to fourteen pounds.

He spent some of that cash buying land in Greenville District, accumulating, sometimes briefly—because he sold almost as often as he bought—more than five thousand acres. He was appointed a justice of the peace and, in 1805, was elected a judge in the Court of Equity. In 1824, he was elected chancellor, one of the state's two most senior judicial positions.

Chancellor Thompson was Greenville's most distinguished resident, but others were almost as equally well known. George Salmon, for example, was a farmer and surveyor. In 1783, he was appointed deputy surveyor for the north side of the Saluda River, soon to be Greenville County. In addition to surveying dozens of claims, he also filed for his own six hundred forty acres. In

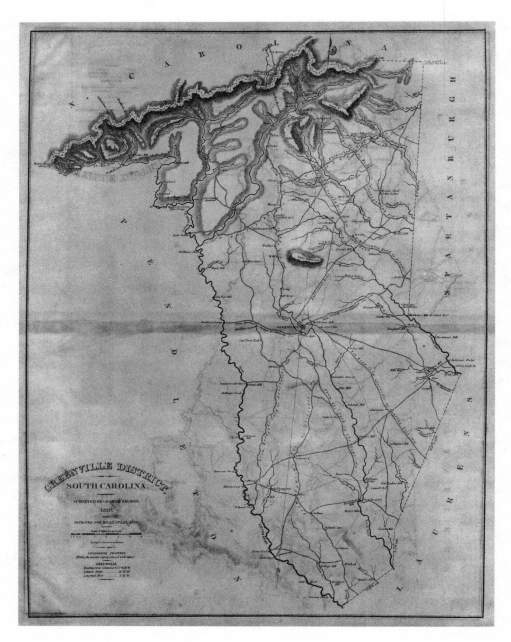

Greenville District, South Carolina. Surveyed by George Salmon, 1820.
Improved for Mills's *Atlas of South Carolina*, 1825. Courtesy David Rumsey
Map Collection.

1785, he married and built a log cabin on the site of a former Cherokee village north of Travelers Rest. The house, the oldest still standing in the county, has been modified and restored.

In 1791, he was elected to the General Assembly, returning for another two-year term in 1816. After 1811, he was a "free school" commissioner, responsible for the pitiful amount of money the state allocated to build schools and employ teachers at "pauper schools," for students whose parents were too poor to pay for tutors. Salmon was also a skilled mapmaker who drew the Greenville District map for Robert Mills's *Atlas of South Carolina*.

As the village of Greenville Courthouse grew slowly, plantation communities gathered along its waterways. The land around the Saluda, for example, was the home of more than a dozen large plantations by 1800. Others were planted around Golden Grove Creek and near the White Horse Road, a former Indian trail, not far from the Saluda. John Blassingame, who fought for the Patriots at the Battle of Kings Mountain when he was twelve years old, bought eleven hundred acres in 1792 and later purchased twenty-five hundred more acres near the White Horse Road where he established "Tanglewood Plantation."

He leased seven acres of land to Alex McBeth, who built a store on the White Horse Road. McBeth's account book for 1797 shows that he sold staples—salt, harnesses, whiskey—as well as luxury goods such as dinner plates, a blue teapot, and a looking glass. Because there was no school or church in the vicinity, the store became the center of a loosely knit plantation community.

The district's climate appealed to summer visitors. In 1812, Blassingame sold two hundred acres of land to former Governor Joseph Alston and his wife. Alston built a substantial summer retreat where Theodosia probably spent some months in 1810 and the entire following summer. "My neighbors," she wrote to her father in May 1811, "are plain good people, the poorer sort particularly. I mean those who live comfortably but work for it. Grenville [*sic*] pleases me greatly." Her health and that of their son improved. The child came "with bilious fever and returned all roses." She urged Burr to visit her, suggesting he sail to Savannah, go by water to Augusta, and then take "the well-travelled wagon road" (the Augusta Road) to Greenville.

The village attracted Lowcountry visitors fleeing from malaria and yellow fever. Among them was Henry Middleton, the son of Arthur Middleton, a signer of the Declaration of Independence, who had also served a term (1810–1812) as South Carolina's governor. Middleton built Whitehall for his wife and eleven children on land he bought from Elias Earle near the Rutherford Road. Over the next few years, he purchased additional acreage to create a thousand-acre plantation watered by Richland Creek.

Whitehall had no balcony or veranda, but its five large front windows caught the summer breezes. In early 1820, President Monroe appointed Middleton minister to Russia, so he sold the house, acreage, sixteen enslaved people, and all the family's personal property except their clothes to George Washington Earle, a son of John Earle who had married Elias Earle's eldest daughter, Elizabeth.

Two Earle brothers—John and Baylis—knew Richard Pearis and purchased land from him, but unlike Pearis, they were Patriots during the American Revolution. Their younger half-brother, Elias, came in 1787. He was only twenty-five years old when he arrived with his wife, Frances Wilton Robinson, and two children, but he had enough money to start buying land—by 1810, more than forty-four hundred acres in Greenville District alone. "Colonel" Earle (a militia title) built his home, "The Poplars," on a tract of seven hundred thirteen-acres east of Rutherford Road between modern-day Buist and West Mountain View Streets. Although he farmed (with enslaved labor), he was primarily a politician and an entrepreneur who helped build the Upcountry.

A consummate campaigner who plied potential voters with whiskey, he served in the state's General Assembly as both representative and senator and vied with Lemuel Alston for the county's congressional seat. He later was the first US commissioner for Indian affairs. Perhaps his

greatest accomplishment was building the Buncombe Road. As one of the first ironmongers in the state, he hoped to profit from the shallow vein of iron ore that ran under Piedmont soil. In 1815, he received a federal contract to supply ten thousand "stands of arms" (including a flintlock musket, bayonet, and ramrod). However, when he was reelected the following year, he couldn't legally fulfill the contract, so he turned it over to his partner, Adam Carruth, who had come to Greenville in 1800 to make his fortune.

Carruth's father died during the revolution, but his mother's family included at least one ironworker who settled in Greenville. Soon after he arrived, Carruth partnered with Alston to purchase 213 acres around Lafferty's Shoals on the Reedy River. The site, located between modern day Conestee and Parkins Mill Road at the northern end of Conestee Nature Park, was well chosen. Its shoals could provide power and nearby forests offered wood to burn for charcoal.

Although the thin vein of iron that extended from Iron Mountain in York County through Lawson's Fork in Spartanburg into the Pickens District was petering out at the beginning of the nineteenth century, at least three Greenville furnaces or foundries were still being worked. Foundries were essential to communal life because they provided anvils for blacksmiths, nails for builders, pots for homemakers and guns for hunters. Carruth's furnace at Lafferty's Shoals turned out all of

The Whitehall house located at 310 West Earle Street in Greenville, SC. It was built in 1813 as a summer residence by Charlestonian Henry Middleton on land purchased from Elias Earle. Henry Middleton was the son of Arthur Middleton, a signer of the Declaration of Independence. Furman University, Special Collections and Archives.

these goods, but he also explored erecting a cotton factory there. In 1812, the state agreed to lend him and several partners $10,000 to build South Carolina's first cotton mill. It wasn't constructed, probably because of the lack of expertise and isolated location.

Carruth was more successful with guns. The War of 1812 led the General Assembly to contract with him to manufacture five hundred muskets at $20 each. He evidently carried out that contract successfully, because in 1815, the legislature requested five hundred more. At about the same time, according to former Clemson historian E. M. Lander, the Governor of Georgia inquired about purchasing five hundred guns. Even as he was busy making guns for South Carolina, Carruth began thinking bigger. In November 1816, he agreed with the federal government to produce twenty-five hundred muskets a year for four years using the government-pattern "1816 Flintlock Musket." (These guns, now collectors' items, were manufactured in only three armories: Carruth's; Springfield, Massachusetts; and Harper's Ferry, Virginia.)

The Lafferty Shoals armory, the largest manufacturer in the district, was a busy place.

He had fifty-seven enslaved people working for him, making him one of Greenville's largest slaveowners. In addition, about seventy white artisans worked at the armory, including charcoal burners, stockmakers, blacksmiths, barrel makers, grinders, filers, and fitters. In 1818, the village of Greenville had a population of about three hundred. In comparison, about one hundred seventy people lived at the armory, so it was large enough to have its own postmaster—Elias Carruth, the ironmaster's son. It was known as a rowdy place, composed almost entirely of hard-working and hard-drinking men. Its reputation for pervasive drunkenness evidently reached the governor, who grew concerned about Carruth's ability to pay his state debts, and the Episcopal Diocese of South Carolina, which sent a missionary to St. Paul's in Pendleton; St. James in Greenville; and St. Peter's at the Armory in 1820.

A more ordinary settler was Peter Cauble. The young blacksmith and his family arrived in Greenville from Lincolnton, North Carolina, in 1814 with three loaded wagons, one filled with the tools of his trade, and enough money to set up a smithy. C. A. David, who wrote a series of reminiscences for the *Greenville News* in the late 1920s about Greenville in the 1860s and 1870s, described it as "low, frame affair, little better than a partly enclosed shed, that sagged and leaned . . . the side facing Main Street was taken up by a huge door that was

never shut. Along the back was a long hitching post where mules and horses stood patiently while awaiting shoe repair."

The site was ideal. Every drover, every steer, pig, turkey, and horse traveling down the mountains along the Buncombe Road to Augusta passed by the shop. It stood opposite the Last Chance Saloon on East Coffee Street, where a man could conveniently cool his parched throat while his horse's shoes were being repaired. Furthermore, it was distant enough from the central part of town—Court Square—so that its roaring furnace, ringing anvil, and loud bellows disturbed no one.

From the time that Cauble settled in Greenville, he lived simply, saved carefully, and invested wisely. He; his wife, Elizabeth; and their infant son, William, moved into a home on lower Falls Street when they arrived. By 1820, he was prosperous enough so that he could subscribe $5 to the founding of the Greenville Academies. (Since subscribers were promised free tuition for their children, this donation may not have been entirely altruistic.)

Greenville District was growing slowly— from about sixty-five hundred people in 1790 to thirteen thousand by 1810. About ten percent were Black in 1790, growing to eighteen percent by 1810. Most were enslaved, but several families of free Blacks had settled near modern-day Taylors. Most of the newcomers were Scots-Irish, many of them subsistence farmers who traveled down the Great Wagon Road from Pennsylvania through the Shenandoah Valley before settling in the northern portion of Greenville District. Almost all were Protestant, many of them fervently so, and they brought their faith with them and soon began churches.

Baptists at Fork Shoals, where Big (or Rocky) Creek met the Reedy River, claim to be the first, arriving in 1788. Their first services took place under a brush arbor assembled by worshippers. The Reedy River Baptist Church in the northern part of the county is also documented to 1788. These early Baptist churches grew rapidly: Fork Shoals Baptist, for example, boasted ninety-two members by 1802.

Methodism began here when a group of families from Virginia and the Dunklins from Charleston moved into the Ninety Six District in 1784. In 1785, Hulet Sullivant (the spelling later changed to Hewlett Sullivan) and several friends received the first of several state land grants in lower Greenville County. Sullivan immediately set aside land on his Grove Plantation where the group built a log "pole chapel" they called Grove Church. Almost immediately, Mark Moore, a Virginian, moved south to become their preacher and teacher, beginning one of the earliest schools in the county. A few years later, Moore founded Mt. Bethel Academy in Newberry County, which became the nucleus for South Carolina College. Bishop

Portrait of Bishop Francis Asbury, 1813. National Portrait Gallery, Smithsonian Institution.

Francis Asbury visited the area at least twice but obviously wasn't much impressed. He lamented to his diary, "O Reedy River Circuit, spiritually and temporally poor!" It was also Asbury who said, "There is more gold than grace in Greenville."

There evidently wasn't enough gold for Lemuel Alston. The largest landowner in the district was drawn to the rich black earth of Alabama and listed his acreage for sale in early 1815. That sale changed Greenville's history.

Chapter 3

"A NEGLIGIBLE PLACE,"
1815–31

In November 1815, Vardry McBee, a forty-year-old tanner, merchant, and farmer who lived in Lincolnton, North Carolina, bought Lemuel Alston's eleven thousand Greenville acres for $27,000. He couldn't afford the purchase, and his friends advised against it, but he had visited the area several times and liked its waterpower and location. When Alston offered easy terms (he gave a mortgage on most of the amount), McBee bought the property around the Reedy River. He continued, however, to live in Lincolnton until 1835.

Born in Spartanburg County in 1775, McBee had been reared on a farm by Scots-Irish parents. His father had "taken him out of school" (according to the *Annals of Lincolnton County*) when he was twelve and put him to work at a nearby limestone quarry, but he always regretted his lack of further education. In Lincolnton, where he apprenticed to his brother-in-law, he became an expert tanner and saddler and soon went into partnership in a dry goods store.

Although Lincolnton was a growing town, it was very small, so McBee set out in the spring of 1799 to seek his fortune in Charleston. A summer there convinced him to return to the Upcountry. Then he tried Kentucky and Tennessee, but they didn't work either. Again, he returned to Lincolnton, where he opened a general store and his own saddlery. He began wooing Jane Alexander, the daughter of a wealthy and successful Presbyterian farmer in adjacent Rutherford County. By 1813, McBee was clerk of the county court, a prosperous merchant, substantial landowner, married, and the father of five children.

He became the absentee landowner of the South Carolina village. After leasing Alston's home, Prospect Hill, to Edmund Waddell to become Greenville's first inn, he built a brick corn mill at the Reedy River ford on Main Street and expanded Alston's original village plat to North Street. He built McBee Hall, a three-story building on Main Street where he sold a wide range of staples. It had a columned portico and meeting rooms on the second and third floors. He also started a tannery and, in 1829, erected a stone gristmill next to the brick one on the river. As a builder, he needed raw materials, so he established a brickyard at modern-day Hudson Street, a stone quarry, and a sawmill.

He also helped build community. In 1820, when trustees of the village's male and female academies asked him for land on which to site the schools, he gave thirty acres on the northern outskirts of the town. The irregularly shaped rectangle stretched from Buncombe Road to modern-day Townes Street, and from College to West Park Streets, and included a "glorious spring that gushed at the bottom of the hill." Summer visitors had nudged local residents to begin the schools. In a village of perhaps four hundred fifty people, forty-seven residents pledged $4,738 to build them. The funds, which ranged from the $500 subscribed by Francis MacLeod, William Toney, Jeremiah Cleveland, and Tandy Walker to Peter Cauble's $5 gift, were raised "with utmost difficulty and

Vardry McBee, portrait, Furman University Special Collections and Archives.

the greatest exertion, for the town was small and very poor."

The academies were, of course, private. This state's "pauper schools" were miserably underfunded, were poorly taught, and usually met only three or four months a year. In 1824, the annual allocation for the one hundred forty-four Greenville District children whose parents could not afford to educate them was $1,049.

The trustees erected two-story brick houses for the headmasters and spacious one-room

22

A SHORT HISTORY OF GREENVILLE

brick schoolrooms for each school. It took inexperienced bricklayers more than a year to complete these first brick buildings in the village. The school calendars appealed to summer visitors who wanted to keep their sons and daughters occupied during the five or six months they spent in Greenville. Students could enter at any of the four terms, including the popular summer one. Vacation was scheduled for December and January. Although both academies offered elementary instruction, most children had been taught by their parents or tutors to read, write, add, and subtract before they entered. The schools offered more advanced courses. The Male Academy prepared students to enter the junior class at the South Carolina College. At its opening, the school provided instruction in Latin and Greek, algebra, and geometry for $8 a quarter, while arithmetic, geography, reading and writing cost $5.

Principals could barely survive on those fees, so constant turnover was a problem, especially for the Male Academy. It wasn't until 1838, when trustees hired William Leary, M. A., who had been a professor at St. John's College in Maryland and for several years a tutor of Robert E. Lee, that the school gained a modicum of stability. Much loved and admired by his students, he stayed until 1842, left briefly, but then returned in 1848.

At the more stable Female Academy, the first principal was William B. Johnson, a Baptist

minister, who taught from 1823 to 1831. Unusual for a Baptist at that time, he believed that girls should be educated as well as boys. He was followed by D. D. Hallonquist, who remained for a decade. Johnson introduced "the solid branches of learning" to his young ladies, most of whom would leave school at age fourteen or fifteen. He emphasized English grammar and reading in the first two years; the third year included more grammar ("parsing" or diagramming sentences) as well as history, and the final year included natural philosophy (physics), chemistry, logic, moral philosophy (ethics), Latin, and Greek.

The number of students varied over the years. At its highpoint in the late 1830s, two hundred or more students were enrolled in the summer term. Although most students were the sons and daughters of local families, Benjamin Perry later commented that the schools had a "salutary influence on the prosperity of the village" because so many students came from "afar."

Johnson hired the village's first music "professor" to teach piano lessons on the Female Academy's piano, the only one in the village. (A year later, a second piano was installed in the ballroom of the Mansion House.) The music instructor, John Hill Hewitt, a twenty-three-year-old New York native who was wooing a student at the Female Academy, found other opportunities in Greenville, which he called "a pretty district town embedded in the Saluda Mountains like a pearl surrounded by emeralds." He began reading law with Judge Baylis Earle, and became friends with another law student, Benjamin Perry. Then, with the sponsorship of Elizabeth's father and the encouragement of Judge Earle, he decided to begin a newspaper. In 1825, he started the *Greenville Republican*, the village's first newspaper, with himself as editor and chief contributor. The "romantic little town" of Greenville evidently inspired him, for in addition to his frothy *Republican* articles, he also composed and published "The Minstrel's Return from the War," a "parlor ballad" that musicologists consider America's first popular song. He was appointed to chair Greenville's celebration marking the fiftieth anniversary of the Declaration of Independence in July 1826.

However, the young lady had a new suitor, and Hewitt had evidently begun commenting about politics in the newspaper. When he arrived at the Courthouse early in the morning of July 4 to check final arrangements for the planned celebration, he found a stuffed effigy of himself hanging from the courthouse beams. Doggerel pinned to its chest accused "the curly headed poet" of wanting to end slavery. Being parodied as an abolitionist was devastating; Elizabeth turned cold; Mr. Macklin told him that he was no longer welcome in their home. Hewitt left Greenville at the end of the year.

Erecting the academy buildings was one of several major construction projects underway in the 1820s. A toll road over the mountains from Charleston through the Saluda Gap was another. It was supervised by Joel Poinsett, one of the most broadly educated men and certainly the most cosmopolitan in the new nation. After travels throughout Europe and the young Republic, he was elected to the General Assembly in 1816 and appointed head of the state board charged with implementing "internal improvements."

Construction through Greenville District did not begin until the summer of 1820; it was completed in October. Working with Abram Blanding, who was acting commissioner of public works, Poinsett personally supervised the construction of the seventeen-feet-wide state road over the mountain. The bridge he designed over Little Gap Creek still stands, extending one hundred thirty feet across the shallow stream; the Gothic arch at its center is fifteen feet high and seven feet wide. Poinsett, who had traveled widely and was trained as an engineer, is credited with its unusual Gothic design.

A second state project was carried out by Robert Mills, America's first professional architect. For a decade beginning in 1820, first as a state employee and then privately, he created in South Carolina a series of magnificent public buildings, including the Insane Asylum (State Hospital) in Columbia, the First

Poinsett Bridge, built in 1820, is named for Joel Poinsett and is believed to be the oldest surviving bridge in South Carolina. It once formed part of the road through Saluda Gap. Photo: Poinsett Bridge, ca. 1986. Photo by Jack E. Boucher. Library of Congress, Prints and Photographs Division.

Baptist Church and the Fireproof Building in Charleston, and courthouses throughout the state. Later, he was the architect of the Washington Monument. His (almost) lasting mark on Greenville was the courthouse, later called the Record Building. It was not unique; Mills designed a prototype used, with some adaptations, in at least twelve other towns. A few, such as those in Winnsboro, Cheraw, and Lancaster, still survive. Greenville's courthouse reflected the architectural fashions of the 1820s: the ideas of Jefferson; Greek and Roman designs; and the newly popular style of Palladio, the Italian Renaissance architectural master.

Greenville District's Commissioners of Public Buildings signed the courthouse construction contract for $10,000 in late 1821. Built of bricks made from the red clay along the Reedy River, the two-story fireproof structure had a ground floor for offices and storage. The courtroom was on the second floor. Elegant curving exterior stairs framed a first-floor arcade. In 1826, when a traveling artist painted a watercolor of Greenville, he drew the courthouse at the center of the green little village.

The square in front of the courthouse was the site of sales days on the first Monday of each month. These were rambunctious affairs, characterized by drinking bouts, horse trading, and impromptu fights, as well as the disposal of estates and property. The north end of Main Street, past Coffee Street, was the place for informal trades, horse races, swaggering tales, and occasional fist fights. On Court Days on the third Monday of February, May, August, and November, a slightly less rowdy crowd gathered. Lawyers, judges, and large property owners jostled farmers buying, selling, and talking politics at the Mansion House bar.

That bar was deservedly popular. Beginning in 1824, when William Toney welcomed his first guests to his gleaming new hotel, it was at the center of Greenville life. Its location at Main and Court Streets was ideal. As a result, Colonel Toney paid the exceptionally high price of $5,000 (nearly $64,000 today) for two lots opposite the new courthouse. He planned, he said, to build a hotel that would "excel any house in the upper part of the State in appearance and accommodation for the traveling public."

And he did. The brick walls were twenty-four inches thick at the ground level, a wrought iron balcony extended across the second floor, and nearly every bedroom had a fireplace. The floors were heart pine, the roof was tin, and the circular staircase ascending to the third floor was considered a rare piece of workmanship. The basement featured the popular bar (for gentlemen only) and a card room opening on to a courtyard. In later years, a massive crystal chandelier, the first in Greenville, was installed there. Even teetotalers peeked in to gaze at it. The ground floor parlor extended the whole depth of the building and was so large that it required fireplaces at either end. It boasted the only sofa in Greenville and had one of the village's two carpets.

According to James M. Richardson's 1931 *History of Greenville County*, it was famous for its "commodious and artistic design and appointments and the excellent quality of the food and drink served from its tables, but more especially for the aristocracy and wealth of the guests who frequented it." They had to be rich. The Mansion House charged guests $1.50 a day (including meals); horses cost an additional 50 cents daily. Although Colonel Toney sold the hotel for $10,000 in 1830, and it had several later owners, it remained the pride of the town for most of the century.

In 1820, the village was already twenty-five years old, but it had no church. Local residents didn't complain: Methodist, Baptist, and Presbyterian ministers occasionally married couples and preached at the Courthouse, and there were churches outside the village. However, Greenville Courthouse was a summer resort frequented by predominantly Episcopalian Lowcountry vacationers, and they wanted a place to worship. The Diocese of South Carolina responded in the summer of 1820 by sending Rudolphus Dickinson as a missionary. He was successful enough in Pendleton and Greenville that Bishop Nathaniel Bowen visited in the summer of 1821 and appointed Dickinson to serve the tiny congregations. Thanks to his efforts; financial assistance from local Episcopalians Edward Croft, Emily Rowland, and Jane Butler; land donated by Vardry McBee; and a building committee, the cornerstone for the first church building in Greenville was laid on September 15, 1825. Nine months later, the church was unfinished, and funds had run out. It was so poorly constructed that the new minister forced the contractor to reduce its cost by four hundred dollars. The first service was held in the still-unfinished building on June 18, 1826. Services were still being held in the "mere shell" in 1827. In 1828, still incomplete, St. James Mission was admitted to the Diocese and consecrated as Christ Church, Greenville.

Local residents (not Episcopalians) called it "the snap bean church," because it was open only during the summer, when beans were ripe. Its ministers presided at Lowcountry churches in the fall and winter and came to Greenville in late spring. Christ Church did not create a hotbed of high church fervor in Greenville. In the 1830s, winter services were attended by five to ten worshippers, swollen to fifteen or twenty in the summer. In 1841, the Rev. C. C. Pinckney reported fifty-one white and three Black communicants.

Perhaps it was the building of the Episcopal church that led "the most respectable, most wealthy, and numerous inhabitants of this rising town" to finally erect a Baptist church. In 1822, Vardry McBee had donated a lot (one hundred twenty square feet) on Avenue Street for a meeting house that would also be open to other "Ministers of the Orthodox faith." (That meant Presbyterians and Methodists.) Fundraising began when William Bullein Johnson came to town to head the Greenville Female Academy. By 1826, the committee had raised $1,294 and had hired contractors to construct a sturdy brick building with glazed (glass) windows, an interior balcony, and two doors. Building costs ran $350 over budget, but the committee pled for community understanding in an accounting published in the *Greenville Republican* on February 24, 1827.

"Forgive us this wrong," they began, yet, after listing every expense, they confessed that they had seen the "liberality" of the town in building the Male and Female Academies, and they had the duty of building a place of worship "suitable in its decency and propriety" for the whole town. The new meeting house hosted the community's Independence Day services in 1831, and ecumenical Bible Society meetings were held there, but it was primarily used for Baptist sermons. The congregation, however, wasn't formed until after Johnson moved to Edgefield in January 1831.

The number of Lowcountry visitors increased during the decade, probably because of the opening of the Mansion House and other hostelries. Among the new summer residents was Thomas Lowndes, a wealthy political leader who owned extensive plantations in Charleston and Colleton Districts. His home combined the luxuries of a Charleston plantation with the style of a simple Upcountry farmhouse of the period. With views of the distant Blue Ridge, it was about five miles from the village but convenient to the home of his friends, the Butlers. Cypress columns lugged from the Lowcountry by mules and enslaved men fronted the stucco-covered four-room dwelling.

Another new, but permanent, resident was Edward Croft. He purchased one hundred thirty-three acres (eventually expanded to six

Postcard of the Record Building (Robert Mills Courthouse) that once stood in downtown Greenville. It was notable for its distinctive architecture. Postcard, ca. 1910, Curt Teich & Co. South Caroliniana Library, University of South Carolina.

hundred acres) to create Oaklawn Plantation at the foot of Piney Mountain and ten additional acres as a site for his village home on North Street. Perry described him as "a genial and friendly man, who entertained "with dining and dancing parties that contributed greatly to the sociability of the place." He was primarily involved with establishing Christ Church, and he was chairman of the board of trustees of the Academies from 1824 until well into the 1830s.

Parties like those Croft hosted were frequent during the summer, and so was drinking. Brandy made from local peaches and apples, hard cider, home-distilled whiskey, sherry, and rum were most popular. Coffee and tea were expensive; milk (unrefrigerated and unpasteurized) was dangerous, and water wasn't always pure. Gentlemen drank at home, at afternoon dinner, and throughout the evening. Many of our most distinguished early settlers spent their days, according to Benjamin Perry, lazily "drinking toddy" (the first cocktail, concocted of rum and

hot water) and rocking in chairs at the front of Main Street stores. On sales days, farmers from outlying parts were well fortified with a dime's worth of whiskey from the popular Last Chance Saloon or from their own private stash.

Greenville in the early 1820s may have been, as a Charleston reporter noted, "a negligible place," but it was growing, thanks to Vardry McBee, its Lowcountry visitors, and its climate. In his 1826 *Atlas of South Carolina*, Robert Mills described the village as "rapidly improving." He went on to say, "It is the resort of much company in the summer, and several respectable and wealthy families have located here on the account of the salubrity of the climate. These have induced a degree of improvement, which promises to make Greenville one of the most considerable villages in the state."

Chapter 4

"A FLOURISHING LITTLE TOWN,"
1831–60

The village of Greenville was officially chartered in 1831. Chartering meant that residents could elect an intendant (mayor), aldermen, have a policeman, and had boundaries established a mile in every direction from the courthouse. That summer, *Mountaineer* editor Benjamin Perry boasted that the "flourishing little town" had about six hundred residents (swollen to perhaps eight hundred during the summer), sixty-four houses, and sixty-nine families. There were, he said, "9 merchants, 6 tavern keepers, 37 mechanics, 9 stores, 6 first rate public houses, 3 tailors' shops, 3 milliners' stores, 2 carriage making establishments, 2 tanyards, 2 grist mills, 1 sawmill, 1 silver smith, 1 cabinet maker's shop, 1 shoemaker's shop, 2 tinsmiths, and 1 printing office."

Greenville was "flourishing" because it was a summer resort, an agricultural center, and a courthouse town. Its popularity as a resort had recently grown because of the politics of nullification and increasing northern opposition to slavery. As a result, Newport, Rhode Island, and Saratoga Springs, New York, longtime summer refuges for plantation owners, were less welcoming than they had been in the past. In June, Perry noted, "Our village is beginning to wear the appearance of life and gaiety. Three of the largest Hotels in the place are pretty well filled with visitors from the low country. Dancing parties and Balls are becoming very frequent."

The grand event of that summer was the celebration of the fifty-fifth anniversary of the Declaration of Independence. Activities included thirteen (for the original colonies) rounds of artillery fire at dawn; a military parade by militia companies; a service at the Baptist Church at 11 a.m., a "sumptuous dinner" at 3 P.M., concluding with thirteen regular toasts and thirty volunteer ones and ending at the ballroom of the Mansion House where, "overflowing with beauty and fashion," ladies and gentlemen danced all evening.

Editor Perry, then twenty-seven, was becoming one of the most important men in the antebellum village. His father and an uncle had come south to Charleston from Massachusetts after the American Revolution and ended up running a general store in an isolated spot near the Tugaloo River. An itinerant Pennsylvania schoolmaster triggered young Ben's love of books and reading. At fifteen, Perry crossed the mountains to study classics at the Asheville Academy. Two years later, in 1823, he came to the newly opened Greenville Male Academy to learn mathematics and natural philosophy. He didn't have enough money to attend South Carolina College, so in 1824, he began reading law with Judge Baylis Earle. A year later, he passed the bar and immediately began a legal practice at Greenville Courthouse. Within three years, he was doing well enough as an attorney to speak out against the politics of nullification preached by John C. Calhoun of nearby Fort Hill. To promote his Unionist

views, he became editor of the Greenville *Mountaineer*. His persuasive editorials built support for democracy and made Greenville the most Unionist stronghold in the state.

Unfortunately, most of his friends were nullifiers. They soon became his enemies.

The pen wasn't his only weapon. He almost drew pistols to duel with his longtime friend Waddy Thompson; with Dr. Frederick Symmes, the editor of the Pendleton *Messenger*; and with wealthy landowner Henry Townes. And he stabbed William Choice, who was also hot tempered, during a newsroom encounter. Nullifiers began a Greenville newspaper to oppose him, choosing Turner Bynum, a brilliant young writer from Columbia, to edit their *Southern Sentinel*. Within months, the editorial battle between the two men grew so hot that Perry challenged Bynum to a duel. They met on August 16, 1832. Bynum's first shot pierced Perry's coat; Perry's return shot killed Bynum.

Nullification and the "tariff of abominations" that sparked it, were hotly debated in newspapers, at the Mansion House bar, and around family firesides. Women even got involved. The *Mountaineer* carried a report that "Miss Wells of Spartanburg has managed to braid common crop grass that can be woven into 'anti-tariff hats'" that looked as good as imported leghorns, although they cost $10 to $15, the modern equivalent of $300. Other ladies found ways to clean and reuse their hats for another season rather than paying the 35-cent tariff duty on new ones.

While villagers were arguing politics, the town's first industry began. In 1835, Ebenezer Gower from Maine and Thomas Cox of Charleston opened the Greenville Coach Factory. Their operation was housed in an unpainted but serviceable wooden building that stretched along the Reedy's north bank above its upper waterfall. It was adjacent to the narrow pedestrian bridge over the shallow ford that linked the village with trading routes to Augusta and Pendleton. A huge, slowly revolving water wheel provided power from the river's shoals and immediately became a Greenville landmark.

The partners advertised in the Greenville *Mountaineer* for "sober and industrious" mechanics who could help build wagons for nearby farmers. They were evidently not successful. They were still advertising two years later, although they had dropped "sober" from the requirements. The business expanded in the next decades as younger relatives joined the business. Eben's brother, Thomas Gower, made his way south from Maine to join the company in the early 1840s, and Cox's nephew, Henry Markley, became a partner in the 1850s. By that time, it was the largest coach and farm wagon business south of the Potomac, employing more than eighty workmen.

The district too had its first industries. Entrepreneurs from Rhode Island, where America's textile industry began, made their way to South Carolina with disassembled looms and spindles. After landing in Charleston, they headed for the well-watered Upcountry. In 1820, William Hutchings, a Methodist minister as well as an experienced mill operator, purchased three hundred seven acres of land and set up a small (one-hundred-forty-spindle) wooden yarn factory on the banks of the Enoree. He also started preaching at the nearby home of William Moon, creating one of Greenville's earliest Methodist meeting houses. Ebenezer Methodist Church in Pelham traces its roots to Hutchings's fervor. The mill was a success, and a year later he built a second larger one adjacent to it. He also built a grist mill and sawmill on the property. However, money problems (to build the second mill, he mortgaged the first mill to one man and its machinery to another) and fire—the twin banes of the early textile industry—did him in.

In 1825, the second mill burned down; three years later, hopelessly in debt, Hutchings sold his property for $500 and moved on. Philip Lester, a local farmer who was probably one of Hutchings creditors, operated it in partnership with Josiah Kilgore. Buena Vista Mill (usually called Lester's Factory) functioned until 1853, when it once more burned. Employing twenty-five men and women, it produced cotton yarn worth $12,000 annually in 1850. After the fire, Lester bought out Kilgore's half interest, rebuilt the mill (this time of brick), installed five hundred new water-powered spindles, and started carrying fire insurance. He also reorganized the company, bringing his sons in as partners. By 1860, the mill was earning a profit of about $6,000 a year, a paper mill had been built to take advantage of the waterpower of the Enoree dam, and mill operatives lived in the village of Buena Vista across the Spartanburg line.

William Bates, another Rhode Islander, joined Lester and Kilgore as part owner of Lester's Mill in 1830. In 1833, Kilgore purchased three hundred acres around a grist mill at Rocky Creek, less than a half mile away from the Enoree, for $800. Three years later, Kilgore sold the land to Bates for $810. The Rhode Islander then moved used machinery into the grist mill to spin cotton. By the 1840s, his Batesville Mill was flourishing. Because the area was isolated, local planters used the mill as a kind of bank, depositing their money there. Bates bought six mules, a Conestoga wagon, and hired young William Thackston to peddle five-pound bunches of Batesville yarn throughout the Carolinas. Thackston exchanged the yarn for money, rags (to be sold to paper mills), tallow, furs, hams of venison or pork—anything that could be sold or traded.

In 1847, Thomas Cox, who had started the Greenville Coach Factory, became a partner. A year later, Bates's new son-in-law, Henry Hammett, a former schoolmaster and storekeeper, bought into the company, and the firm became William Bates & Co. With these infusions of cash (capitalization nearly tripled between 1840 and 1860, and employees increased from twenty to fifty-five), Bates built a new two-story mill, ordered looms and new spindles, and began producing shirting fabric. When the Civil War came, Batesville was the largest mill in the county. The Confederate government commandeered most of its production, with just one day's output allowed to civilians. As a result, said a local newspaper, "the rich and poor, high and low, came in splendid carriages, in sulkies, in wagons and in carts, to buy cloth but only ten yards allowed to each purchaser regardless of wealth or station."

The third and longest operating mill was Vardry McBee's factory on the Reedy River seven miles south of the village. When McBee opened it about 1834, it was the first cotton mill in Greenville District to make use of the waterpower of the Reedy. In the 1850s, the *Keowee Courier* reported that the village had a "neat appearance," and workers lived at no charge in "attractive and comfortable houses" with ample room for gardens. According to McBee's biographer, the company store sold a variety of merchandise—combs, shovel handles, nails, wash pans, socks, shoes, tallow, cider, but no alcohol.

In 1843 McBee appointed his son, Alexander, and his millwright, John Adams, to run the factory. Adams, a canny and ingenious Scot whom McBee had known since 1835, unfortunately allowed the river to undermine the mill's water wheel, but he also shored up an already existing dam at the shoals to increase the mill's power. In 1851, according to the *Southern Patriot,* V. McBee & Son included a cotton factory with fifty operatives, a paper mill, a gristmill, a sawmill, and a community of about one hundred fifty people. McBee's Factory produced seventy-five thousand pounds of cotton yarn and manufactured "linsey-woolsey," a cheap warm fabric manufactured from a combination of wool and linen. In March 1856, according to the same newspaper, Adams designed and built a new octagonal meeting house for the Methodist congregation that had formed in 1841; Alexander McBee paid for it. McBee Chapel on Main Street in Conestee is among only three extant octagonal brick churches in the nation and the only one located in a former mill village.

Mills and their equipment were expensive. Without banks, men like Josiah Kilgore provided important initial capital and later expansion. Kilgore's father was a plantation owner in southern Greenville District, and Josiah followed in his footsteps. After graduating

McBee Chapel, one of only three known octagonal brick churches still standing in the United States. Greenville County Library System, South Carolina Room Archive.

from South Carolina College in 1813, he was immediately named state surveyor. He resigned from that position in 1819 and returned to Greenville District, where he became a planter and engineer. By the time he was thirty, he was farming one thousand acres of land, had married and fathered two sons, enslaved fourteen African Americans, and was representing Greenville in the General Assembly. During the next twenty-five years, he amassed another thousand acres of land, fifty more slaves, three more children, and a home in the village. In May 1838, he purchased a full acre of land bounded by Buncombe and Academy Streets.

The house he built there was impressively tall. Massive granite steps over a partially raised cellar level led to a veranda, room ceilings

The Fountain Fox Beattie House is a large Italianate home, built ca. 1834. The Beattie family lived in the house until 1940. It later served as the Greenville Woman's Club. Photo by Bill Fitzpatrick.

on both floors were twelve feet high, and it was topped by a full attic. With solid poplar columns rising to a pediment, heart of pine floorboards four inches thick, a copper roof, and a dining table that could seat thirty people comfortably, the Kilgore house was not just an Upcountry farmhouse come to town. It was a showplace. Greenville welcomed it.

Although it wasn't quite so elegant, Fountain Fox Beattie's new home was almost as impressive. Beattie came from Virginia and started building "in the eastern suburbs" on what is today East North Street just opposite Christ Church. He was newlywed, twenty-seven years old, and had enough money to make a splash when he arrived in Greenville in 1834. By October of that year, he was a partner in a general store at Main and Coffee Streets and had purchased a $400 lot on which he would build a fitting home for his bride, the former Emily Edgeworth of Charleston. The house had elegant detailing with carved mantels for each fireplace and an elaborate stairway that must have taken months to complete. Its design, however, was simple—probably four rooms on each floor with a kitchen building behind the house. The house grew over the years, with one-story wings and a columned porch with elaborate Italianate style decorations that were added as their family and wealth grew.

In addition to elite homes, churches were built and rebuilt during the years after charting. The Methodist Church, for example, started in 1832 when Vardry McBee conveyed a small lot—just one hundred by one hundred twenty feet—on the eastern boundary of the village opposite Christ Church "for the promotion of religious worship in order that a suitable church may be erected for the Methodist denomination . . . as well as in consideration of one dollar" paid by the trustees of a church that did not yet exist. Two years later, according to S. S. Crittenden in the *Greenville Century Book*, five women and a lone man met at Mrs. Maria Turpin's Main Street home to organize the Greenville Methodist Episcopal Church. Like many Methodist churches of the time, the building was deliberately plain. It looked like the boarding house it became after Methodists constructed their more imposing edifice on Buncombe Street in 1873. Because its benches were free, according to Crittenden, "most of the schoolgirls attending the Female Academy and boarding in the village attended that church, and as a natural consequence, the young men did also."

The Episcopal and Methodist churches were forbidden by McBee's deed to establish burying grounds, so the city needed a cemetery. A public burying ground was established by Francis McLeod on his property at the top of Main Street in 1829. The first burial there had been 1812, when Elizabeth Blackburn Williams, the mother-in-law of Waddy Thompson, who then owned the property, was buried in the garden under her favorite tree. In 1833, McLeod conveyed the property for one dollar to the village's Commission of Streets and Markets for the "sole and exclusive" use as a graveyard. It was one of the first municipal cemeteries in the state. In 1834, Edward Croft conveyed land adjacent to Christ Church for burials, reserving a large site for his family.

Presbyterian women established the fourth church in the village in 1847. Mrs. Charles Stone raised nearly $50 from among ladies of her acquaintance and invited the well-known Presbyterian minister Benjamin Palmer of Columbia to spend the summer in Greenville and preach to them. That experiment was so successful that, in October, she asked the presbytery for "a supply of preaching." The church leaders dismissed her request as "only a woman's idea," but because she hadn't asked for money, they grudgingly agreed. They arranged for the Rev. S. S. Gaillard, then at Mt. Tabor Presbyterian Church south of Greer, to occasionally preach at Greenville Courthouse.

Beginning in February 1848, he did so. The first officially scheduled Presbyterian services were held in the Lyceum Building of the Greenville Academies. Soon a congregation of sixteen formed, seven of whom had been members of Mt. Tabor. About a year later, John Adams, who was lured from Fairview Church to be presiding elder, L. C. Cline, and Whiteford Smith asked Vardry McBee for land on which to build a church. They had a distinct advantage: Mrs. Jane McBee was a member of their small group.

McBee had given land for the Academies and for Greenville's first three churches, but the village was growing, and land values had risen. That may be the reason why he initially asked the trustees of the Academies to return an acre of the land he had granted them in 1820 for the new church. They responded (firmly but very politely) that he had given it for educational purposes, and they could not do so. Instead, he

gave the Presbyterians an acre at the northwest corner of Washington and Richardson Street where, in 1851, they dedicated a small, columned brick and stone building topped with a (short) tower and a "sweet-sounding bell."

While the Presbyterians were building, the Baptist congregation began considering rebuilding. By 1849, the church membership had grown to about a hundred people, and the little church on Irvine Street was crowded. Women's newly fashionable hoop skirts took so much room that pew doors had to be removed, but that didn't help enough when, a few years later, students and faculty from Furman University crowded into its pews. Furthermore, the tree on which the church's bell hung was rotting, and the building was unheated. Elders, urged on by the women in the congregation, decided to rebuild. It wasn't until 1853 that church leadership decided to take the bold step of purchasing a new site on West McBee Avenue (the Irvine Street property was far too small for the edifice they envisioned) and started raising funds for a new $10,000 church building.

Fundraising was difficult. It took a year to obtain the pledges. And when church leaders—principally, James Boyce, head of the building committee—engaged the nationally known Philadelphia architectural firm of Sloan and Stewart to design an appropriate building, their estimate came in at $12,000. The news that Christ Church was spending $16,000 on its new church, however, evidently opened Baptist purses. Their new Church was completed in 1858.

Episcopalians had initially asked summer resident Joel Poinsett to design plans for their new edifice. When he presented a design for an elaborate (and expensive) gray stucco sanctuary in 1848, they decided to find a cheaper plan. Church rector T. S. Arthur turned to J. D. McCollough, rector of Spartanburg' s Church of the Advent, who had designed several Upstate churches, for a less expensive design in 1851. They consecrated their new building in 1854.

Poinsett, who had become a summer worshipper at Christ Church after he purchased a two-hundred-acre "mountain homestead" in 1834, was Greenville's most famous summer resident. He hired a neighbor to farm his land and employed free white men as laborers. A firm federalist who was deeply and bitterly opposed to Calhoun and his ideas of nullification, Poinsett had served as ambassador to Mexico and as secretary of war under President Martin Van Buren. In 1841, after Van Buren was defeated, Poinsett returned to South Carolina to spend summers managing his Greenville farm. Like most Lowcountry visitors, he usually arrived in May and left the first week of November. Poinsett was deeply interested in agriculture (he wrote frequently about fertilizer), in the Episcopal Church, and in bringing a railroad to Greenville. He became friends with Vardry McBee and vied with him at the district agricultural

Plans to replace the original Christ Church building began in 1845, and Joel Poinsett, a vestryman in the church, drew up plans. They were too elaborate to execute, however, and construction of the new building did not begin until 1852. Though expanded through a series of building campaigns, the original church continues to stand on North Church Street. Image: Christ Episcopal Church, 1934. Historic American Buildings Survey, Library of Congress Prints and Photographs Division.

fair. He and McBee were not, however, the only ones pursuing agricultural experiments.

In 1848, a Connecticut native, Junius Smith, came South looking for the ideal place to grow tea. He brought seedlings with him, and, after inspecting land in Alabama and

Joel Roberts Poinsett. Lithograph on paper by Peter S. Duval, 1838. National Portrait Gallery, Smithsonian Institution; transfer from the Library of Congress.

Georgia, settled in Greenville. Smith planted an experimental garden in 1849. It was such a success that, in the following year, he purchased two hundred sixty-nine acres of land at Golden Grove, where he began tea cultivation. In 1851, he boasted in a letter published in both Greenville and New York that he was able to drink a pot of tea brewed from his own leaves. He also grew oats, buckwheat, peas, and beans

and planted a fine orchard. However, Smith was attacked at his home in December 1851 and beaten so badly that he died a year later. His biographer cited evidence that the beating occurred because of his abolitionist views.

Golden Grove still attracted large plantation owners. The best known was attorney Richard Gantt, who first purchased land there in 1818. Over the next fifteen years or so, he added to that first purchase, eventually owning nearly two thousand acres, most of which he eventually conveyed to his sons. In 1834, he bought six hundred eighty-three acres from the executor of Humphrey Hall's estate. That "Hall Plantation" became his home. If it wasn't a large house, it must have been crowded, because the 1850 census lists the other residents as his daughter Eliza, her three children, and his son Edward and his wife and two children. He lived there on the Grove Road (now Piedmont Highway) for more than a quarter of century.

The land north of Taylors around Milford Baptist Church drew other landowners. Crittenden described it as "a notable settlement of intelligent and refined, as well as thrifty and industrious farmers." "It is," he wrote, "one of the most beautiful sections of the country with the South Tiger [sic] flowing between its undulating hills and fertile valleys." Among those attracted to its "moral, religious and industrious character and healthful climate" was Judge John Belton O'Neall, who purchased a nine-hundred-acre summer place there in 1849. In 1832, a Baptist congregation had been constituted with Samuel Gibson as its first minister. Like O'Neall, a Newberry native who was president of the Greenville & Columbia Railroad and a distinguished jurist, Gibson was a teetotaler. Although most Milford residents were firm Baptists, many of them distilled and sold whiskey to supplement their income. Devout churchgoer Washington Taylor, for example, recorded making fourteen gallons of corn liquor from seven and a half bushels of corn in 1835 and selling every drop to neighbors. In the late 1840s, however, Gibson's preaching converted Taylor to prohibition and sobriety ruled in Milford.

Many summer residents, such as Poinsett, were Huguenots from the Lowcountry who had immigrated a century or more earlier, but in the 1840s, new and more permanent immigrants began coming from Germany. Simon Swandale, for example, was a travelling "merchant tailer [sic]" who, beginning in 1842, advertised "superior French and English broadcloths, doeskins and cassimers [cashmere] as well as rich satin cravats, silk and cotton undershirts and gentlemen's accessories including canes and umbrellas" in the pages of the *Mountaineer*. Throughout the 1840s, he made frequent trips to New York to buy fabrics and "fancy goods" to sell in Greenville. He settled full time in Greenville in 1852 when he

married Deslain Tupper, a graduate of Emma Willard's famous Female Academy, at a wedding presided over by a Baptist minister.

The Tuppers were Baptist; Swandale, however, was among the thousands of German Jews who immigrated to America between 1820 and 1840. He started as a peddler, became a retailer, and eventually became manager and owner of the Mansion House. It seems likely that he was the pioneer Jewish businessman in the village. The religion of the "quiet, quaint and loveable little man" was no secret. A priest visiting Greenville during the Civil War referred to him as "a kind Israelite." He certainly welcomed other Jews who ventured into the Upstate. Abraham Isaacs, for example, lived at the hotel and with Swandale ran a men's furnishing store in the 1860s.

The village prospered from summer visitors, but Greenville District also became the home of substantial plantation owners, although only one, T. E. Ware, qualifies as a "great planter" as defined by historian Chalmers Davidson in the *Last Foray*. These four hundred plantation owners had immense wealth, land (at least a thousand acres) and enslaved more than a hundred people; they led the state into the Civil War. In addition to being a plantation owner, Ware was a political power and, more unusually, a convicted murderer.

Born in 1808, Edwin Ware grew up in a landed family in northern Abbeville District.

He increased his wealth dramatically when he married Mary Williams Jones of Greenville, whose father owned seventeen hundred acres of farming land and a substantial plantation house in southern Greenville County. The young couple moved into the large home that Jones had erected in 1824. In the 1840s, Ware served three terms in the South Carolina House of Representatives and four more terms in the state senate. After her mother's death in 1851, the relationship between Mary Ware and her father deteriorated. Arguments between father and daughter were finally so violent that Ware decided to move the family to Greenville. On the February morning in 1853 when the couple planned to leave, Jones, who was sixty-four years old but six feet, four inches tall and sturdily built, began drinking heavily. As Ware got up to leave, Jones seized a pair of iron fireplace tongs and attacked him. When Ware put up his arm to guard his head, Jones smashed it with the tongs. Ware then pulled a pistol from his pocket, and before his father-in-law could strike again, he shot three times. Jones fell to the floor, dead.

Fewer than eight weeks after the incident, newspapers across the state headlined news of "A Melancholy Homicide" trial in Greenville. Lawyer Benjamin Perry argued that Ware had acted in self-defense; if Jones's tongs had hit Ware's head, Perry pleaded, he would have died. The jury found Ware guilty of manslaughter but recommended mercy. The Judge heard them: He fined Ware $500 and sentenced him to three months in prison. He was incarcerated in the Greenville County Jail ("Siberia") on Falls Street, where his stay was made more pleasant by constant visits from friends. After a week's imprisonment, Ware had "the interesting spectacle" (according to the Greenville *Mountaineer*) of his wife's appearance with a pardon from the Governor clutched in her hand.

Perry Duncan was almost as wealthy as Ware. He and his wife, Mary Ann, had a town house in Greenville, six miles (about an hour and a half by horse-drawn buggy) away from their nineteen-hundred-acre homeplace off the Buncombe Road. It produced all they needed: butter, milk, and beef from their herd of cattle; pork from pigs; mutton from sheep; fowl, including chickens, turkeys, peacocks, and guinea hens; and corn, wheat, oats, beans, and potatoes in abundance. Devout Methodists who conducted daily devotions in their rambling two-story home near the modern Furman campus, Mrs. Duncan had a wooden chapel built on land close to Buncombe Road in 1847. Perry Duncan had been a Unionist during the nullification controversy, but by 1860, he too supported secession; he was one of the five Greenvillians who signed the Institutes of Secession.

Visitors "resorted" to two new Greenville hotels in the 1840s and 1850s. Dr. J. P. Hillhouse constructed the Paris Mountain House near the mountain's summit. That hotel was "plain, neat, and furnished in country style." The charter authorized Hillhouse, a pharmacist, to lay out and construct (at his own expense) a toll road "beginning on the Rutherford Road and passing along the crest of Paris Mountain to terminate at the hotel." It reduced the time involved in reaching the top of the mountain from Main Street to about two and a half hours, but it was expensive: The toll for a single horseman was fifty cents; a coach with two horses cost a dollar.

Even more popular and luxurious was the resort at Chick Springs. Beginning in 1840 and continuing for almost a hundred years, despite wars and fires, the bubbling mineral springs near Taylors attracted ailing, marriageable, and leisured South Carolinians to its hotels and cottages, its lake, and its shady groves. Long before the resort was dreamed of, Cherokees knew its healing powers. In his 1826 *Statistics of South Carolina*, Robert Mills praised the water's efficacy in treating "desperate cases of ringworm." However, it took Dr. Burwell Chick, a Newberry physician, to see the commercial value of the potent sulfurous water. While he was hunting on land owned by Asa Crowder, Indian guides led him to Lick Springs; they also told him that its water cured sores. Within a year, Chick had purchased one hundred ninety-two acres from Crowder and, in 1840, opened Lick Springs Spa. In 1842, he completed a "large and

commodious" sixty-room hotel, where board was a dollar a day, with children, servants, and horses charged half price. By 1849, the resort—then generally known as Chick's Springs or Spa—had become, under the direction of Chick's son Ruben and "his lady," one of the most popular summer retreats in the state, with frequent balls and card parties, exciting evening excursions to Greenville, hunting with the hotel's pack of hounds, and games (gambling strictly prohibited) of billiards and ten pins.

Although many Greenvillians partook of the water whose "particular flavor and villainous smell" was so popular, most long-term visitors came from a distance, arriving, after 1853, on a special stagecoach from the Augusta Street depot of the Greenville & Columbia Railroad. They included Father J. J. O'Connell, a Catholic priest from Charleston who was a regular summer guest. The Masses he said at the hotel in the late 1850s were probably the first Roman Catholic services in Greenville County.

One Sunday, he and "a Baptist at the Furman University" had a preaching competition. He gave a twenty-minute sermon as a part of a morning Mass, and the Baptist minister spent an hour that afternoon condemning dancing in the hotel ballroom. (The priest won.) There would be no more dancing or preaching competitions in the years that followed. Vacant and isolated, both hotels burned to the ground during the Civil War.

Chapter 5

DECADE OF DECISIONS,
1850s

Decisions—corporate, institutional, and communal—changed Greenville in the 1850s from a lighthearted mountain resort village and Unionist stronghold to a more somber "Athens of South Carolina" that embraced secession.

The first decision was to create a railroad. In 1845, Benjamin Perry, Waddy Thompson Jr., John T. Coleman, Joel Poinsett, and Vardry McBee called a public meeting. With a committee of thirty potential subscribers, they agreed to seek a preliminary charter for a Greenville & Columbia Railroad, on the basis of the assumption that they could raise $300,000 in subscriptions locally within a year. They were not successful, but they renewed their charter the following year. Their plan was to build a line one hundred nine miles long from Columbia, which was already tied to

Charleston by rail, going up the east side of the Saluda River through Newberry and Laurens directly to Greenville. The thirty commissioners sought subscribers from Columbia and all the surrounding counties.

By May 1847, they had succeeded. However, when all the stockholders met in Columbia, those from the capital city and from Abbeville and Anderson Districts—urged by local property owner John C. Calhoun, who wanted a different route that would eventually lead over the mountains to Tennessee—voted to build a line one hundred forty-seven miles long on the west side of the Saluda with its terminus in Anderson. Greenville stockholders, and especially McBee, the largest single subscriber, cried foul. They wanted their money back. The majority stockholders refused, so the Greenvillians promptly

chartered the Greenville Railroad Company
and threatened to build a separate railroad from
"Dr. Brown's place," near modern-day Belton,
directly to Greenville, and thus to shift freight
and passengers away from Anderson.

Furthermore, McBee put up $50,000 of his
own money to make the branch line possible.
(To put that amount in context, the president
of the United States earned $25,000 a year.)
The other stockholders reluctantly agreed to the
branch and elected Judge John Belton O'Neall
of Newberry, McBee's hand-picked candidate,
as president of the Greenville & Columbia Railroad. However, it soon became clear that, if the
line to Greenville was to be successfully completed, McBee would have to build it. His son,
Pinkney, a civil engineer, surveyed the route; his
sawmill provided the timber; he coaxed hard-
to-find iron from distributors. He even used
stone from his granite quarry (on modern-day
McDaniel Avenue) for the foundation of the
Greenville freight terminal. It was, said his
daughter, a "monstrous task."

By August 1852, the line had been completed to Greenwood. But then a flash flood washed
out bridges, embankments, and tracks along the
Broad River. The legislature refused to pay an
assessment on the stock it held. Judge O'Neall
threatened to resign. But McBee somehow per-
suaded the doubters and the judge to continue,
and by November 27, 1853, according to Roy
McBee Smith in his biography of his ancestor,

Greenville & Columbia Railroad stock certificate. The
Greenville & Columbia Railroad went bankrupt in 1872
due to financial malfeasance. It was later reorganized and
sold in foreclosure, eventually becoming incorporated into
the Southern Railway.

the tracks were laid to within three miles of
Greenville. Ten days later, on December 8, the
first train arrived in town to general rejoicing.

At the low cost of $14,000 a mile, Vardry
McBee had constructed the rail link. From the
beginning, it was a "rickety road," but he had no
choice: The difficult-to-procure iron was poor

James Clement Furman. Furman University, Special Collections and Archives.

quality, and funds were pitifully limited. Within a year after its completion, the railroad had to be mortgaged for $800,000, but the legislature guaranteed the debt and took a lien on the road. The company tried to buy fifty prime acres overlooking the Reedy River for $15,000 as the site for its Greenville terminal, but McBee was saving that land for another purpose. Instead, the line bought twenty-two acres on Augusta Road close

to the current site of Greenville High School. It became the "Depot Green," and the house on the property became the passenger depot, with offices in former upstairs bedrooms. The freight terminal was built nearer Pendleton Street.

The coming of the Greenville & Columbia Railroad meant that Greenvillians could "board the cars" at 5 A.M. and be in Columbia by 3:30 P.M. for a cost of $5.75. (In 2022 dollars, $193; nobody said it would be cheap.) On the following day, they could be in Charleston. For a journey that had previously taken two weeks, this was modern transportation at its best!

For Lowcountry residents who enjoyed summers in "the mountain city," but not the strenuous journey there by stagecoach, the Greenville & Columbia Railroad was extremely desirable. In addition, it had the advantage of attracting Furman University to the city. In 1850, the South Carolina Baptist convention decided to transform their struggling theological institution in Winnsboro into a liberal arts college with a theological department and to relocate it. James Clement Furman, a professor at the school, was appointed to find a new site. He was the son of Richard Furman, the college's namesake, a Baptist minister in Charleston during the Revolution, and as the first president of the Convention had urged the establishment of a school before his death in 1825.

J. C. Furman chose "the considerable village" of thirteen hundred, he said, because the

Old College, pictured here ca. 1956, was the first building completed on the Furman old campus. This two-room cottage housed the first classes at the newly chartered Furman University in the early 1850s. Furman University, Special Collections and Archives.

cost of living was cheap, Baptists abounded, the climate was "salubrious," and the railroad terminus was planned. The Furman University was chartered in December 1850. Sixty-eight students began classes at McBee Hall on Main Street in February 1852. The first on-campus classes were held in a two-room wooden cottage (now "Old College" on the university's campus) on grounds above the Reedy River while a handsome main building was under construction. Charles Judson, a Connecticut native and University of Virginia graduate, was

Main Building, or "Old Main," was completed in 1854 and represented a substantial upgrade in the physical plant of the newly chartered Furman University campus in downtown Greenville. Furman University, Special Collections and Archives.

the first professor hired. The first chairman of the faculty and later president was James C. Furman. By 1854, when workers finished the main (for many years only) building, the university, complete with preparatory school and seminary, was enrolling about two hundred students. Those "from away" came primarily from towns along the railroad.

That summer, delegates to the South Carolina Baptist Convention voted to begin a college for women. After considerable discussion, they agreed to accept Greenville trustees' offer of the campus and buildings of the Greenville Academies for its site. The Greenville Baptist Female College opened in February 1855. Without any endowment, it was governed by Furman's trustees, who rented the institution to their appointed president, who paid the bills and faculty salaries from student tuition. With support promised from prominent Baptists as well as wealthy Greenvillians, within three years, it had a "commodious and impressive" central building, and more than a hundred girls were enrolled in primary, academic, or college classes at this "nursery of knowledge and piety."

In 1855, trustees hired James Petigru Boyce, a graduate of Brown University and Princeton Seminary whom Furman historian A. S. Reid described as "scholarly, eloquent, debonair and rich," to head the university's religion department. In 1859, it became the Southern Baptist Seminary, with Boyce as president. The Baptist Convention agreed to raise $100,000 (including $26,000 from Furman's endowment), provide a library of two thousand books and rent-free accommodations, and cover faculty salaries if the seminary were located in Greenville. The town proudly became "the Athens of the Upstate"; Furman officials, delighted with

Greenville Woman's College as shown in a vintage postcard from the early twentieth century. Furman University Postcard Collection, Furman University Libraries.

their new location, inscribed "Greenville, South Carolina," at the base of the new college seal.

Professor Albert Sanders was undoubtedly correct when he wrote that Furman's coming brought a new sobriety to village life. That increasingly somber tone came in part from ministerial students who were, generally, serious-minded young men. They were also politically conscious and mostly secessionists. President James Furman believed that slavery was biblically ordained. He preached secession at Baptist churches throughout Greenville District, which had long supported the federal union. The University became what a recent

writer calls "a seedbed" of secession with a student rifle company founded in 1856 that drilled in enthusiastic anticipation of war.

But it was not only Furman that edged Greenville District away from its longtime Unionism. It happened gradually. William H. Campbell, a young secessionist from Edgefield, became editor of the old Unionist newspaper, the *Mountaineer*, early in 1850 and promptly spoke out for secession. Attorney Benjamin Perry, a member of Greenville's all-Unionist legislative delegation, immediately set up the *Southern Patriot* to answer his editorials. A third newspaper, the *Greenville Enterprise*,

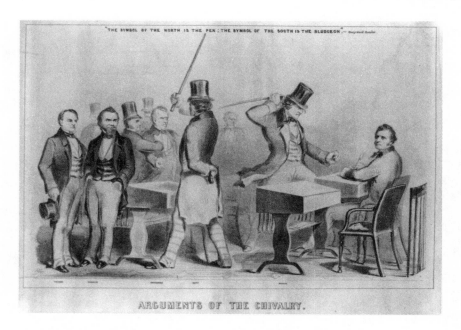

"THE SYMBOL OF THE NORTH IS THE PEN; THE SYMBOL OF THE SOUTH IS THE BLUDGEON."

ARGUMENTS OF THE CHIVALRY.

South Carolina Representative Preston Brooks of Edgefield attacked Charles Sumner on the floor of the United States Senate, bludgeoning him over the head with his cane. It became a symbol of sectional tension between North and South and the splintering of the nation over the issue of slavery and its expansion. Lithograph, probably printed in the shop of John H. Bufford, Boston, and possibly the work of artist Winslow Homer. Library of Congress.

attempted initially to avoid the issue but drifted toward secession at the end of the decade.

War and military posturing were in the air. The Butler Guards, a company of elite young Greenville men, began in 1855. State Adjutant General William King Easley, whose plantation was on the Saluda River, was a busy attorney, newspaper editor, and frequent orator. His oratory was directed at convincing militia members, whom he reviewed on horseback in full uniform with plumed hat and brandished sword, that secession and war were manly and that compromise with the North was effeminate and slavish. While James Clement Furman preached secession from Baptist pulpits, Easley did so at militia musters.

Although dueling editorials and sermons sharpened attitudes, they did not shake established voting patterns. Then, in May 1856, when the US Senate was debating the

Kansas–Nebraska Act, arguing whether Kansas should be admitted to the Union as a free or slave state, Massachusetts Senator Charles Sumner began a thoroughly rehearsed two-day speech. About halfway through, the abolitionist senator launched into an intemperate and remarkably ugly attack on South Carolina and its senior senator, Andrew P. Butler. The state, he said, "wallowed in its shameful imbecility from slavery." Butler, he lamented, had chosen "the harlot slavery" as his mistress and also criticized the elderly man, who had suffered a stroke that affected his speech and who had returned to South Carolina to recuperate, for his "loose expectoration." Even the Northern press called the address excessive.

The next day South Carolina Representative Preston Brooks, Butler's nephew, retaliated. He entered the floor of the Senate at the end of the day; confronted Sumner at his desk; and, raising his cane, attacked the seated man, beating him on the head and shoulders with about thirty strokes (by his count) of his gold-headed gutta-percha cane. It finally splintered into bits. Senators gasped in horror as Sumner, bleeding copiously, fell to the floor.

The press, Northern and Southern, abolitionist and proslavery alike, had a field day. Northern antislavery newspapers condemned Brooks's actions as barbaric, brutal, and uncivilized, an unconscionable action on the floor of the Senate. For Southerners, says Sean Wilentz, "Sumner

had committed an unpardonable offense that deserved the meanest sort of punishment." Southern editorialists, even those who were Unionist, unanimously applauded his stand for the honor of his family and his home state.

When the cane's splinters became "sacred relics [*sic*]" throughout the South, the severity of the attack and Brooks' pride in it further inflamed the North. The blows that Brooks rained down on Sumner's head reverberated throughout the nation, hardening attitudes along regional lines rather than political positions.

In Greenville, they had a personal impact. Both Preston Brooks and Andrew Butler lived in Edgefield, just sixty miles away. Butler's brother, Dr. William Butler, and his wife had lived in Greenville near Lowndes Hill for many years. Their son, Matthew, who had attended the Male Academy, had lived with his uncle in Edgefield after his father's death in 1850. Emmalia Butler, A. P. Butler's sister, had married Waddy Thompson, one of the richest men in town. Mrs. Thompson had reared her niece, Harriet Butler, who had married Vardry McBee's son, Pinkney, in 1846. Preston Brooks was Mrs. McBee's cousin and had attended her Greenville wedding. (Pinkney named the street in front of their home "Butler Avenue" in honor of his wife and her family.)

These local and family ties created intense support for the caning, even—or perhaps especially—among families such as the McBees and

Waddy Thompson, lithograph on paper, 1842. Artist
Charles Fenderich. National Portrait Gallery, Smithsonian
Institution.

Thompsons, who were opposed to secession,
but even the humblest local resident resented
Sumner's vile characterization of his state. To
show their support for Brooks, Greenville
gave a grand party. On September 8, several
hundred people attended a "Brooks Ball" at
the new courthouse, "beautifully and tastefully
decorated and ornamented" for the occa-
sion. The guest of honor was the "gallant and

distinguished" caner and his lady, who danced
"quadrilles, waltzes, scottishes, and ending with
a Virginia reel" until 2 A.M. The ball followed a
festive dinner at the Mansion House. Pyramids
of sweet cakes were offered for dessert, one
decorated by a flag depicting a hand holding an
upright cane labeled "This Conquers."

And if that display of support wasn't enough
to show that Greenville's loyalties lay with the
home side, staunch Unionist Benjamin Perry,
commenting on what he called "a genteel caning," said that "Mr. Brook's [sic] gallantry, spirit,
and patriotic course in Congress have made
him a hero worthy of the respect and admira-
tion of his State."

The caning of Charles Sumner wasn't
enough to make Greenville District a secessionist stronghold, but the personal—the
local—involvement may well have done as
much for creating an emotional climate recep-
tive to secession as all the debates in Washington, the speeches in Columbia, or even the
sermons of James Clement Furman. It would
take John Brown's attack on Harpers Ferry in
1859, and the fear of local slave insurrections
that it aroused, together with the election of
Abraham Lincoln, the "Black Republican,"
in November 1860 to finally convince most
Greenvillians that secession was both inevita-
ble and essential.

Chapter 6

WAR AND RECONSTRUCTION,
1860–76

In November 1860, Greenvillians prepared for Christmas. Main Street bustled with shoppers. They patronized John Kraus's Ice Cream Eating Saloon opposite the Mansion House. They bought remedies for liver disease and "female complaints" at John W. Grady's store and purchased brandies, whiskey, and rum (for medicinal purposes) at J. H. Dean's pharmacy. They browsed among goods from all over the world: coffee from Colombia, Chinese tea, molasses from Cuba, English sauces, New York buckwheat and millinery, even a Paris-made organ at W. Hovey's dry goods store. But they mostly bought Southern products. "In consequence of the impending crisis," a large advertisement for Carr's Store began, "we have received a stupendous stock of goods." "Buy Southern!" it ended.

They talked, though, less about Christmas (characterized more by feasting than gift-giving) than about the "impending crisis": secession. According to the *Greenville Mountaineer*, the small Upstate town (population, fifteen hundred) "greeted with joy the irrepressible conflict." On November 17, 1860, at a "Glorious Mass Meeting" at the courthouse, J. C. Furman, William King Easley, Perry E. Duncan, James H. Harrison, and William Campbell were elected Greenville's representatives to the Secession Convention in Columbia a month later. On November 29, secessionists gave a "Resistance Party" at McBee's Hall, the largest gathering place in town. Newspapers advertised that all ladies of the town were invited to the "last party to be given in our community in the United States of America."

"The Palmetto State Song," composed by George O. Robinson and published in 1860, was dedicated to the signers of the Ordinance of Secession. It was an early anthem of the Confederacy. Library of Congress, Prints and Photographs Division.

On December 3, Unionists (called "cooperationists") ignored stormy weather and proposed an opposition Convention slate. Among their nominees were James Boyce, the financial genius and Southern Baptist Seminary president, who was convinced that the South could not win. John Belton O'Neal, the president of the Greenville & Columbia Railroad, and landowner T. C. Bolling thought that South Carolina should not act independently. Benjamin Perry, who had been a Unionist for thirty years, was totally opposed to secession. Boyce and O'Neal withdrew their names. Convinced that they could not win, Perry and his colleagues did not bother to campaign before the election on December 6.

Most Unionists did not vote. Greenville overwhelmingly elected the secessionists' slate. James Clement Furman led the ticket with thirteen hundred forty-two votes. Benjamin Perry, who had represented the county in the state legislature for nearly thirty years, received only two hundred twenty-five.

The next week, secessionist Jordan Pool shot Unionist Edward Jacobs in front of the Courthouse. Pool was found innocent; the killing was self-defense, the jury ruled, because he was defending the honor of the state.

On December 20, South Carolina seceded from the Union. Benjamin Perry commented, "I have tried for thirty years to save this state from disunion. Now they are going to the devil, and I will go with them." The rest of Greenville celebrated.

That evening, for the first time, gaslights illuminated Main Street. On December 21, a great torchlight procession thronged Main Street. Greenville "Minute Men," with blue cockades in their hats, marched from the West End Hotel on Augusta Street to the Female College on

College Street and ended at Goodlett's Hotel at the corner of Main and Washington. There were speeches and fireworks; the ladies of the town presented a flag inscribed "We Conquer or We Die." Christmas came and went. Talk continued. When Citadel cadets fired on Fort Sumter in April, the nation's most devastating war began.

Greenvillians responded enthusiastically. The Butler Guards immediately joined the "Palmetto Regiment," commanded by Col. Joseph Kershaw. In addition to the Greenville men, it was made up of "the flower of chivalry" from across the state, with companies that included the Lancaster Invincibles, Columbia Greys, Camden Light Infantry, and Sumter Rifles. The University Riflemen, Furman's military unit, offered their services to Governor Pickens. He declined, saying that the war would be fought in Virginia so they would not be needed. Instead, they and most other Greenville men enlisted in Captain Wesley Brooks's troop, which became Company B of the Sixteenth South Carolina volunteers. Benjamin Perry immediately embraced the Confederate cause. His son, William Hayne, who had just completed Harvard Law School, enlisted. Perry himself contributed $50 and raised two companies of men from the Dark Corner, a Union stronghold for thirty years.

It wasn't only the men who responded enthusiastically to the call to arms. In July, Mary Ann Duncan, whose husband had been a delegate to the Secession Convention, organized thirty friends, and together they formed the Greenville Ladies Association in Aid of Confederate Volunteers. Their goals were "to relieve the sick and wounded among the soldiers, by forwarding to them linen, underclothing, cordials, bed ticks, etc. & etc. and to make winter clothing." At the end of July, after the Battle of Manassas, they sent boxes by railway express to wounded men in Virginia and to those suffering from typhoid, malaria, and measles in Columbia, Charleston, and Coosawhatchie, where militia were protecting the coast.

In August 1862, Greenville authorities asked the ladies of the volunteer association to provide lodgings for soldiers arriving by train. The Female College offered the old Male Academy classroom on its property as a "Soldiers' Rest." It became a place where soldiers, some wounded, most not, could find a bed, a hot meal, a change of clothing, and a few dollars to help them on their way. They hired a matron at $12 a month and provided an extra dollar for fuel. During its first three months of operation, the women hosted one hundred twelve soldiers. Town Council members contributed $20 a month to cover the cost of transporting soldiers from the depot.

By mid-1862, association membership had expanded to two hundred forty-five ladies and twenty gentlemen ("patrons" who supplied cash), including students at the Female College, and many of the refugees who were crowding into the Upstate after federal troops invaded the Lowcountry coast. In 1863, the quartermaster reported the town's population as about three thousand, which included these refugees—primarily children, women, and old men—who arrived, usually by train, with as much furniture as they could transport as well as, often, house servants from their coastal plantations.

Furman did not reopen in the fall of 1861, because most of its students and faculty had enlisted in the Confederate army. The Female College remained open, however, and flourished. Trustees appointed James Clement Furman, jobless after the closing of the university, to its presidency. He remained in the position for less than a year. Charles Judson, the first professor appointed to the Furman faculty, became president in 1863. Judson initiated a "postgraduate" class to serve the many young women among the refugees.

Greenville soon became one of the breadbaskets—and clothes closets—of the Confederacy. Far from the battlegrounds in Virginia and the West, the Upstate district supplied food, fabrics, and footwear—not to mention horses, mules, and wagons—to the Southern cause. The Confederate States of America quartermaster arrived in the fall of 1862 and immediately leased a thirteen-stall stable and set up

office. He estimated that local sources could potentially produce a million bushels of corn, a good sweet potato crop, and the twenty-five local tanneries could manufacture two hundred pairs of shoes a day. The Gower, Cox, and Markley coach factory could turn out three ambulances or wagons daily, but if the former workmen (including owner Thomas Gower) returned to Greenville, the output would double. In addition, cotton jean material, yarn, and linsey-woolsy were available from Lester's Factory (later Pelham Mill), McBee's Factory (Conestee Mill), William Bates & Company, and Samuel Morgan & Co. (the forerunner of Apalache Mill in Greer). The quartermaster also commandeered mules and horses, but in January 1863, when he had one hundred ninety-four animals in his stable yard, he couldn't send them to Columbia because no iron was available to shoe them.

Greenville also provided guns. In the spring of 1862, Vardry McBee donated twenty acres of land near the Anderson Road to the state of South Carolina as a site for an arms manufactory. Until the last weeks of the war, the "State Works" there was the primary source of the state's munitions. South Carolina's first armory had been set up on the statehouse grounds in Columbia, but that location was unsatisfactory. When McBee offered land bordering the Greenville & Columbia Railroad tracks, former Governor William Henry Gist, who was in charge of the state's wartime manufacturing, immediately accepted. The ammunition, rifles, and bayonets produced at the Works were not, however, a part of the Confederate supply line. Officials in Columbia didn't trust the Confederate government in Richmond and were focused on keeping South Carolina safe.

By late 1863, the slogging reality of warfare, increasing hardships at home, and orders to go to Mississippi led numbers of Upstate farmer-soldiers to desert. In August, Upstate Conscription Officer John Ashmore reported that desertions were increasing daily and that nearly a thousand deserters were holed up along the North Carolina border. Many had probably planned to return to their units eventually, but when they saw crops to be harvested and local need, they stayed home. Groups of forty to fifty, said J. T. Otten in a scholarly study of disloyalty in the Upstate, set out guards and worked their farms, distilled liquor, and mended fences. To protect themselves from conscription officers, they erected a fort at Gowensville, a heavy log building with loopholes for guns. Major Ashmore requested a six-pound cannon to destroy it, and the governor sent Boykin's Rangers to capture deserters, but the Rangers met, says A. V. Huff, with little success.

By 1863, all local stores had closed, and necessities of the past had disappeared. Coffee was a memory, tea was made with herb roots, and salt was scraped from the floor of

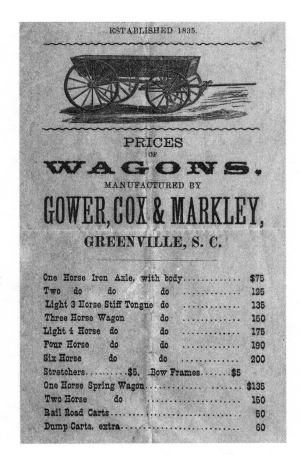

Advertisement for the Gower, Cox, and Markley coach factory showing wagon prices in 1860. South Caroliniana Library.

smokehouses and reused. Although some farms still produced cider, most distilleries had closed. Even paper had become a luxury. The *Enterprise* and the *Southern Patriot* had closed at the beginning of the war, and the *Mountaineer* was reduced to a single-page broadside.

Because newsprint was in such limited supply, Presbyterian minister Edward Buist, said to have the most sonorous voice in town, read aloud lists of men dead or wounded in battle to the crowd gathered at the platform of the Greenville and Columbia Depot. Confederate dollars, however, were all too available. Because the Confederate government realized that taxation would not work, officials issued more than a million dollars in bonds without gold to back them. As a result, inflation in the Confederacy was nine thousand percent, and prices for staples soared.

Late in November 1864, Female College President Charles Judson notified the Ladies Association that he would soon need the old Male Academy building for his students, so the volunteers requested the use of two rooms at Greenville's Wayside Hospital, housed in the Gilreath Hotel at the corner of Washington and Main Streets. The Rest Home remained on the college grounds until early in January, however, when the "directoress" reported that it had housed only sixteen soldiers since December 12. In late February, however, after Sherman's troops invaded the state, the situation changed. Even though trains had stopped running, sixty soldiers arrived during the last week of the month. The ladies then moved beds, mattresses, and supplies to the Wayside Hospital. In the weeks that followed, the matron and porter quit. The porter's replacement

got drunk on "spirits" stocked for soldiers. In the last days of the war, more than two hundred soldiers came seeking help.

Alexander Townes, who had walked all the way from Appomattox, announced the surrender of Robert E. Lee to the town just three days after the Army of Northern Virginia laid down their guns. On May 1, the town had its only taste of war. Stoneman's Raiders, a federal cavalry troop searching for Jefferson Davis, his Cabinet, and the Confederate treasury, rode down the Buncombe Road to Greenville. They stripped the Rest Home of whatever had been left after the move, confiscated horses and guns, found $30,000 in gold specie sent from the Bank of South Carolina in Charleston that Hamlin Beattie, their Greenville agent, hid in the cellar of his dry goods store. They rifled through warehouses of the Greenville and Columbia Railroad, emptying cases of wine into Augusta Street, then set fire to Wesley Brooks' home on Augusta Road before moving on toward Abbeville. Two men, one of whom was drunk, were killed.

Greenville had been distant from both battlefields and the destruction brought by Sherman's march, so it was in better shape than the Midlands and Lowcountry. (In mid-May, local citizens got together a wagonload of supplies to send to Columbia, where people were desperate for food and clothing.) After Lee's surrender, civil authority vanished. Governor Andrew McGrath was imprisoned; law and order collapsed.

Bushwackers (Confederate desperados) and renegade federal soldiers terrorized the area. Torrential rains, Sherman's men, and Confederate troops had destroyed Greenville's railroad access to Columbia in late January, when Greenville & Columbia Railroad tracks were torn up south of Abbeville and railroad bridges destroyed. Almost no mail came through for several months, and no goods were available in local stores. It wasn't until the late summer of 1865, when Frank Porcher, who had refugeed in Greenville, borrowed $200, drove a wagon to Charleston, loaded it with "coffee, herring, soap, dry goods, [and] two dozen round hats trimmed with deep blue and magenta," and set up a stand in Court Square. He was sold out within a few hours. Train service to Columbia was not restarted until September 1866.

Late in May, US Commanding General Quincy Gilmore divided South Carolina into two military districts. Western South Carolina Subdistrict One included Anderson, Pickens, and Greenville Districts. Gilmore stationed garrisons in every district. Col. Charles Trowbridge, commanding Company A of the Thirty-third US Colored Troops (USCT), settled into subdistrict headquarters in Anderson, where lawlessness was a particular problem. In early June, seventy-five of his soldiers arrived in Greenville and moved into the Goodlett Hotel.

On June 30, President Andrew Johnson appointed Greenville lawyer and Unionist Benjamin Perry the state's provisional governor. Perry immediately called for white citizens to take the oath of allegiance to the federal government. He also called for a constitutional convention that fall to ratify the Thirteenth Amendment. Only eight hundred fifty Greenvillians voted on delegates to the convention, as most eligible voters had not yet taken the oath. The Greenville delegation were all former Unionists: T. C. Bolling; James Petigru Boyce; Dr. J. P. Latimer; and William Hayne Perry, Perry's son and private secretary.

To white residents, the uniformed and armed Black soldiers represented the complete destruction of the social order, while to freedmen they were an inspiration and example. They were reasonably well accepted. A. V. Huff notes that several attended the Methodist Church one Sunday, and quotes from a July letter by Louisa Porcher, saying that "the Yankee garrison are here & although it is galling in the extreme to see them, yet they are very quiet and orderly & they put down the complaints of the Negroes in a very summary manner." A student at the Greenville Female College recalled years later that the "Yankees made themselves disagreeable in many ways, but they did nothing to interfere with our school attendance or commencement exercises."

However, racial violence in Edgefield, Chester, and Newberry, as well as the resistance of most whites to the "colored" troops, led

The Thirty-third USCT had its origins in the First South Carolina Volunteer Infantry, one of the first full regiments of Black soldiers that were mustered into US Army service in November 1862. Dress parade of the First South Carolina Infantry (later the Thirty-third USCT) in Beaufort, SC. Library of Congress, Prints and Photographs Division.

Governor Perry to plead with President Johnson and General Gilmore to withdraw them from the interior of the state and station them along the coast. The officials agreed. The USCT soldiers left Greenville about September 1. The federal presence continued, however, in the form of a provost marshal, responsible for legal issues and recording oaths of allegiance. After March 1866, the local Freedman's Bureau (technically the Bureau of Refugees, Freedmen, and Abandoned Lands) assisted former slaves and starving whites and adjudicated some Black-white issues.

The Constitutional Convention delegates, meeting in Columbia, quickly repealed the

Ordinance of Secession and abolished slavery. "But," Perry said, "This is a white man's government." His statement enraged the North, as did his support of a Black Code to govern freedmen's lives that was little better than bondage. In October, Greenvillians once again went to the polls to elect a governor. James Orr of Anderson was elected, and George Townes, Alexander Townes's father, became state senator. Perry was elected US senator by the legislature. (America did not yet have direct election of senators.)

In the fall of 1866, John William De Forest, a writer and Connecticut native, was appointed the major in charge of the Greenville's Freedmen's Bureau. He described Greenville in an article for *Harper's Weekly*, as "the third town in South Carolina, ranking next after Charleston and Columbia. It boasted an old and a new courthouse, four churches and several chapels, a university (not the largest in the world), a female college (also not unparalleled), two or three blocks of stores, one of the best country hotels in the South, quite a number of comfortable private residences, fifteen hundred whites and a thousand or so of other colors." It was, he went on to say, "an upland region, a country of corn rather than of cotton, cultivated by small farmers and middling planters. Its poverty derived from the leanness of the soil, the imperfection of agriculture, the loss of hundreds of young men in battle, the exhaustion of stock and capital during the war, the lack of

intelligent and zealous labor, and the thriftless habits incident of slavery."

Radical Republicans in Congress were unhappy about the direction and pace of change in the South as well as angered by Perry's comments. In March 1867, they passed their own Reconstruction bill over the President's veto, and they refused to seat Perry and other Southern senators. New state governments were suspended, and Southern states were divided into military districts. New constitutional conventions were called that gave freedmen the right to vote, and whites who had held office before the war and who had supported the Confederacy were disenfranchised.

A South Carolina Union Republican party was formed. Among its leaders were two Greenvillians, James M. Allen, who had come to town in 1860 and who was considered a northern "carpetbagger," and Wilson Cooke, a "very genteel mulatto" who had been enslaved by Vardry McBee. They both played important roles in Greenville politics in the next few years. Allen, a stone carver, became state senator. He was later indicted for construction fraud and fled from the state in 1872. Cooke continued to play a political role in the town for fifteen years. He was a remarkable man.

He had come to Greenville with Vardry McBee in the late 1830s. McBee had evidently planned to free him and set him up in business as a barber, but the Town Council, following laws that forbade the rental of property to slaves, refused to allow him to do so. As a result, Cooke worked as a barber in a shop owned by McBee but retained the profits—about $1,500—for himself. When Malinda McBee became his owner in 1860, she allowed him to marry a free woman from Charleston whose father had also been white and who was a successful mantua (cloak) maker. Because enslaved people could not own property, Alexander McBee purchased a lot on West Coffee Street "as trustee and friend of Wilson and Margaret Magdalena Cook." (The final "e" appears and disappears in the public record.) After the war, he transferred the property to them.

Although he had been unable to obtain freedom, when emancipation came, Cooke had cash to begin his new life as a freedman and skills to earn an income. J. W. De Forest described him as "the most notable colored man in the district, a person of remarkable intellect, information, and high character." By 1870, Cooke owned a general merchandise store, a tannery, and considerable property. The census that year listed "the genteel mulatto's" wealth at $5,000. It had climbed to $6,000 by 1876, and in 1881, Cooke paid $2,300 in property taxes and was the most affluent Black taxpayer in the county. He was wealthy enough to send his son, William Wilson Cooke, to Voorhees College and then to study architecture at Columbia University and Massachusetts Institute

of Technology (MIT). He was also politically influential. When South Carolina's Republican Party formed in 1867, he was the only Black among Greenville's three-man delegation to the Columbia meeting at which it was organized, and he was appointed a member of the new party's Central Committee.

That summer, the most controversial political issue in the state was another proposed Constitutional Convention, opposed by conservative white Democrats. In October 1867, Cooke spoke in support of the party and revising the constitution at a Republican-sponsored meeting to register new voters. The *Greenville Enterprise* reported that he "avowed himself a Republican, with kind feelings for all, white and colored; advised all who voted, to vote for the best man, even if such were a former master." That constitution established public education for all children and allowed women to hold property and sue for divorce (a right previously restricted to men). It also provided for universal male suffrage and changed the state's local organization from "districts" to "counties." In November 1868, Wilson Cooke became the first Black man to represent Greenville in the state legislature. It would be more than a hundred years later before the second (Theo Mitchell in 1974) would be elected. He was "a quiet but efficient member," who voted to ratify the new constitution and to charter Greenville as a city. His efficiency, however, could not overcome the increasingly bitter and racially divided political climate two years later.

In 1868, Republicans won all positions in the new legislature from Greenville, but Democrats eked out local victories. The next year, Republicans split into two factions, Regular Republicans and Union Republicans, whose platform included shared power with white Democrats. As result, the vote split so that Allen, a Regular Republican, was elected to the senate from Greenville, but a reform ticket of white Democrats was elected to the house, and Cooke was defeated. In 1872, Democrat T. Q. Donaldson was elected state senator: political Reconstruction was over in Greenville.

Poverty gripped the city in the years immediately after the war. Newspapers were full of foreclosure notices; once wealthy men were bankrupt. Peter Cauble, one of the town's most substantial citizens before the war, was "insolvent" by 1870. George Townes sold his comfortable home. James Clement Furman advertised Green Farm, now Cherrydale Alumni House at Furman, for sale. Many Greenvillians emigrated to find a better life. Waddy Thompson Jr. sold nine hundred acres on Paris Mountain and moved to Florida. The son-in-law of Senator T. Edwin Ware declared bankruptcy and moved to Mississippi. The Female College was so deeply in debt that Furman's trustees, who owned the school, feared for the university's solvency and decided to sell off seventeen of its twenty-two acres, leaving the college with a five-acre campus.

Some of the land sales went to freedmen who were trained as artisans and had a regular income. When Dorcas Green's thousand or so acres were auctioned off at Court Square, seven Black men became the owners of what would later be called Nickeltown. John Buckner had been enslaved to Thomas Gower before the war and had been a painter at the coach factory; his wife was "mammy" to Gower's children. He had the funds to purchase three acres of land off Stone Avenue; other Coach Factory employees bought land nearby in what was soon called Bucknertown. (It became Viola Street in 1945.) Brutontown formed around the blacksmith shop of Benjamin Bruton at the corner of Rutherford Road and Paris Mountain Road. Freetown, settled first by squatters, formed west of the river near the Easley Bridge Road during the first years of Reconstruction.

At about the same time, the Ku Klux Klan came to Greenville. In March 1868, the *Southern Enterprise* said that it was "something new" that was "striking terror into the Loyal Legions. Its object is announced to be Conservative and hostile to extreme Radicalism." The editor went on to say that he "would not be surprised if the 'Ku Klux Klan' has a great run." "Extreme Radicalism" referred to the "Radical Republicans" in Congress who pushed for a punitive Reconstruction; its "Loyal Legions" were the Blacks, carpetbaggers, and Southern whites who voted the Republican ticket. In Spartanburg, Union, and Newberry Counties, the Klan flourished, but no evidence was presented about its activities in Greenville when federal hearings were held in South Carolina in July 1871. It was one of the few Upstate counties where, as a result of the hearings, President U. S. Grant did not suspend habeas corpus laws.

Many Blacks left the county. Its population grew only 1.7% between 1860 and 1870, from 21,892 to 22,262, while the Black population declined by 1.7%. Droughts in 1865 and 1866 hurt, but the primary problem was the total lack of cash. Confederate dollars and bonds were worthless. Assets, which had included both land and enslaved people, no longer had cash value; farmland lay fallow. The old order had changed. The Freedmen's Bureau had been established to deal with refugees, freedmen, and property, but John De Forest had many other problems as well. Among his responsibilities was negotiating labor contracts with new freedmen that soon turned into a tenant farming system. He also dealt with Black complaints against whites, which De Forest and his successors had little power beyond persuasion to adjudicate and which he generally left to local courts. He had a high opinion of local judges. He wrote that "New York City would be fortunate if it could have justice dealt out as honestly and fairly as it was dealt out by the plain, homespun farmers

who filled the squire arches [*sic*] of Greenville, Pickens, and Anderson."

Among the Bureau's major responsibilities was creating schools. Greenville's first one for formerly enslaved people was begun by Charles Hopkins, a Black man from the Lowcountry. He first taught classes in the Goodlet House on Main Street. Then he had a wooden warehouse from the Green Avenue armory moved to Laurens Street to become a school. By 1868, four hundred thirty students were enrolled. In 1869, the schoolhouse was moved again, this time to Elford Street on land that later became a part of Springwood Cemetery. It was renamed the Allen School, in honor of Senator James M. Allen, the New York carpetbagger. On October 20, 1869, the *Enterprise and Mountaineer* (the papers had merged) noted that two acres of land at the northeast corner of Springwood Cemetery "adjoining the Colored School" had been "appropriated to the burials of colored persons." Greenville's first public school became a part of the new state system, although most funding continued to come from the Northern Methodist church.

Education for white children had nearly ceased. For two years, the Peabody fund, established by northern philanthropist George Peabody to educate Southern white children, helped fund a primary school for boys and girls in the old Male Academy building on the Women's College grounds, a female school in the college, and a school for boys at the former Gaillard School in the West End. By 1870, however, Basil Manly commented that all the schools were dead or dying.

Black men and women also started their own churches. Black members of the Methodist Church were the first to separate. Under the leadership of James Rosemond, a Black lay preacher before the war, and with the help of funding from the Northern Methodist Episcopal Church, they purchased a lot for a church in 1866. They worshipped at Allen School while their church, Silver Hill Methodist Episcopal, was being constructed. Rosemond would later begin thirteen other Upstate congregations. Black Baptists followed. (In the county near Taylors, a white minister had established a Black Baptist congregation, Jubilee Church, before the war's end.) In 1868, sixty-five freedmen led by Gabriel Poole requested dismissal from the Greenville Baptist Church to begin their own congregation. Initially, they met in the church's basement, but by 1871, they had their first service at Springfield Baptist Church on East McBee Avenue. Matton Presbyterian was organized in 1878 and Allen Temple African Methodist Episcopal (AME) Church in 1879.

The last new church to be established during Reconstruction was Roman Catholic. Greenville, like most of the rest of the Upstate, was virulently "anti-papist." During the Civil War, city officials had refused to allow a Catholic priest to hold Mass in the courthouse, and children had thrown stones at worshippers who held services in McBee Hall. The *Enterprise* commented in 1870 that "Whilst we regard Romanism . . . as having been a great curse to mankind by its perversion of the plain and simple teachings of Christ, its intolerance to Jew and Gentile Protestant Christians, and all who do not bow to the infallible Pope, we have no unkind feeling or want of respect for sincere individuals of that faith, be they bishops, priest, monk or layman." By 1875, local attitudes, ever pragmatic where business was concerned, had changed, at least among community leaders. The town desperately needed (white) immigration. A Catholic church, leaders thought, would encourage settlers to choose Greenville. As a result, the community responded with "alacrity and generosity" when "two Protestant gentlemen of great respectability" (one was Vardry E. McBee) set out to raise funds for a Catholic church. In two days, they collected $2,000. McBee also donated a lot at the northeast corner of Hampton and Lloyd Streets for a Catholic church, as his father had for the Protestant ones. On October 15, 1876, Bishop Lynch dedicated the two-hundred-thirty-seat church to Our Lady of the Sacred Heart of Jesus. (By 1885, it had become St. Mary's.) According to the *Enterprise and Mountaineer*, its two services that morning were filled with "Catholics, Baptists, Presbyterians,

St. Mary's Catholic Church. The original section was built in 1903 and replaced an earlier sanctuary first dedicated in 1876. It was later enlarged in subsequent building campaigns. Greenville County Library System, South Carolina Room Archive. Postcard Collection.

Episcopalians, and Nothings." It was, said Father O'Connell, "a great day for Greenville."

Another great day came when a bridge finally spanned the Reedy at Main Street. In 1870, Thomas Gower ran for mayor on the single issue of building it. (His opponent argued that if God had wanted a bridge there, He wouldn't have created a shallow ford). Residents may have called the town "Slowhole," but the bridge, a second railroad, and a bank helped lure the first downtown cotton mill to Greenville and start its recovery. The Charlotte to Atlanta Airline, with direct connections to the north, was the most important. Residents voted overwhelmingly (1,618 "for" vs. 324 "against") for the bond issue of $200,000 that funded local construction, with the condition that the railroad would pass

through the municipal limits of the city. It just barely did so. The railroad company built a small wooden passenger depot and a larger freight one along the tracks on John Westfield's farmland exactly a mile from the Courthouse. Westfield, who had just purchased about eleven hundred acres from the McBee estate, then extended Washington Street from Richardson Street to the depot. It soon became the most fashionable address in town. The railroad merged with others over time, becoming the Richmond & Danville and the Piedmont Airline before it became a part of the Southern Railway System in 1894. As it made its way south from Charlotte, it established depots—and future towns—on Manning Greer's farm and Alfred Taylor's property in eastern Greenville County.

In 1873, O. H. Sampson and George Hall of Boston came south on the Charlotte to Atlanta Airline searching for a cotton mill site. They found it in a grist mill owned by the McBee heirs on the Reedy, just east of Main Street. After shipping spindles from Boston, Sampson, Hall & Co., began turning out cheap cotton thread. Within three years, they were doing so well that they leased a far larger sawmill across the river and expanded it dramatically. In 1876, they opened Camperdown Mill Number Two there, and the original factory became Camperdown Number One. (The "Camperdown" name evidently referred to a highly successful woolen mill in Scotland.) With a boarding house and "tenements" for mill workers, the city's population tripled between 1870 and 1876.

Although Sampson and Hall had cash from a Boston insurance settlement, their mills succeeded because the National Bank offered financing for expansion. In 1872, dry goods merchant Hamlin Beattie, one of the town's few solvent citizens, had received a charter for the state's first national bank. (Its charter, granted in January, beat out the South Carolina National Bank by six months.) Beattie had the assistance of South Carolina's senators as well as wealthy board members. Early in 1873, Beattie moved the operation into the new two-story brick "Cleveland Range" near the corner of Main and Avenue Streets ("Avenue" became "McBee" in 1882). Besides "elegant furnishings," it boasted "one of Hall's burglar-proof chests with the latest triumph of American genius, the time lock." It was the only bank in Greenville until 1885.

By 1876, cotton was prince, if not yet king, in Greenville County, thanks to newly discovered phosphate fertilizer. The first bales were shipped out in 1869. Both the Camperdown Mill and Henry Hammet's Piedmont Mill, some twenty miles west, began producing sheeting. Thomas Gower had started a mule-driven street railway, transporting both people and freight from the Airline Depot on Washington Street to the Greenville and Columbia terminus on Augusta Street, but

Camperdown Mill as viewed from above the falls, ca. 1908. From the Camperdown Historical Society Collection, Greenville County Library System.

even with this business activity, about the only newspaper advertisements in the new paper, the *Greenville Daily News*, were for attorneys, bankruptcy sales, and fertilizer.

In August 1876, South Carolina's revered war hero (and largest antebellum owner of enslaved people in the South) General Wade Hampton finally agreed to serve his "prostrate state" and run as the Democratic candidate for governor. Political heat, already intense, rose to fever pitch. Hampton's candidacy led to massive intimidation of Black voters and deaths at Cainhoy, Ellenton, and Marion. Soldiers from Greenville's federal garrison were sent to Laurens and Blackville to maintain order and protect Black citizens; in October, the newspaper reported that twelve thousand federal troops, one-third of the army, were coming to South Carolina. The actual number was twelve

Wade Hampton III, depicted around the time that he became governor of South Carolina in 1877. Library of Congress, Prints and Photographs Division.

hundred, but that was bad enough for Democrats. "Hampton and Home Rule" became the Democrats' motto; "waving the bloody shirt" (remembering the Civil War) was their campaign strategy.

Hampton campaigned in Greenville in September. After a parade and fireworks, he spoke to thousands of people, both white and Black, on the grounds of Furman University. November 7 was Election Day. City voters, standing outside, cast their ballots into a box inside the northeast window of the Record Building, as

three election commissioners, two Republicans and a Democrat, and challengers from each party looked on. By 3 P.M., most ballots had been deposited, but a huge crowd—about two thousand people—lingered around the building, "entertaining themselves by reading genuine and bogus telegrams" reporting on returns from nearby cities.

After a "rumpus" involving two Black voters, soldiers from the garrison were summoned to keep order. There was, the newspaper reported, less intoxication than usual, and after the polls closed and the votes were counted, more jubilation. The city had delivered nine hundred sixty-four votes for Hampton and eight hundred twenty-six for Chamberlain. The county voted Democratic by a twenty-five-hundred-vote majority—but the outcome of the election of 1876 was still in doubt.

While the national decision between Rutherford B. Hayes and Samuel Tilden occupied the rest of the country, South Carolinians were far more concerned about whether incumbent Republican Daniel Chamberlain or Democratic challenger Wade Hampton would be their next governor. It wasn't until spring that politicians made a deal: South Carolina electors cast their ballots for Republican Hays, turning the vote in his favor. Federal troops were withdrawn from the state. When Hampton became governor, Reconstruction in South Carolina was over.

Chapter 7

JOINING THE NEW SOUTH,
1878–1900

The election of Wade Hampton and the end of federal Reconstruction triggered a wave of Greenville building. The mansions built at the end of the 1870s were not the columned colonial plantation homes of the antebellum years; they were Gilded Age modern—with Mansard roofs, bay windows, and towers that boasted wealth. William Wilkins erected his on Augusta Road, Charles Lanneau built a fine home on what became Belmont Avenue, Benjamin Perry moved into elegant Sans Souci near the Buncombe Road—and Greenville constructed a city hall.

It was not a distinguished structure. In 1873, aldermen had purchased a site at the northeast corner of West McBee Avenue and Laurens Street from the McBee family, but it took six years—until February 1879—to erect a small,

two-story, brick building there. Mayor Samuel Townes, whose municipal budget derived almost entirely from taxes on saloons and billiard parlors, had finally gathered sufficient cash to construct a town hall appropriate "to a city of Greenville's wealth and importance." (Its population then topped six thousand.)

By the 1880s, that population was divided by the Reedy River into the East End, the original downtown, and the growing West End. Linking them was the wooden Gower Bridge. It had so much wear from farm wagons, coaches, and carriages that, in 1891, it was replaced by an iron bridge, the latest technology. (The wooden one was moved to River Street.) Those bridges stimulated business around the West End intersection of River, Main, Pendleton, and Augusta Streets near the Furman campus and provided more convenient access to the elegant homes along Pendleton, River, and Augusta Streets.

But there was conflict. After schools for both East and West Ends were built in the late 1880s, their students battled daily. Stones and snowballs caused so many injuries that the schools had to have staggered closing hours. The rivalry between the two parts of town was so strong in the late 1890s that West End residents briefly considered incorporating. Residents argued that, although the west side of the river had a smaller population, it had several blocks of brick stores, a large cotton seed oil factory on the depot green, several cotton warehouses and an ice mill, not to mention Furman. It also boasted of churches (St. Paul's Methodist, Second Presbyterian, Pendleton Street Baptist, and St. Andrews Episcopal), as well as a bank.

The American Bank at the "smoothing iron" intersection of Pendleton and Augusta Streets had been established in 1890 by three West End businessmen. Capitalized at $75,000, it was substantially smaller than the National Bank and Peoples Bank in downtown Greenville, but it was set up to serve the brisk West End cotton trade and neighborhood residents.

Both sections of the city were part of New South Greenville. Atlanta *Constitution* editor Henry Grady proclaimed in 1880 that the future of the South was industrialized, modern,

entrepreneurial—he didn't say "Yankee"—and rigidly based on white supremacy. Those modern innovations—telephone, running water, electricity, public education—as well as the entrepreneurs who made them possible, came to Greenville during the next twenty years.

The telephone was first. In 1882, Thomas Gower, who, according to the *Greenville News*, was "largely instrumental" in the deal, made extravagant promises, including fifty subscribers within a year, to induce the Southern Bell Telephone Company to set up a switchboard in the city. Furthermore, Gower offered a one-room office above Gower & Reilly's livery stable on Laurens Street and provided the system manager, his son, Arthur Gower. On May 16, 1882, the switchboard opened with sixteen subscribers.

There was no long-distance service (phone lines served only the city of Greenville), the wooden telephones had to be cranked, and all service went through an operator. Calling, however, was easy. Number one was Southern Bell, two was the Greenville National Bank, and three was for Lipscomb and Russell wholesale groceries. Of those first sixteen subscribers, only two were residential: the pioneer home-phoners were Ellison Smyth and Jeff M. Richardson of the *Greenville Daily News*.

The newfangled boy-toy (most women refused to use it until well after the turn of the century) was soon accepted by businesses, especially local mills. Henry Hammett paid to extend the line to Piedmont in 1883; by 1890, a line reached Batesville and Pelham Mills. In 1885, when the company had finally grown to the promised fifty subscribers, it moved out of its manure-scented headquarters and reestablished itself on the third floor of a building at Washington and Main Street above Capen's Cigar Store. The aroma must have been nicer. These subscribers paid an outrageous $50 a year for service. Telephones were clearly for the rich. In the same year, Southern Bell hired its first "lady operator," because customers complained that male operators were rude.

Running water arrived in 1887. Grocers Ferguson & Miller became locally famous because they installed pipes from their "Gaol Spring" on Spring Street and pumped its water to a tank on the roof of their new building on the corner of Main and Washington Street. Within a few months, they were supplying the Mansion House and a Main Street fire hydrant. Greenvillians loved the innovation. Within a year, a City Council committee negotiated with the American Piping Company of Philadelphia to lay pipes from Paris Mountain to supply the city with water. That arrangement lasted until 1918, when the private system was purchased by the city. Water lines required sewers. Although many Greenvillians did not tie into the relatively expensive water and sewer connections, established in 1892, sewer pipes were installed to empty the untreated sewage into the Reedy River.

Electric lights took a bit more time. In 1875, the city contracted with Reuben Asbury to operate the city's gaslight system. On September 4 of that year, the Enterprise and Mountaineer joyfully reported that "the bright lights burned brilliantly from one end of the city to the other."

An 1884 advertisement for the Huguenot Mill boasted of producing "plaid cloth under electric light," and the Mansion House bragged in the 1888 City Directory that it had electric lights, electric call bells, and fire alarms in every room. (These buildings had individual generators.) Furthermore, Columbia had just electrified its street lighting. So the City Council went into the illumination business, using a coal-fired, steam-powered engine to power generators and erecting a powerhouse on Broad Street to house the machinery. That 1888 powerhouse still stands.

The city's foray into utility ownership was brief; in 1890, officials sold the franchise to R. R. Asbury and his son, who formed the Greenville Gas, Electric Light, and Power Company. They agreed to supply "Moon Schedule" electricity to forty electric lights for fifteen years at a cost of $100 per light a year. When there was a full moon, the lights were not turned on, but if clouds hid the moon, the chief of police notified Asbury and Son, and the company had

The Greenville Gas and Electric Light, and Power Company complex was built ca. 1890 and is one of the few remaining Victorian structures in downtown Greenville. Photo by Bill Fitzpatrick.

an hour to light up the town. Although lighting dark streets was initially the main public use of electricity, in 1898, George Bunting purchased the Asburys' power franchise and began planning an electric trolley system. The Greenville Traction Company ran its first streetcar on January 12, 1901. Four years later, the "beltline trolley" connected every mill village with downtown. Power poles and electric lines joined telephone wires to create a steel web above Main Street.

Three entrepreneurs began innovative businesses in the 1880s. Jeremiah Harris, who had taught all the science classes at Furman, began a cotton seed oil and fertilizer plant on Depot Green in the West End in 1882. It was the first one in South. Initially, it just pressed

cotton seed to make cooking oil. Then chemists realized that, after the first pressing for oil, if the seeds were even more tightly compressed, three pounds would yield a one pound "cake," which could then be further ground into meal to be used for fertilizer that was especially good for tobacco plants and cotton and also be used for cattle feed. Harris discovered that the hulls could then be used for fuel. According to the *Richmond Times-Dispatch* at the time of Harris's death in 1919, "his discoveries of the value of hulls added millions to the wealth of the South."

Charles Lanneau was another of "our enterprising men." He had learned the cotton mill business at the Reedy River Factory and Camperdown Mill, and with wealthy attorney T. Q. Donaldson as president, he started the

Huguenot Mill in February 1882. Backed by some of the wealthiest men in Greenville, it took just four months to construct the two-story, one-hundred-fifty-foot-long building and adjoining dye house and to secure the "newest and most improved" machinery from Philadelphia. The Huguenot Mill used electric lights so that its forty "operatives" could see to match the plaids in the cloth they were weaving. Workers' housing—a dozen six-room houses hardly qualify as a mill village—was immediately adjacent to the mill on Broad Street and along the east side of Jackson Alley, the site today of the Peace Center. Yet even with the support of Greenville's wealthiest residents, the mill struggled to survive, and it closed for several years after the panic of 1893. At the end of the decade, it was sold to two North Carolina cotton men who operated it for several years before selling to Alan Graham, who also bought the Camperdown Mill.

John Marshall made money in ice, a necessity in Southern summers. Greenville was expanding and modernizing, and he expanded and modernized along with it. The ice factory, which only employed two men initially, was located on the north bank of the Reedy River. By 1898, the "ice mill" was producing ten tons of ice a day. Four years later, production had increased to twenty-five tons. In 1908, it was forty tons. He sold the operation in 1909 for $60,000 (about $1.5 million today).

Huguenot Mill, ca. 1895. Greenville County Library System, South Carolina Room Archives.

Public education was another beneficiary of New South (or at least "New Greenville") thinking. By 1884, both the white school (Thompson School, named for Hugh Thompson, a former schoolmaster and then state superintendent of education) and the Black school (the Allen School) enrolled more than three hundred pupils and met for ten months, an innovation because most county schools, which were a part of the state system, offered only four or five months of instruction.

Support for taxes and bond issues for public education was stirring throughout the state, but in Greenville, it took a shove from Maine native Thomas Gower. After a public meeting in support of education in 1885, Gower and others petitioned the legislature for the right to tax for schools. The General Assembly said no because so many prominent Greenvillians objected. Gower kept pushing.

Elected president of the school board, he spent his own money to buy a central school site. Then Columbia established city schools. That decision helped change local minds. Finally, in 1887, Gowerand—public education—won when, after legislative approval, Greenvillians approved a bond issue of $18,000 for school buildings. Construction began immediately on Central School on Westfield Street, adjacent to Lemuel Alston's old Prospect Hill mansion. The West End School—later called Oaklawn—was constructed on Pendleton Street near Perry Street. It opened about 1889. The Allen School on Elford Street became the East End Colored School, and a West End school for Black youngsters was established in the Gaillard Building, owned by Allen Temple AME Church, before construction started on Union School on Markley Street in 1890.

While public schools were beginning to serve the city's children, Furman and the Female College struggled. Furman's situation was awkward. The university had been established in part to train Baptist ministers, but when the Southern Baptist Seminary was established in 1859, taking nearly half of the university's endowment, Baptists throughout the state supported the "dearly loved" seminary with far more vigor than they did their liberal arts college. The rest of the school's endowment went to the Confederate cause. The university could not afford to print a catalogue when it

reopened in 1866, and by 1872, it had only forty-five students and owed faculty members $4,000 in salaries. The Seminary moved to Louisville in 1876, taking its eminent scholars and students.

Then Furman's president, James Clement Furman, and Charles Judson, its treasurer, who was also president and proprietor of the Female College, decided to raise $200,000 to make the university tuition-free to white males. This plan was an abysmal failure. The university, bankrupt, closed in June 1880; its five faculty members resigned. After some relatively successful fundraising among Baptists that summer, trustees reopened and reorganized it in the fall, hiring Charles Manly as president. He rehired Furman and Judson, but not the other professors, and worked during the following decade to restore some degree of financial stability to the school.

The financial hardships of the times also reduced the Female College to poverty. It had no library, no laboratory, and only part-time teachers until 1878, when Charles Judson appointed his sister, Mary, the Lady Principal (or dean) of the institution and subleased the school to Alexander Townes. Miss Judson believed that a woman deserved an education equal to a man's. She began instruction in calisthenics so girls could loosen their corsets and become healthier and elocution lessons to give them confidence to speak in public; she started the college library; and she organized the Judson Society, the first women's organization in Greenville. She served as Lady Principal until 1912.

The college was among the first women's colleges in the South to stress physical activity. Dressed in flowing, toga-like garments, the girls swayed to music, swinging banners, wands, and Indian clubs. Without corsets, stays, or bustles, they gained poise and confidence. At commencement each year, the calisthenics class put on a public performance that was considered the highlight of the festivities. Baptist ministers complained that it was dancing, but the school's president, Alexander Townes, queried how a Baptist minister could recognize dancing if he saw it, and for twenty years, Miss Judson's students performed intricate movements to the delight of appreciative audiences. Those exercises even brought a critic from the Charleston paper, who commented, with some slight acerbity, "Greenville is wont to be vainglorious, but it can take honest pride in the institutions in which the rising generations of both sexes may imbibe knowledge with the mountain air."

In 1894, when Alexander Townes was forced out of the college presidency by Furman's trustees, who wanted to tie it more formally to the Baptist Convention, he immediately set up a competing college, the Greenville College for Women, in his adjacent home. Many students and some teachers went with him, and

the Female College faced a crisis. Miss Judson loaned her life savings of $3,000, saved from her salary of $50 a month, to help the school survive.

In addition to Townes's new college for women, a third woman's college opened. In 1893, the Presbyterian Synods of Upstate South Carolina and Western Georgia purchased Alexander McBee's West End farm, "McBee Terrace," on River Street in the West End. McBee's former wheat fields became the college campus. They converted McBee's River Street home into the president's residence, built a central administration building, a "Study Hall" with classrooms, an adjacent dormitory, and a twelve-hundred-seat domed octagonal auditorium. Offering elementary instruction for both boys and girls, high school preparation, and a four-year college curriculum for women, Chicora College (the name meant "Carolina" in Cherokee, the 1897 catalogue explained) was not overrun with students. Three years after its opening, only seventy-eight students were enrolled in its three departments; by 1909, total enrollment had risen to two hundred thirty-five.

Railroads had contributed to the town's prosperity since the first Greenville and Columbia locomotive had chugged into the city in 1853. Greenville was never the hub that Spartanburg was, but in 1886, the coming of the Greenville & Laurens Railroad, soon to be the Charleston and Western Carolina, changed

Railroad cars bearing the "Greenville & Northern" company name. This shortline railroad operated until 1998 and was later converted for use as the Swamp Rabbit Trail. Photo from Marsh Photograph Collection, South Caroliniana Library.

the county and, in later years, the city as well. In 1881, Thomas Gower, lawyer William Earle (representing the Airline Railroad), former Mayor W. L. Mauldin, and three other officials made a visit to Laurens, a cotton county eager for a link to Greenville. Within a year, a railroad was born. Mauldin was president, and he and his colleagues began beating governmental bushes for funding. By 1882, they had city

and county commitments totaling $150,000 and began buying rights-of-way through the countryside. As tracks were laid for the thirty-six-mile stretch from Laurens, they spurred the growth of Fountain Inn and created Simpsonville and Mauldin.

In January 1886, Fountain Inn had three stores, an elementary school, a Baptist church, a graveyard and about a dozen homes. Although the tracks went through the cemetery, forcing two graves to be moved, citizens were so excited that they chartered the town on Christmas Eve 1886 and made the depot agent the mayor. In September, the first Greenville & Laurens locomotive had steamed into the new terminal at East Court Street. By 1888, two cotton platforms, a substantial freight warehouse, and Gower & Reilly's building supplies warehouse were next to the passenger terminal.

A rail link to Knoxville and the West had been a Greenville dream starting in the 1840s, so the Carolina Knoxville & Western was enthusiastically welcomed when it began laying tracks in 1888. Enthusiasm waned when it suffered bankruptcies and the dismantling of its tracks, becoming (in order) the Greenville & Knoxville; the Greenville & Western; and, in 1920, the Greenville & Northern. Unofficially, it was called "the Swamp Rabbit," because its unevenly laid tracks edged the swampy banks of the Reedy River. Fifteen miles long (it never got close to Knoxville), for many years, it was a freight line with excursions to River Falls and flag stops along its "Swamp Rabbit" route. Its office depot was near River Street.

Although New South ideology was distinctly urban, Greenville remained an agricultural center until after the turn of the century. In the 1880s, more than one hundred twenty thousand acres were under cultivation. The county led the state in the production of wheat; cotton, corn, barley, rye, and potatoes flourished. Growers were beginning to ship apples and peaches to statewide markets. But even in agriculture, there was innovation. Townsend Smith, for example, grew rice on twenty-five acres of marshy land along the Reedy near present-day Greenville Country Club. In 1883, according to the *Historical and Descriptive Review of the State of South Carolina*, he sold more than sixteen thousand pounds. Although sugar cane, associated with a far milder climate, did not flourish here, twelve hundred fifty gallons of syrup were produced.

Among other new agricultural products were carp, imported from Germany; grapes, planted by a French winemaker; and Jersey cows for commercial dairies. H. C. Markley, the owner of the Coach Factory, was as interested in farming as in turning out sturdy farm carts and planters' buggies. He had an orchard and vineyard on Paris Mountain and had developed five spacious carp pools near Lowndes Hill to breed goldfish for both food and decoration.

By 1884, there were five vineyards in and around the city. The largest, with one hundred acres, had been planted with grapes for wine-making by an enterprising Frenchman who spent $20,000 beginning a vineyard in the Tanglewood section because, he said, Greenville's soil and climate were so well adapted to wine production. Agricultural innovator Hugh Buist planted grapevines and fruit trees on the east side of Rutherford Road. In town, Dr. S. S. Marshall had a ten-acre vineyard on his property behind the Female College near Buncombe Road, and the Garraux family had terraced vineyards off North Main Street. Two years of late frosts ruined crops, however, and by the early 1890s, the vine growers had given up.

The first commercial dairies opened in 1880. One owned by Wash Howell was located on an extensive pasture on the south side of Spartanburg Road about three miles from Greenville. Howell's milk wagon delivered raw milk, buttermilk, and butter to the east side of town and had a reputation for square and honest dealings. Across town on the Augusta Road, O. P. Mills and New Yorker James Walker established a three-hundred-twenty-five-acre dairy, Millsdale, with prize-winning Jersey cows that produced rich cream and butter in the most sanitary conditions. In addition, more than eleven thousand sheep and lambs gamboled on the slopes of Paris Mountain, and Greenville-bred mutton became renowned (locally, at least) for its tastiness.

The overwhelming political issues of Green-ville's Gilded Age were prohibition and Black voting rights. Baptist and Methodist churches had supported temperance before the war, and that support increased when the Wom-en's Christian Temperance Union (WCTU) opened a reading room in 1884. In 1880, responding to a statewide referendum, the state legislature banned the sale of liquor outside of cities. A year later, in a closely watched "hot municipal election," Greenville city voted wet, but dry votes were increasing.

After 1880, women and Evangelical Chris-tians (Lutherans, Episcopalians, Catholics and Jews remained uninvolved) were supported in their anti-liquor campaign by textile mill owners such as Ellison Smyth, who wanted a sober and reliable workforce. At the same time, however, "moonshine," untaxed corn liquor, was being distilled in great quantities in the hollows and hidden valleys of northern Green-ville County. It became one of the few sources of profit for former subsistence farmers who had difficulty eking out a living from the tired soil of the Dark Corner. From all accounts, it flowed easily into thirsty city throats.

The prohibition question was complicated by finances and racism. About eighty percent of the city's budget derived from liquor stores and the seventeen Main Street saloons. Aldermen saw no way to replace those funds. Prohibition wasn't a specifically partisan issue—neither wets nor drys were consistently Democrats or Republicans—but some white political leaders worried that the issue might give Black voters political power, because it was their votes that gave wets the edge.

In 1892, Greenville, together with the rest of the state (except Charleston) voted in favor of prohibition. However, Governor Benjamin Tillman, worried that the government couldn't operate without liquor taxes, ignored the refer-endum, and instead initiated "the Dispensary System," which gave the state a total monopoly on alcohol sales. Special "liquor constables," most untrained but eager prohibitionists, were hired to enforce it. One result was "blind tigers." While selling liquor was illegal, giving it away was not. Saloons promoted "performanc-es" of (imaginary) blind tigers with entrance fees and then served alcohol to patrons who were "waiting" for the performance.

The liquor constables, arrogant in their power, tangled with local citizens in Darlington in an incident that led to three deaths. Tillman called out the state militia to stop a somewhat exaggerated rebellion. (The young men in Greenville's Butler's Guard, who were among those summoned to put down the "insurrec-tion," reportedly had a swell time.) In Green-ville, the system led to a standoff between Sher-iff P. D. Gilbreath and the liquor constables who threatened to search a Main Street home for hidden liquor. A crowd of pistol-toting residents protested the search, and the sheriff refused to enforce the search warrant. The constables and the governor finally backed down.

It wasn't until the election of Greenvillian Martin Ansel in 1906 that the state monopoly was replaced by local options. Greenville and thirty-five other counties, all in the "dusty Piedmont," were dry by 1909. (A county's vote was generally determined by its number of Baptists and Methodists and its distance from "wringing, sopping, dripping wet" Charleston.)

Prohibition was deeply imbedded in local morality; so were "blue ordinances." In 1875, Greenville's City Council passed its first one. It forbade merchants, shopkeepers, vendors, barrooms, saloons, and barbers from operating on the Lord's Day as well as the "sale, gift or barter of spirituous or malt liquors, wine or cider." It did allow drug stores and apothecaries to remain open, but they couldn't sell wine or liquors except for medicinal purposes. (There were a lot of those.)

But "indigo Sundays" had challenges. The first was baseball. Introduced in the 1870s, it was fun, attracted noisy crowds, and could be (and often was) enjoyed by "lower class elements." Gallons of ink were spilled in explaining the evils of the sport. If baseball was the work of the devil, then what about the new game of golf? Some people defended it, because it was played quietly and out of sight by gentlemen. However, said a *Daily News* editorial

in September 1900, both sports were signs that the South was becoming "Yankeeized." If play kept up, the editorial warned, "We shall soon have no Sabbath at all."

"Yankees" and the federal power associated with them did make one positive physical imprint on the city. In 1889, the federal government agreed to replace the aging and dilapidated wooden post office on the east side of Main Street. They paid $12,000 for a lot at the southwest corner of South Main and Broad Streets and assigned a treasury architect to design a $75,000 structure to include mail-handling functions, a federal courtroom, and offices. James R. Lawrence, an architect and contractor from Wilmington, North Carolina, was hired to supervise its construction. The result was a substantial Romanesque structure costing $11,000 more than the estimate, complete with two battlemented towers, huge deep-set round-headed windows, and an entrance resplendent with terra cotta ornament. Its walls were two feet thick. Although the federal building was three stories tall, had a finished basement and two fourth-floor tower rooms, by 1905, it was too small and was extended.

Maintaining white supremacy was the prime impetus for rewriting South Carolina's constitution in 1895. Post-Reconstruction politicians hated the state's 1868 "Yankee" state constitution, which was based on Ohio's. Greenville's Constitutional Convention delegation included Attorney Harry J. Haynsworth, who served on what A. V. Huff called "the all-important" Committee on Rights and Suffrage, headed by Governor Benjamin Tillman. It was evidently Haynsworth who drafted the legislation for poll tax and property qualifications—$300 in assessed value—for voting. The new constitution, which mandated segregation, became the basis for Jim Crow legislation and practice in South Carolina. It also greatly increased the power of legislative delegations.

Greenville's delegation—indeed, the entire county—supported the war with Spain. Two months after the battleship *Maine* exploded in Havana Harbor in February 1898, war was declared, and President McKinley called for volunteers to fight the Spanish oppressors of Cuba. Greenville responded with alacrity. (David Hackett Fischer points out in *Albion's Seed* that there never has been a war that the South hasn't loved.) On May 4, 1898, "a date," the *News* stated portentously and unprophetically, "that would have a conspicuous place in the history of Greenville," two companies of Greenville volunteers, the Butler Guards and the Greenville Guards, departed from the Southern Railroad Station to join the fray. All schools were dismissed for the day so that students could bid them farewell; young ladies from the Greenville Female College presented flowers to officers; a brass band played. Their first stop was Columbia, where volunteers had

physical examinations. Nearly half failed, but others rushed to take their place. As Companies F and H of the First South Carolina Volunteers, they eventually made their way to Florida's Camp Cuba Libre, where they were still stationed when the war ended four months later. They never got to Cuba.

In the meantime, rumors began to circulate in Greenville that the city was a possible site for a potentially profitable war camp. On June 15, Mayor James Williams, Alderman James Richardson, and business leader Alester G. Furman set out for Columbia to persuade the site selection committee that Greenville would be an ideal location. The committee, they learned, had gone to Augusta to inspect that town's land offer; Greenville's delegation followed by train. By the time they got to Augusta, the site selectors had gone on to Charlotte. The persistent committee followed, and this time they were successful in arranging a meeting.

In September, the army committee visited Greenville; they were impressed with the sites shown them and pleased with the availability of water piped from Paris Mountain. In October, after Williams, Richardson, and Furman met with President William McKinley, the government announced that two brigades, ten thousand men, would be stationed in Greenville. Spartanburg, also vying for a camp, was envious, but Greenville's water supply had been the deciding factor. Local residents were assured that "gentlemen of good social standing whose families would accompany them and no Negro troops" would be sent to the town. Although the conflict in Cuba had ended in August, the United States was still involved there and in the Philippines, and future military action was possible.

Camp Wetherill, named for Capt. Alexander Wetherill, one of the first men killed during the battle for San Juan Hill, was set up on two sites. The First Brigade was stationed on land north of Earle Street, extending from Buncombe Road almost to modern-day Wade Hampton Boulevard. The property, owned by the Stone family, had only one house, Whitehall, which became a nurses' residence. The Second Brigade camped on land south and east of Anderson Street, including acreage that later would be the Dunean Mill village, with brigade headquarters on the Dunbars' farm close to the future location of Greenville General Hospital. They plodded through the mud of the Mills Mill village to get to town.

Those soldiers brought a brief rush of Christmas prosperity to merchants, and for the first time since the Civil War, they opened the small mill town (population, about eleven thousand) to the larger world. Pennsylvania troops arrived during the first week in November to begin construction of wooden mess halls and headquarters buildings; soldiers would be housed in tents. On November 14, the Second

West Virginia regiment arrived, marching up Main Street to the strains of "Dixie." A few days later men of the Fourth Missouri unloaded at College Station near Anderson Street on a "particularly disagreeable day." Then came the well-trained and disciplined Fifth Massachusetts regiment, which marched through town in perfect order during a heavy rainstorm. A New Jersey regiment completed the contingent.

These troops' knowledge of Greenville's climate was nonexistent; assuming that they were coming to the "Sunny South," many had discarded blankets and overcoats issued to them because they anticipated palm trees and balmy temperatures. Instead, they faced one of the coldest winters in Greenville history. (The only one worse was in 1917–18, when World War I Camp Sevier was located here.) Rain, sleet, and snow made life miserable for the troops and created quagmires of red mud along Greenville's notoriously bad unpaved streets.

Greenville jubilantly greeted the men and their money. The Mansion House flew a thirty-foot long US flag, the largest ever seen in the town. With a payroll of $150,000 a month, $120,000 of which was spent in Greenville, merchants were ecstatic; residents, however, complained that Christmas gifts and cards could not be found. But Camp Wetherill brought unexpected problems. A beggar was found dead near Springwood Cemetery, and authorities decided that a soldier was responsible. When the Governor of New Jersey came to town, he reviewed his state's troops on a Sunday afternoon, and several local citizens complained that he had "desecrated the Sabbath." There was, in fact, a good bit of Sabbath desecrating, including camp band concerts on Sunday afternoons, secular entertainment frowned upon by pious Greenvillians.

By early March, it was clear to federal authorities that troops would not be needed, and the soldiers departed, not at all reluctantly, for the North. The weather immediately turned springlike. The two camp sites, cleared of underbrush by the army, became home sites. Real estate developer Alester Furman hired an auctioneer from Charleston and led a brass band down Main Street to the former First Brigade Camp on Earle Street where house lots were auctioned off; in one day, lots worth $15,000—a huge amount for the time—were sold. Black citizens

moved in increasing numbers to the land around the center of the Second Brigade Camp, where Sterling High School would soon be established.

The Spanish-American War was one of the first steps in the United States' becoming a world power; for Greenville, it initiated a new relationship with the nation. It restored Independence Day celebrations, which had ceased with the Civil War. (In 1894, the *News* referred to the Fourth of July as "The Day we do not celebrate.") Southern boys enthusiastically volunteered for active duty and communities throughout the region followed the progress of the conflict with patriotic fervor that spread to observance of the nation's birthday. But the time was also right: the generation that had had directly known civil war, defeat, and Reconstruction was passing away, and the South—or at least, the Greenville portion of it—was ready to claim its place among the United States.

Chapter 8

BUILDING THE TEXTILE CRESCENT,
1895–1915

Greenville District's rivers and streams provided a source of waterpower for early settlers. By the time of the Civil War, mills at Pelham on the Enoree, Bates Manufacturing on Rocky Creek, and McBee's Factory on the Reedy were major sources of woven fabric for the Confederacy. Afterward, Camperdown (1873) and Piedmont (1876) mills helped Greenville recover. Although Piedmont president Henry Hammett noted that a well-run cotton mill could return twenty percent a year on investment, a solid inducement, aside from Huguenot Mill (1884), Greenville businessmen were slow in joining the New South textile surge. Equipment was expensive, ready capital unavailable, cash flow a problem. Huguenot and Camperdown Mills closed for several years after the national recession of 1893, which also made new mill ventures difficult.

In fact, in February 1895, a private railroad train carrying seventeen New England textile executives came to inspect southern cotton mills with an eye for investment. The trip, organized by entrepreneur Daniel Tompkins of Charlotte, visited mills in the North Carolina piedmont and then traveled into South Carolina to see Piedmont, Pelzer, and Pacolet Mills. Lewis Parker invited them to stop in Greenville; they refused, politely. There was nothing to see here.

Sampson Mill, officially American Spinning Company, began Greenville's postbellum textile rush. Oscar Sampson, the Boston selling agent who had organized Camperdown

Mill, started the mill with thirty-five-year-old equipment and about $60,000 in cash. He purchased more than a hundred acres of farmland east of Buncombe Road near the Southern Railway tracks. Needing local backers, he turned to James Orr, Henry Hammett's executor, son-in-law, and successor as head of Piedmont and Camperdown Mills; and to Orr's brother-in-law, James Morgan, a successful local merchant, known as an "energetic, pushing, and high-toned gentleman."

Sampson Mill operations began in September 1895, with Morgan as president. The first mill was a two-story wooden building, a "greenhouse" with huge windows providing natural light on all sides. It was cheap but well-built and lasted into the 1960s. The village housed two hundred fifty men, women, and children. A pasture for their cows was sited nearby.

The second mill to be completed was Poe Manufacturing Company. In 1895, Francis Poe purchased a sixty-acre knoll called "Governor's Hill," adjacent to the American Spinning property. The main line of the Southern Railroad ran nearby, and the White Oak Branch of the Reedy flowed just beyond the tracks. Established to manufacture finer quality goods, Poe Mill was initially regarded as a foolish experiment but proved to be one of Greenville's most profitable mills. F. W. Poe had been the Southern representative of a New York clothing company, so he knew fabrics, and his friends

provided much of the early funding for his company. The site was laid out by twenty-five-year-old J. E. Sirrine in his first assignment for Lockwood, Greene and Co. of Providence, Rhode Island, which built many Southern mills. When it began operating in March 1896, Poe was steam powered and equipped with electric lights.

That April, the Greenville *Enterprise and Mountaineer* enthusiastically applauded the announcement of Otis P. Mills's new cotton factory. One of the "oldest and richest" Greenville entrepreneurs (he was fifty-four), Mills owned more than three hundred acres of land from Augusta Road to Brushy Creek. He had money, land, and a new son-in-law, Walter Moore, who had textile expertise. But while Mills was wealthy, he found mill construction hard going. He had to raise additional funds from the "best and staunchest" Greenville businessmen, convince the Southern Railroad to put in a siding, buy textile machinery, and erect a mill and an adjacent village.

The first brick, fired from clay from the banks of nearby Brushy Creek, was laid in September. Winter rains interrupted construction. The rolling site on the north of the creek became a sea of red clay. When the mill finally began operations in the spring of 1897, its two hundred operatives had no school, no church, and no store. But with the Spanish-American War raging, the mill, even with untrained workers and only five thousand spindles, made money. By 1900, Mills and Moore were ready to expand. They doubled the mill's size, added houses, and commissioned J. E. Sirrine to design a brick YMCA building.

The initial successes of these operations led J. Irving Westervelt to plan for a mill of ten thousand spindles and four hundred looms off the Pendleton Road. That summer, the Brandon community of sixty-six cottages was nearly complete. Construction then began on the mill. The Greenville *Mountaineer* predicted would be "one of the prettiest cotton mill settlements in the state." J. E. Sirrine, who had just completed work on Poe and Abbeville Mills, designed the village. The impressive iron-framed, fire-resistant mill two miles south of downtown Greenville was finished in January 1901. Westervelt raised $220,000 to begin Brandon, and the directors increased its capital to $450,000 and its spindles to forty-one thousand in 1903. Between 1908 and 1909, they added a $1.4 million addition and announced a 100% dividend on original investments.

The surrounding community grew with the mill's expansion. One hundred fifty "operatives" were employed at its opening; by 1907, Brandon employed four hundred twenty men, women, and children (only six under the age of twelve, owners boasted). More than nine hundred people lived in the village. Between 1900 and 1903, four hundred fifty homes were built there.

Brandon Mill village, ca. 1930. From the Brandon Historical Society collection, Greenville County Library System.

Agents from all the mills were sent out to scour the glens and hollows of the Appalachians to find dispossessed farmers and struggling sharecroppers who might be lured to Greenville. When a Brandon Mill agent arrived in Newport, Tennessee, for example, he convinced Jessie Lee Carter's family to move to Greenville. All of the family's possessions were loaded into horse-drawn wagons; a cow was tied to the back of the last one. It took them a week to get to Greenville; immediately after their arrival, her grandfather, father, and uncles went to work at the mill.

The village they moved into had far more "luxuries" than their Tennessee mountain home: space for a large garden and pasture for their cow; an elementary school; a church financed by the mill; electric lighting—one

Brandon Mill Elementary School was built to serve the children of mill operatives who worked in the mill and lived in the surrounding company-owned village. From the Brandon Historical Society collection, Greenville County Library System.

outlet per house—supplied by the company; a bank (by 1907, it had $9,000 in operatives' deposits); a social worker; and, below the first line of mill houses, the field where the great hitter and controversial baseball player "Shoeless" Joe Jackson began his career in 1903. The mill seemed successful, but in 1914, Westervelt had "financial reverses," and Aug W. Smith of Spartanburg was named president of both Brandon and nearby Carolina Mill.

Carolina was an anomaly. It was high above the Reedy River within the city limits, and it was housed in a factory originally constructed to build desks. Located off Birnie Street, its thirteen-acre site was wedged on a bluff near

the tracks of the Southern Railway, convenient for transportation but making expansion to the north impossible. Its capitalization was only $50,000, compared with Brandon's $300,000, and its initial workforce was just eighty men, women, and children.

In 1901, George Norwood, who owned the desk factory, remodeled the facility to spin cotton into yarn and appointed his son, a graduate of the University of Chicago, to be the president. The makeshift operation did well enough to expand and build cotton warehouses along the railroad siding within a few years. Then young Norwood resigned and was replaced by J. Irving Westervelt, who was then profitably running Brandon. In 1907, the mill had thirteen thousand spindles and an annual payroll of $35,000. A church built by management on Birnie Street was also used as a weekday school for the forty-two children living in the village of about two hundred people.

The following year, directors doubled capitalization and began constructing a two-story weaving building west of the older factory. In 1910, however, Westervelt accepted the presidency of a new million-dollar mill on Easley Bridge Road while he tried juggling the finances of Carolina and Brandon. In 1912, the board of directors increased Carolina's capitalization to $600,000 and, in January 1913, purchased sixty-five acres of land across the Southern trestle at Queen Street to expand the mill village. Before

Group portrait of the Brandon Mill baseball team. Ball fields and Mill League baseball games were among the amenities and attractions that mill owners used to convince mill hands to move from the countryside and work in the textile mills. Photo: Clemson University Libraries.

they had a chance to build, however, Westervelt resigned, bankrupt. He had overestimated his ability to manipulate finances and underestimated the cash flow problems that he would face. He lost all three mills. Three years later, Carolina Mills was auctioned off and acquired by a group organized as Poinsett Mills for $205,000.

Union Bleaching and Finishing Company came to Greenville in 1902 with little fanfare. "An Important Enterprise Quietly Incorporated," said the *Greenville Mountaineer*. J. B. Duke and a group of northern investors chose Greenville as the site of the second bleachery in the South because of the county's eleven

Postcard showing Monaghan Mill along with the YMCA building, which was the first industrial YMCA in the South. From the Monaghan Historical Society collection, Greenville County Library System.

"up-to-date" cotton mills, access to Southern Railroad freight lines, and availability of water. They purchased one hundred sixty acres of swampy land bordering Langston Creek on the Buncombe Road. Investing $250,000, directors predicted that initial production would be one hundred thousand yards of cloth daily, and one hundred twenty-five workers, "nearly all grown men," would be hired. Not a cent of Greenville capital was involved. The stock was entirely held by Duke and his New York friends.

But the company's income depended on local mills' using the facility, and their executives had no financial incentive to do so. Business was slow. Men reported for work and, often finding none, would go fishing in the creek until a train delivered a shipment of cloth. Although the wealth of the stockholders,

the *Mountaineer* had boasted, "was almost unbounded," they lost almost their entire investment the first year. The board turned to John White Arrington, an experienced textile manager from North Carolina, whom they appointed company treasurer in 1904 and president in 1906. He insisted that the northern directors retire and be replaced by Upstate mill presidents. They responded with orders.

By 1907, according to a reporter, Union Bleaching and Finishing Company was "doing a remarkably successful business and has practically all the work it can undertake." He exaggerated. Only seventy-five workers (five under the age of fifteen) were employed, and only two hundred fifty people lived in the mill village. By 1910, however, conditions really were better. The company increased its capacity by fifty percent and its capital stock to $400,000, it and installed electric generating equipment. It also improved the mill village, building a new three-room schoolhouse, a union church for Baptists and Methodists, and a boarding house for visitors and unmarried workers. Union Bleaching also started its own farm and provided employees, most of whom were former farmers, with garden plots, a cow pasture, and pigpens.

Lewis and Thomas Parker were cousins, the grandchildren of Thomas Fleming, a successful merchant in Charleston and Philadelphia who had immigrated to the United States from

County Monaghan in Northern Ireland. In the late 1890s, Lewis Parker was the partner of Greenville attorney Harry J. Haynsworth, president of the Bank of Greer, and receiver of the financially distressed Victor Manufacturing Company in Greer. Thomas Parker, five years older, was raised in Linville, North Carolina, and was working for his grandfather's firm in Philadelphia.

As receiver, Lewis Parker had discovered that, given careful management, cotton mills could make money, and he invited his cousin to return to the South to manage a new Greenville operation. In February 1900, they incorporated Monaghan Mill with the advice of F. W. Poe and the financial support of their grandfather. Thomas F. Parker was president, and Lewis was the treasurer of the company, which began with $450,000 in capitalization. They hired Lockwood, Greene & Co. to build their mill and its surrounding village on three hundred twenty-five acres west of Greenville along a country lane lined with cedar trees. They also hired Harlan Kelsey, a Boston landscape architect, to lay out the rolling site on the Reedy River to include space for playgrounds, a medical clinic, and the first industrial YMCA in the South.

The mill opened in 1902. From its very beginning, Parker made Monaghan an example of community services. He hired Dr. Fletcher Jordan, later one of Greenville's most beloved physicians, to supervise his medical clinic and employed a visiting nurse to care for mothers and their babies. I. E. Umger, a former missionary to China, was employed as director of the mill YMCA; in 1905, he hired Lawrence Peter Hollis, president of the student YMCA at the University of South Carolina, as assistant director at a salary of $40 a month. Umger left his job just a few months later, and the inexperienced Hollis was made director. For the next three summers, "Pete" Hollis attended programs at Lake George, New York, the national YMCA training headquarters. There he was introduced to the newly invented game of basketball; to soccer; and to Lord Robert Baden-Powell, who had begun the scouting movement in England. He purchased a basketball in New York City on his way home and introduced that sport, soccer, and the Boy Scouts to "the young men who have good red blood in their veins" at Monaghan and to South Carolina. Because recreation programs encouraged worker loyalty, he built a baseball field and gymnasium.

Hollis made the Monaghan YMCA the center of the community, reporting in 1907 that the sixteen hundred mill village residents had made 47,168 individual visits to the YMCA that year. With two hundred ten houses and one hundred twenty-five cows, the community was still rural, but its programming was distinctly urban: adult education classes, basketball, bowling alleys, pool tables, moving pictures every two weeks, Bible study, and a dramatics club. With a large school building, which the mill built and to which it contributed $850 a year, a union church, a library with a thousand books and periodicals, and no children under the age of twelve employed in the mill, Monaghan was the model textile village.

Five years after it opened, the mill's capitalization was increased to $700,000 and its spindles increased to sixty thousand; seven hundred people were employed to manufacture print cloths, fancy dress goods and shirting, and shade cloth. Although the Parkers lived in Boyce Lawn in downtown Greenville, the superintendent, all overseers, the five teachers at Monaghan School, and Pete Hollis lived in the village, shopped in the mill store, and attended local churches (the union church was soon replaced by churches built by Baptist, Methodist, and Presbyterian congregations). Residents could even be buried in Monaghan's private cemetery.

Thomas Parker said in a 1910 address, "If mills could afford a yearly average expenditure of 1 percent of their capital for adequate building and competent welfare workers, with active support by the presidents the villagers would quickly become revolutionized, and not only would they retain a true friendliness toward the management, which is decreasing, but would escape the future control of demagogues and labor agitators." If the Parkers supported "welfare work" to avoid unionization, they were disappointed, for in 1914, the International Workers of the World formed a local at Monaghan and established a meeting hall in downtown Greenville. They spearheaded a walkout at the mill over work rules and overtime and led a labor parade down Main Street. Lewis Parker, however, took personal charge and appealed to workers' sense of white identity and distrust of both Blacks and "outsiders." He promised to address the specific reasons for the strike only if workers returned to work.

Meanwhile, he had become president of the "Whaley Group," which included four Columbia mills in addition to Victor in Greer. In December 1910, he organized the Parker Cotton Mills Company with sixteen mills and a combined capital of $15 million dollars; he controlled a million spindles, more than any other single individual in the nation. However, even for the talents of the Parkers, the business was too large, and when the price of cotton fell precipitously at the beginning of the war in Europe, the business failed. In January 1915, Lewis Parker announced that he would reopen his legal practice, but he died of cancer before he could do so; Thomas Parker began selling real estate.

In 1901, it took John T. Woodside just thirteen days to get commitments of $85,000 from local businessmen—enough money, when combined with his own savings and cash from Northern investors, to charter the Woodside Cotton Mill. A native Greenvillian, Woodside had been employed by his uncle, J. D. Charles, at the Reedy River Factory at Conestee between 1884 and 1891. This apprenticeship, begun when he was twenty, included working at the company store, where he "kept books, weighed cotton, bought and paid for cotton, worked in the mill, sold cloth on the road and collected for same, ditched, grazed the cows, and fished."

By the time he was twenty-seven, he had saved enough money to invest in a store of his own at Pelzer, where he came to know supply merchants and cotton buyers. In 1894, Woodside opened a grocery store in downtown Greenville, which he ran with the help of his younger brother. In January 1902, he sold the store and began to concentrate on building an eleven-thousand-spindle mill, which opened in 1903 with one hundred operatives and $200,000 in capital. The four-story brick building was sixty feet long, had ten rows of windows, a two-story support building, and a one-story cotton shed. Situated on a ridge overlooking Long Branch, it was located between the new Brandon and Monaghan Mills and was bordered on the east by Southern Railroad tracks. A new street, Woodside Avenue, linked these westside mills, and the new Beltline

Woodside mill under construction, ca. 1903. From the South Carolina Room Archives, Greenville County Library System.

Trolley soon ran along it to provide easy access to downtown Greenville.

In late 1904, Woodside's capacity tripled; by 1907, it had increased again, to 45,120 spindles and six hundred employees (only seven under the age of twelve); twelve hundred people lived in the expanding mill village. With a three-teacher schoolhouse attended by one hundred fifty of the village's three hundred children; a full-day kindergarten; a "union" church built by the company, which contributed one-third of its expenses; and an "excellent brass band," the Woodside Mill was flourishing.

In 1906, the Woodside brothers purchased controlling stock in the Fountain Inn Manufacturing Company, and in 1908, they built

90

Dunean Mill. From the Richard D. Sawyer Historic Greenville Collection, Furman University Special Collections.

the twenty-five-thousand-spindle Simpsonville Cotton Mill. But Greenville's Woodside Mill was their major enterprise, and in 1909, they added a mill building, cotton storehouse, mechanical building, and seventy-five additional houses across Woodside Avenue on the western side of their property. In the same year, the brothers merged their Greenville, Simpsonville, and Fountain Inn operations to establish Woodside Cotton Mills, with capital of $1.2 million, and began planning an immense expansion in Greenville operation. By 1913, the mill was one hundred eighty feet long and operated one hundred twelve thousand spindles; it had become the largest cotton mill under one roof in the nation.

The final two textile crescent mills were much larger operations than the earlier ones. On January 1, 1911, the *Greenville Daily News*

announced that three hundred acres had been acquired between Easley Bridge and Anderson Roads for the first fine goods textile mill in the South. The price of the "Westervelt Mill property, which commands a fine view of the city," was not revealed, nor was the fact that J. Irving Westervelt, who lent the considerable prestige of his name to the risky enterprise, was a figurehead. Early in 1910, a coalition of Northern textile machinery companies had decided to gamble on a Southern mill. The "Pawtucket Syndicate" needed an experienced Greenville man with a solid reputation to raise local funds and run the plant. J. Irving Westervelt was a reasonable choice. With twelve years of experience at the Pelham Mill and eight as president of Brandon, Westervelt had both friends and expertise. He convinced the landowners to accept stock in "his" new enterprise rather than cash for their land. He also chose the site on a "well-watered plateau" near Brandon.

The mill's original capitalization was a million dollars. The Northern group took fifty-two hundred fifty shares and sold (or traded) the remainder to Greenvillians. The plant opened in March 1912. Its first fabrics were fine-quality linen handkerchiefs. Because of its sophisticated machinery, most of the two hundred operatives recruited by Westervelt Mill were experienced. The seventy-five houses in the village, constructed at a cost of about $100 a room, were set on smaller lots than at older mills, but there was community garden space and a cow pasture.

Building a Southern mill to produce linens, "Indian lawns," and other fine fabrics was a gamble. J. I. Westervelt had sunk every penny he had in Brandon Mill; he soon faced great financial difficulties. The syndicate dismissed him a year after the mill was completed and made Bennette E. Geer the president. Geer, a wealthy native of Belton, held a bachelor of arts degree and a master of arts degree from Furman University, where he had taught English and then had been dean from 1901 to 1911. His mentor was Charles Judson, the university treasurer. After Judson's death, Geer also ran the university's finances, but he also had experience running Easley Mill when his brother, John, the president, became ill. His first move was to rename the Westervelt Mill in Judson's honor.

Rumors of another "million-dollar mill" had been circulating in Greenville for several weeks before the New Industries Committee of the Board of Trade met in late December 1910 to learn the details. Captain Ellison A. Smyth, whose Pelzer Mill was one of the largest and most successful cotton mills in the South, presented the idea of a "fine goods manufactury" to a large and enthusiastic audience of businessmen on the evening of December 28. The project was clearly destined for success: $700,000 had already been raised in the North; all Greenvillians had to do was pledge $100,000, and the mill was theirs. They did so quickly.

The idea, it was said, was James B. Duke's. Always alert to economic development opportunities, especially when they promised profits to his electricity-generating Southern Utilities Company, it may have been Duke who encouraged organizers to seek sufficient capital to make a success of a mill that would produce high-quality goods that were expensive to manufacture. Smyth's Northern backers, who formed half of the mill's first board of directors and the majority of its stockholders, were those who saw future profits for themselves in the Southern experiment.

Two months later, the new mill was chartered. It was named Dunean by Captain Smyth in tribute to his great-great-grandfather's Irish linen mill, which had been located on the Dunean River in County Antrim, Ireland. In March 1911, the principal stockholders met in Greenville and elected J. Adger Smyth, Captain Smyth's son, a graduate of the Alabama Agricultural and Mechanical College at Auburn, president. Smyth had been trained at his father's mill at Pelzer and shared both his outlook on management and his antipathy toward dogs, banned at both Pelzer and Dunean. (They were "99 percent worthless and troublesome.")

The new corporation purchased two hundred thirty-seven acres of land between Mills Mill and Anderson Road. It was near a spur of the Southern Railroad's old Greenville & Columbia line, and James Duke's proposed new electric railway also planned to serve it. The "particularly beautiful" site was fertile and had an abundance of water from Brushy Creek on the southern edge of the property where Camp Wetherill had been located during the Spanish-American War. The land cost more than $50,000. Dunean's organization and structure—with Northern suppliers and agents the dominant stockholders and prominent Green-villians providing textile expertise and local reputation as minority shareholders—precisely paralleled that of the Westervelt (Judson) Mill announced just weeks earlier. The two large mills, near neighbors, both set up to weave fine fabrics, were immediate competitors.

Construction of the fifty-thousand-spindle mill began in May 1911. Built of unusu-al-for-Greenville buff brick with black mortar, it had concrete floors and pillars in the main building and a one-story, wooden-floored weave shed. All of the mill's machines were driven by individual electric motors. The one-hundred-eighty-house village around the mill was unusual. Its layout combined a curving and picturesque main street with the usual textile mill grid design. Three different housing styles alternated on relatively large lots. The overseers' street, the first block of Smyth past the mill, included only six large homes; the east side of Wallace was reserved for cow barns and pig pens. Alongside the mill ran Allen Street, later Highway 29, and for some years, the Atlanta Highway.

Greenville's mill village population—all living outside the city limits—grew dramatically between 1895 and 1912. That growth brought new social pressures and antagonisms. City people referred to mill workers as "lint-heads," because of the cotton lint that lingered in their hair. They were a class apart, isolated from the increasingly urban city center, made to feel unwelcome in Main Street stores, and uncomfortable at downtown events. They were poor—mill wages were notoriously low—and they couldn't afford city prices. Even in death they were separate; mill workers could neither afford nor desire a burial at Springwood Cemetery. Seeing an opportunity, Alester Furman opened Graceland Cemetery for mill workers on the White Horse Road in 1916.

The cotton mills also drew a new class of white-collar workers—textile salesmen, accountants, lawyers, and engineers—to the city. It was primarily these men, newcomers and Southern representatives of Northern textile machinery manufacturers, who, together with J. E. Sirrine, bet against heavy odds that Greenville could successfully host a textile exposition. Biannual expositions of mill equipment and programs had been scheduled in Boston for at least two decades, and at the turn of the century, Atlanta businessmen had tried unsuccessfully to organize an exposition. By 1913, it was clear, however, that a Southern show would be profitable and possible. (Greenville was not the only Southern city with an expanding cotton industry. Spartanburg, Augusta, and Laurens all claimed to be "the Lowell of the South," referring to the huge conglomeration of textile mills in the Massachusetts town.)

However, the economy as well as the world situation was shaky, and after war was declared in Europe in 1914, Atlanta, which had agreed to fund an exposition, backed off. It took expertise and experience as well as facilities to put on a huge and complex multiday exposition. Greenville businessmen had neither experience nor facilities, but they had nerve. Even though the city's population was about seventeen thousand (Atlanta's was approximately one hundred fifty-five thousand), it boasted only three modest hotels and had no large indoor space. A group of "wide-awake go-getters" got together and offered the South Carolina mill town as the site for the first Southern Textile Exposition, scheduled in fall 1915. The Manufacturers Association reluctantly agreed.

A nine-member Greenville Executive Committee supported by the Chamber of Commerce immediately began planning for a four-day exposition of textile equipment, supplies, and services. They hoped to attract perhaps five thousand mill presidents, superintendents, and overseers, as well as students,

Dunean mill village with curving streets and electrical transmission lines. From the Richard D. Sawyer Historic Greenville Collection, Furman University Special Collections.

faculty, and exhibits from the South's premiere textile engineering programs at Clemson and Georgia Tech.

As the Southern Textile Exposition Number of *Cotton Magazine* for October 1915 admitted, Greenvillian Joseph E. Sirrine, "ostensibly a mere member of the executive committee and chairman of the sub-committee on halls and buildings, is really the Godfather of the exposition." As another Greenvillian said, "Just let Joe have Saturday afternoon for golf and he is well content to spend the other six and a half days planning for the exposition." And plan he did. He borrowed $100 and began begging space—twenty thousand square feet of it—for exhibits. The Piedmont & Northern Electric Railroad offered three relatively new warehouses on Washington Street near its depot for exposition use.

By June, it was clear that twenty thousand square feet was insufficient, so the railroad provided two additional warehouses for exhibits. The City Council's contribution was clean streets decorated with flags and banners. All hotel rooms at the Ottaray, the Imperial (now the Greenville Summit), the old Mansion House, and every boarding house in town were booked by mid-summer. When they weren't sufficient, organizers pleaded with Greenvillians for rooms in their homes. More than a hundred people offered beds.

The show was a roaring success. Not only had Greenville received "pecuniary benefits" estimated at $50,000 for visitors' housing, food, clothing, and cigars, but the Exposition itself had also made a profit. It confirmed in the minds of local citizens that the Chamber of Commerce's new slogan: "Textile Capital of the South" was true.

Chapter 9

STIRRING THE CIVIC CONSCIOUSNESS, 1897–1916

Fear of disease, influence of the City Beautiful movement, and perhaps a whisper of national progressivism stirred Greenville's civic consciousness at the turn of the century. The impulse arose in part from churches but extended far beyond them. In 1888, the all-female Altar Guild opened the Christ Church Hospital for the Sick Poor. It was located in a rambling house belonging to Mrs. Sarah Coxe across from the church on East North Street. Doctors donated their care at the "public" facility, open to sick white people regardless of income. The Altar Guild ladies covered the cost of food, medicine, and the matron's salary. After serving seventy-nine "gratuitous" patients, it closed in 1896.

Even while the Episcopal hospital was open, there was no place to house poor people with infectious diseases. When two itinerant workmen were diagnosed with typhoid and were quarantined at their boarding house in the fall of 1895, the possibility of contagion worried community leaders. In February 1896, James Mackey of the Knights of Pythias called a meeting of representatives of "every organized body" in Greenville to officially begin the Greenville Hospital Association.

However, after a few futile attempts at fundraising, members gave up and turned the job over to an "auxiliary" Women's Hospital Board. By 1901, the ladies had raised a little over $2,000 through strawberry festivals, fairs, and "silver teas." That sum couldn't build a hospital. Instead, they reserved two cots at the Earle Infirmary for $10 a month. Then they, too, stopped trying. In the meantime, Greenville suffered a smallpox outbreak. The city's Public

Health Bureau opened a "pesthouse" for quarantine on Chick Springs Road near Earle Street in 1897. That first small house was for whites, but a year or so later they erected a second one nearby for Blacks. That was probably the first time that the City Council committed funds (however limited) for free health care.

The coming of the Salvation Army changed charity. In 1904, the commander of the Atlanta office announced that Salvationists were ready to invade Charleston, Columbia, and the Upstate. The Spartanburg City Council immediately deemed their outdoor preaching "a nuisance" and refused to permit it. In Greenville, however, Army officials were allowed to erect a tent and to sing tambourine-accompanied hymns in the streets. The community was so welcoming that, in October 1906, the post commander announced that the Army had raised enough money to start construction of a Greenville citadel. Its site next to the county jail on Broad Street near Falls Street was perfect for the Salvationists, although not especially desirable for anyone else. Located on the edge of Greenville's "industrial area," (Camperdown Mill and gas and electric generating plants were nearby), it was only a block or two away from the city's "Red Light District" on East Court Street.

In May 1907, two thousand people gathered for the dedication of the Broad Street Citadel. The Greenville building cost $8,500 and was the first Salvation Army citadel (a headquarters building owned, rather than rented, by the Army) in the South. Thanks to generous contributions, the mortgage was paid off in less than two years. They also began a "Rescue Mission" for "fallen women," those pregnant without the benefit of marriage. The Mission served women from across the Upstate, many of them painfully young, some the victims of rape or incest. With a casualness that is a bit shocking today, from time to time, the nursing staff would mention in a newspaper article that a baby was available for adoption to anyone willing to take it in.

In the summer of 1908, Army officers opened a medical dispensary at the Citadel. Working with Dr. J. W. Jervey, who donated his time and expertise, they offered free medical care and medicine for poor people with illnesses of the ear, eye, nose, and throat. In 1910, thanks to the Charity Aid Society, that dispensary included five hospital rooms for tuberculosis patients. City Council members were so grateful for the free medical assistance that they willingly appropriated $15 a month to help cover costs.

Charity became "women's work." Some elite women, such as Mrs. W. E. Sirrine (a trained nurse) and Mrs. W. W. Burgiss, began the Charity Aid Society in 1908, which supported all the Salvation Army charity programs, including the Rescue Mission and the Bruner orphanage.

In 1906, Sara H. Davis, a not-very-wealthy fifty-year old spinster, began caring for three parentless children in a tiny house on Lawton Street. She did so with the help of friends who supplied vegetables from their gardens and occasional dollars from their purses. Her first major donor—with a gift of $50—was Nell Bruner. Miss Davis showed her gratitude for that gift and Mrs. Bruner's continuing support by naming the Bruner Industrial Home, Greenville's first orphanage, in her honor. During the next eight years, it expanded into larger houses. With the generous support of Mr. and Mrs. W. E. Sirrine, who helped create a board of trustees (chartered in 1909), within five years, enough money had been raised to purchase a large home on Rutherford Street that had formerly been a home for Baptist missionaries' children.

Miss Davis, the Bruner superintendent, was nearing sixty. Overseeing two dozen children was tiring, so just two years after relocating the facility to Rutherford Road, she turned to the Salvation Army, asking them to operate it. Although they initially refused because they did not have sufficient staff, they promised to reconsider her request later. In May 1917, they agreed to her offer, and in August, the Salvation Army took charge.

The Charity Aid Society also spearheaded the local drive to help tuberculosis patients. Tuberculosis was the leading cause of death nationally during the first decade of the twentieth century. More than one hundred fifty thousand tubercular Americans died annually. "The white plague" hit urban areas, especially poor ones, with devastating frequency. In Greenville, the plague devastated mill villages and Black neighborhoods—places and people who had no political clout and, thus, no support or funds from state, county, or city government. (In 1913, the South Carolina legislature allocated $40,000 to eliminate cattle ticks but refused funds for tuberculosis. Paupers, legislators pointed out, could always go to the County Poorhouse.)

The Charity Aid Society helped initially by providing "out of doors aid"—food, clothes, fuel, and medicine—to the very poor, but that was insufficient; so were the five rooms at the Citadel. In January 1911, realtor William Goldsmith learned that the private forty-bed Corbett Sanitarium (for "nervous diseases," often caused by alcoholism) on Arlington Avenue was for sale for $20,000. He tried to get the medical society interested in beginning a hospital there, but their board refused. Then he went to the women's auxiliary, who had by that time raised $4,000 for a future hospital. They agreed to use the money to buy the sanitarium, if the men could raise $16,000 additional dollars.

With the leadership of Goldsmith, W. E. Sirrine, and Charles Hard, the Hospital Association sold shares in the hospital and raised the additional dollars to purchase and renovate it. The City Council contributed $2,400 for local charity patients, and the legislative delegation pledged $500 for county cases. The shareholder-owned

Greenville Hospital (with a board that, amazingly, was half female) opened in January 1912. Although it lacked an operating room, maternity ward, and X-ray machine, the community was proud. However, as the *Greenville News* pointed out, "every city of any consequence in the country owns its own hospital."

With nudging from the newspaper, the City Council finally purchased it in 1916, proudly changing its name to "City Hospital." Two bond issues for $100,000 allowed for expansion to one hundred beds. It was, as the *News* pointed out, the "conscience of the community" that should "provide for its sick, both rich and poor. ("Rich" was new.) Immediately after it opened, the City Council (and three patrons) withdrew their support from the emergency tuberculosis rooms at the Citadel.

So the ladies erected two tents on an adjacent Broad Street lot for a "tuberculosis camp." That location was hardly ideal, so a Society "investigating committee" and two doctors went to the legislative delegation to ask for funds. The delegation refused. They did, however, agree to allow the Society to use land "in a grove" across Rutherford Road from the County Home to build a shack and to allow the Society's trained nurse to live at the Poor House and prepare food from its kitchens to carry to sufferers across the road. That arrangement began in August 1913. It lasted only until the following April, because the commissioners also insisted that only

Poor House residents (paupers) with tuberculosis could be treated. Families of any size with any member earning anything were ruled out.

Mrs. Harry J. Haynsworth and Mrs. Mary Gridley then formed the Hopewell Tuberculosis Association and immediately opened one of the pioneer tuberculosis "camps" in the state in a tent on the County Home property. The organization soon reconstituted itself as the Anti-Tuberculosis Society, with male members, mostly doctors, including Dr. Davis Furman and Dr. C. E. Smith, the county health officer. When they returned to the delegation this time, they were successful, getting legislators to deed five acres of land on Rutherford Road and appropriate $1,000 annually for maintenance. It opened with space for twenty-five patients in August 1915. Society members begged for contributions. Within a year, the city had agreed to supply $50 annually, and the county gave $200 (amounts that increased dramatically within a few years). Additional funds came from the Salvation Army and the sale of Red Cross tuberculosis seals at Christmas.

The high point of the week for patients was the Monday morning weigh-in. Because weight loss was a sign of the disease, patients looked forward to the scale to see if they had gained any ounces. Because weight was so important, Dr. George B. Wilkinson, who volunteered his services, wanted to tempt patients to eat, so he ordered cooks to fry large quantities of bacon

An example of a tuberculosis camp from the early twentieth century. Before effective vaccination, tuberculosis was an incredibly deadly disease. Although it had existed in human populations for thousands of years, it is thought to have reached its peak between the late eighteenth and late nineteenth centuries. During that time, it killed one in seven people then living. Photo: Library of Congress, Prints and Photographs Division.

and open all the doors and windows so that the aroma would waft out to the sufferers. President Rhoda Haynsworth reported with pride in October 1916 that the Hopewell "family"

had gained one hundred ninety-eight pounds since January.

These patients were all white. Although some thought had evidently been given to

Viola Neblett was a champion for both temperance and woman suffrage.

the Thursday Morning Club, the Rotary Book Club, and others that considered social problems with "sprightly conversation and tempting dainties." They shared books; discussed foreign lands; and learned about artists, writers, and musicians. And they honed their advocacy and organizing skills. Members vocally supported separate reform schools for wayward girls, the establishment of juvenile courts, and college education for women.

Viola Neblett is an exemplar of these early activists. She had been a WCTU organizer before she moved to Greenville in the 1880s. She had supported the city's first bond issue for public schools and was a founder of the Thursday Club. She also began the state drive for women's suffrage. Working with Virginia Durant Young, the editor of the *Fairfax Enterprise* in Allendale County, and Greenvillians George and Sarah Sirrine (he was a Connecticut native, manager of the Coach Factory, and the father of attorney W. E. Sirrine and engineer Joe Sirrine) and Mary Putnam Gridley (the only woman president of a cotton mill in the South) they formed the South Carolina Equal Rights Association in 1890. It was not, however, a success: By 1894, it had only one hundred seven members.

Neblett and Young focused their attention on the state's 1895 Constitutional Convention. There they buttonholed delegates and pushed hard for the inclusion of middle-class white women among SC voters, which, they argued,

allowing Negro sufferers to use the shack where Hopewell had begun, that possibility doesn't seem to have worked out. It wasn't until April 1922 that St. Luke's, the Black hospital, began offering tuberculosis clinics, where many white women brought their cooks before allowing them in their kitchens.

Elite women's first local steps outside their gilded parlors were the WCTU and the United Daughters of the Confederacy (to which no husband could object). In the 1880s, they also began organizing clubs: the Thursday Club, would diminish the impact of Black male voters and millworkers. (They were as racist and classist as the official delegates.) Mrs. Neblett also emphasized that "the presence of a few ladies in the polling place is equal to a whole squad of police officers."

Although they were heard politely, few Convention delegates supported them. Afterward, discussion of women's suffrage disappeared in South Carolina for almost two decades. By 1912, women in nine western states were voting. Here, however, ministers, editors, and politicians almost universally opposed equal suffrage. They argued that it would lead to "the total downfall of the already tottering domestic fabric," was non-Biblical, and would increase political rancor and bad feeling. When a bill allowing women to vote was introduced in the General Assembly in 1914, "a ripple of laughter" wafted through the legislature.

Women's suffrage, however, was not a laughing matter for some Greenvillians. At the Greenville Female College, longtime Lady Principal Mary Judson believed that God had given women brains and expected them to use them; she (discreetly) supported equal suffrage. When the Greenville Equal Suffrage League formed at a meeting at the Women's College in May 1914, among its forty-two members was Eudora Ramsay, the daughter of College President David Ramsay, an English instructor and confirmed feminist. She said in an interview

MISS MARY C. JUDSON, Lady Principal.

Mary Camilla Judson was born in Connecticut in 1828. She moved to Greenville in 1857, where her brother, Charles, taught at Furman University. She was the lady principal of the Johnson Female University in Anderson, 1857–1859, and later taught at the Greenville Baptist Female College. She also founded the Judson Literary Society, the first women's club in Greenville. In addition to her commitment to education, she was also a champion of women's suffrage. Photo: Furman University, Special Collections and Archives.

with the school newspaper that her goal was "to educate girls who are staunch advocates of Women's Rights."

And there were other women, many well educated, who shared her concerns. Suffrage

League President Jessie Stokely Burnett, for example, was a Tennessee native who held a master of arts degree from Smith College, studied at Yale, and later taught history at Furman. Eleanor Furman had graduated from Hollins and was the daughter of business leader Alester Furman. Vice President Andrea Patterson's brother, State Senator Niels Christensen of Beaufort, introduced the suffrage amendment to the legislature and was a spokesman for women's rights.

Although she was in California when the Greenville Suffrage organization began, James M. ("Miss Jim") Perry, who had graduated from the Women's College in 1913, was South Carolina's first woman lawyer. After earning her law degree from the University of California, Berkeley, in 1917, she was the first woman to pass the state bar exam three months later and to win her first case for Haynsworth and Haynsworth in 1918.

While women were focusing on the vote, men were building a new YMCA. For many years, the organization had "rooms" in the old Record Building, but with expanding needs and population, a new facility was essential. In the fall of 1911, they finished a new building on East Coffee Street. The city was so proud of it that they paved Coffee Street. Its first floor featured separate libraries for boys and men, a writing and a game room, and a huge swimming pool with changing rooms and locker area. A second-floor gymnasium had all the latest gymnastics equipment, two basketball courts, as well as classrooms where a newly hired a "physical culturalist" taught skills and techniques in a hundred classes a month. The top floor offered dormitory rooms.

Other men who wanted to improve Greenville took a different approach, forming the Municipal League in 1904. The leaders, Alester Furman Sr. and Thomas Parker, hired Harlan Kelsey, a Boston landscape architect and expert on Appalachian plants whom Parker met when he was developing Linville Falls in North Carolina. Kelsey wrote, and the Municipal League published in 1907, *Beautifying and Improving Greenville, South Carolina*. (Kelsey also designed landscape plans for Columbia; for Parker's East Washington Street home, Monaghan Mill; and later for Overbrook and Cagle Park.)

Clearly influenced by the City Beautiful movement, Kelsey suggested expanding City Park, creating a park around the banks of the Reedy River at Main Street, and developing athletic grounds near Hudson Street. He also suggested garbage pickup, abolishing downtown slaughterhouses, and creating beltways around the city. Both Kelsey and the *Greenville News* lamented the ugliness created by industrialization. Springwood Tannery and a nearby abattoir north of Springwood Cemetery provided Greenville markets with leather and fresh meat.

"The stench," Kelsey reported, "was frightful, and hundreds of buzzards lazily arose to join the black cloud already in the air, while a nearer view revealed large numbers perched on rotting piles of bones, hair and offal, still gorging." It had to go, and it did, three years later. Other recommendations included broadening and extending streets, planting trees, establishing parks, improving sanitation, and removing safety hazards. Greenville did not become a "city beautiful" because of Kelsey and the Municipal League, but the study did set a farsighted and practical pattern for future development.

City officials helped. Since 1887, a board of health had forbidden the raising of hogs within a mile of City Hall, and insisted on garbage pickup and the disposal of dead animals. It had instituted regulations for registering births, deaths, and marriages; reporting and, later, quarantining people with infectious diseases. Starting in 1907, however, the City Council prohibited pharmacies from selling opium, morphine, and choral hydrate (knockout drops) and approved the appointment of a garbage officer. National fear of contaminated meat triggered by Upton Sinclair's expose of slaughterhouses in *The Jungle* was reinforced by photographs in Kelsey's 1907 plan and those that young attorney James Price published frequently in the *Daily News*.

Price, a twenty-three-year-old graduate of George Washington Law School, had worked as an investigative reporter for the *Washington Times*. When he returned home to Greenville in 1908, he visited and photographed local slaughterhouses and petitioned the board so often about closing them that the mayor, as a kind of joke, appointed him to the Health Board. With the urging of Price and the leadership of Dr. Davis Furman, the board hired a health commissioner who had a city abattoir built in an isolated location (near today's Cleveland Park). They also hired a milk inspector to stop house-to-house peddling of unpasteurized "blue milk," a meat inspector who checked on butcher shops and abattoirs, and an inspector to examine sanitary conditions in schools. Furthermore, they mandated smallpox vaccinations for children entering school.

Aldermen also appointed a tree and parks commission and gave it a (small) budget. Hugh Buist, who had taught horticulture at Winthrop College, was chair; James McPherson, a young engineer, was appointed commission secretary. When Buist died, McPherson became chair and held that position for more than thirty years. He planted trees and shrubs, improved City Park, and created school playgrounds throughout the city.

Education improved slightly. Four elementary schools were built, and in 1910, Central School added a tenth grade. At the turn of the century, the pastor of Silver Hill Baptist Church, the Rev. M. D. Minus, determined to build a boarding

Just before her death, Ann Viola Neblett conveyed her home for use as a library. It operated as Neblett Free Library from 1897–1921. South Carolina Room, Greenville County Library.

and vocational school for Black children. Thomas Parker chaired a biracial board that funded the Sterling Institute (later Sterling High School) and personally contributed $2,500 and a good mule. He also had his bookkeeper teach the principal how to balance accounts and funded the school's president's visit to the Tuskegee Institute in Alabama to study its teaching methods. Parker also purchased and developed land off Anderson Road for Black housing.

Greenville's first "public" library opened, thanks to Mrs. Neblett and the Sirrines, who provided a collection of books for borrowing in their home in 1893. Four years later, six months before she died, Neblett conveyed her home on Westfield Street across from the Central School to Sirrine, E. A. Taylor, and Mrs. Gridley, as trustees, to become the site of The Neblett Free Library.

In addition to books, culture came to the community by way of the Grand Opera House, opened on West Coffee Street on October 17, 1901. Erected by a national company funded by four thousand local subscriptions at $5 apiece, it was modern in every way, with seating for a thousand in a first-floor auditorium complete with a balcony. More than three hundred incandescent bulbs brilliantly illuminated the action, and its ventilation was "well-nigh perfect." The impressive two-story building had an elegant entrance and was designed in the fashionable Romanesque Revival style. And its prices were right: The cheapest seats cost fifty cents; the most expensive, a dollar.

"The Grand" was an immediate success, because Greenville was convenient for shows traveling by railroad from New York to Atlanta, and it was easy to schedule the most popular attractions. Although there were few "grand" operas, large audiences gathered several times a week to applaud operettas, minstrel shows, musical comedies, plays, concerts, and famous speakers. Caruso sang here, Sarah Bernhardt acted, William Jennings Bryan spoke, and two weeks after the *Titanic* sank in 1912, a movie made in New Jersey purported to show the event. The outside world was coming to Greenville.

Chapter 10

THE WAR, THE FLU, AND THE HOMEFRONT, 1916–20

In 1916, Greenville, with a city population of about twenty thousand, was home to the presidents of fifty-two cotton mills, nearly as many churches, twenty-eight hundred telephones, two newspapers, ten banks, two colleges, a high school, and four hotels. Those figures wouldn't change much over the next few years, but much else did, as Greenville, with the rest of the country, mobilized for war.

When the United States joined the Allies to fight the "Hun" in April 1917, the city embraced the war effort. Patriotic fervor gripped everyone. Within days of the announcement, every Furman student pledged to fight; every boy at Greenville High School joined one of two companies organized there. Young men, white and Black alike, rushed to join the army. Most whites joined the Thirtieth "Old Hickory" Division; Black men from throughout the state enrolled in the 371st Infantry.

The Chamber of Commerce, with $600 in pennies raised from local children, immediately erected a huge neon-lit sign over Main Street: "Our Country First, Then Greenville." In the following year (electricity couldn't be wasted), the words were emblazoned on a cloth banner. The sign welcomed troops at newly authorized Camp Sevier, but it also emphasized the city's total embrace of the "Great War."

The conflict and the coming of "a national cantonment"—a war camp—brought new people, new ideas, and new horizons to the

Piedmont textile center. Business leaders had begun exploring the possibilities of a local military training site before President Wilson declared war, lobbying the War Department in March, hoping to ensure that Columbia would not beat out Greenville for an army camp. Cheap land, mild climate, and Southern enthusiasm for fighting made South Carolina especially attractive for military bases. Camp Jackson was eventually established near Columbia and Camp Wadsworth in Spartanburg.

The Greenvillians were so encouraged by the response that Alester Furman, William Sirrine, and Oscar Mauldin took an option on one thousand acres northeast of the city. The Chamber invited General Leonard Wood, commander of the Department of the Southeast, to inspect the site in June. After he addressed a large and enthusiastic crowd in City Park, he announced at a Rotary Club meeting that Greenville had been selected. Greenville's initiative was not wholly patriotic; military camps were profitable, as residents learned when soldiers trained at Camp Wetherill during the Spanish-American War.

Starting in July 1917, army engineers, working with J. E. Sirrine & Co. and the Gallivan Construction Company, began to clear a 2,100-acre site near the Parisview depot. Both the Southern and the Piedmont & Northern Railroads passed through the property. The following year, the city purchased the Paris Mountain Water Company to provide

sufficient water for the installation. A military "city" rose up almost overnight, comprising several hundred frame buildings and thousands of tents. It included divisional headquarters, five YMCAs, a chapel, a bakery, more than a dozen warehouses edging the Southern Rail tracks, a post office, and at least four medical buildings. In October, Army personnel constructed the Remount Station for regimental animals at the eastern end of the camp. The first soldiers to arrive—the Butler Guards from Greenville and engineering companies from Columbia and from Wilmington, North Carolina—moved in on July 29.

By the end of August, about thirty thousand men from National Guard units in North Carolina, South Carolina, and Tennessee were living in tents along the dusty and crowded roads of the new cantonment. It was named "Camp Sevier" in honor of Revolutionary War leader John Sevier, the governor of Tennessee when that state was admitted to the nation. The units became part of the Thirtieth Division, nicknamed "Old Hickory" in honor of President Andrew Jackson, the hero of the War of 1812.

The War Camp Community Service program set up programs and activities at an Enlisted Men's Club at Coffee and Laurens Street; a Colored Soldiers' Club on West Washington Street; and the Poinsett Club, adjacent to the Ottaray Hotel, for officers. Hospitable residents invited soldiers to meals

Camp Sevier, October 1917. Library of Congress Prints and Photographs Division.

in their homes. Despite the war raging in Europe and the rationing of coal and sugar at home, Christmas 1917 was "the most prosperous ever for the Pearl of the Piedmont," reported the Greenville *Daily News*. In December 1917, the newspaper and the newly organized Rotary Club sponsored a Christmas party for twenty thousand men at Textile Hall. Soldiers shopped, ate, attended church, and played in Greenville, shuttled from the camp by thirteen daily Piedmont and Northern trains. Young women met new, uniformed young men whose parents did not know their parents. Romances blossomed at the "very chaperoned" YWCA dances at Cleveland Hall and at tea dances at the Imperial Hotel (now the Summit). So many soldiers buzzed around the Greenville Woman's College that a military policeman had to be stationed there.

As the men, who ultimately numbered one hundred thousand, were training at Camp Sevier, their wives and families followed them, filling boarding houses, hotels, and spare rooms to capacity. Rents rose; so did prices of suddenly scarce commodities. Almost overnight, the price of a loaf of bread doubled from a nickel to a dime. For thirsty and soft-drink addicted Greenvillians, dreadful tidings came in December: Coco-Cola syrup was no longer available. In January, sugar was rationed to a cup a week per person. Shortages continued. By October 1917, gasoline was unavailable. In the coldest winter the county had known in sixty years, coal was in such short supply that federal government announced a five-day closing of all nonessential industries, including textile mills, and Monday closings for the next ten weeks. The county shivered. By autumn 1918, the news from the front was grim: The Thirtieth Division suffered more than eight thousand casualties. Greenville mourned the loss of sixty-eight white and thirty-one Black soldiers.

Building materials became impossible to get. As a result, the completion date for Greenville's new courthouse was pushed back nearly six months. The new Textile Exposition Hall opened without a rear wall. Trinity Lutheran Church had only a finished basement to host Lutheran soldiers. When rats infested the military warehouses at the camp, school children donated their patriotic cats to get rid of the rodents.

Everybody participated in Liberty Bond drives. The first, in June 1917, raised $750,000; of that amount, $200,000 came from the textile mills and their villages. In the second drive, launched in October, Union Bleachery alone contributed $100,000. Funding was essential, but the need for volunteers was extraordinary. The Red Cross, which had been established here in 1915, was reorganized in 1917 with J. L. Mann, the superintendent of education, as head, while Mrs. William G. Sirrine organized the "women's program" and created dozens of smaller Red Cross units across the country. Mrs. Sirrine developed a motor corps of generally pretty and leisured young women who learned mechanical skills, including changing tires, and provided transportation in their own cars to families visiting Camp Sevier, patients needing transportation to the city hospital, deliveries of unexpected provisions to the camp, and officers needing transportation to meetings. She set up units at every church in the city, every mill in the county, and in many neighborhoods.

Units had different tasks: Some made surgical bandages, others assembled supplies. The 144-member Crescent Avenue's unit, for example, supplied eighty-three pillows, one hundred five pillowcases, and one hundred forty-four "garments." First Baptist's contribution was four hundred eighty convalescent gowns, and Conestee Mill was responsible for two hundred eighty-eight scrub clothes. Red Cross functions (and there were dozens in the next year and a half) were announced in the society pages of the *Greenville News*. They included a huge parade down Main Street with male officials in cars and marching women's units, many of them displaying huge red crosses. Even after the armistice, Red Cross workers continuing raising money and supporting the men, many of them hospitalized at Camp Sevier with the Spanish Flu. (City Council purchased thirty burial sites at Springwood Cemetery for unclaimed soldiers' bodies.)

Influenza had arrived in Europe in May 1918. By the time the epidemic hit the battlefields of France and Belgium in June, it had been named the Spanish Flu. Spain, which was not a belligerent, had uncensored newspapers (unlike the combatants) that first reported on the epidemic, thus giving the disease its name. The extent and devastation of the epidemic were initially downplayed. Newspapers in warring countries did not want to lower morale, and although a million people had died in the "Russian Flu" epidemic in 1889–1890, it had passed relatively quickly, bringing death primarily to the weak, elderly, and small children, the usual victims.

This epidemic was different. Not only did it attack people in the prime of life, it came in waves. The first one burned itself out in midsummer, after having ravaged the battlefields in France and Belgium and taken thousands of lives in Western Europe. On September 7, newspapers across America reported that more than three thousand people had died in Boston, and three thousand soldiers had been stricken at nearby Camp Devens.

Influenza is a crowd disease. Any place where people gathered together—in army camps, battlefield trenches, churches, schools, theatres, and restaurants—it could flourish. And it traveled fast. Two days after Furman opened on September 17, the university recorded its first two cases, and on September 24, two soldiers at Camp Sevier were sickened. Just three days later, five hundred nineteen new victims were reported at Sevier, and on the following day, more than a thousand soldiers reported to the camp hospital. A week later, twenty-five hundred new victims had been hospitalized.

Military authorities immediately quarantined the camp. They cancelled all indoor meetings, closed YMCA recreation centers, dining halls, and assembly buildings. When the base hospital was overrun with sick men, they converted two YMCA meeting halls to temporary hospitals. Meals were served outdoors and

chapel services discontinued. Officers whose families were living in Greenville, however, were allowed to visit them.

In the city of Greenville there were so many sick and dying residents—at least five hundred—that on October 4, the City Council unanimously passed a resolution calling on the city's Board of Health to declare a quarantine. But the Board refused. Dr. Davis Furman, its chair, noted how difficult it was to know if someone had typhus, a bad cold, or influenza and how impossible it was to establish a strict quarantine, since stores, mills, and businesses remained open, and trolleys kept running. Furthermore, if schools were closed, children would run loose and carry contagion into the streets.

Local feeling, however, opposed the board. A *Greenville News* editorial argued for a quarantine. So did City School Superintendent J. L. Mann, who explained that his teachers (those who weren't already sick) could ensure that children remained at home.

On the afternoon of October 7, the State Board of Health stepped in, ordering a (limited) quarantine throughout South Carolina, including the closing of all schools, movie theatres, churches, and soda shops. It banned trolleys from allowing standees, limited funerals and weddings to families, and emphasized the dangers of spitting ("expectorating"). Two days later, the *Greenville News* published a letter from Dr. Furman, reiterating his objections

A poster promoting Liberty Bond drives during World War I. Library of Congress, Prints and Photographs Division.

and quoting extensively from a letter opposing "general closings" from a physician at Johns Hopkins. However, within a few days, "Quarantine" signs were posted on hundreds of homes, and people had begun to wear masks to work at banks and department stores.

By October 12, the Spanish Flu had struck nearly four thousand city residents. Although no one knew how many people were infected in the mill villages, so many were ailing at Conestee Mill that a full-time Red Cross worker was assigned there. City Hospital was overrun, and the city's few physicians (many were serving in the army) searched for an additional site. By November 4, the worst of the second wave seemed over, and the quarantine was lifted in the city. Furman and the Women's College scrambled to complete the semester after three weeks of closure, and army draft notices were cancelled—the camps were more deadly than the battlefield. In early December, the head of South Carolina's Board of Public Health said that eighty thousand had been infected and three thousand had died in the previous two and a half months. And people continued to suffer and die. A third wave hit in January: Twenty thousand South Carolinians were infected. Although the epidemic ended in March, it would return annually, but never in so deadly a way.

When the Armistice was signed on November 11, mills and stores closed; soldiers streamed into town. Thousands jammed into Textile Hall to celebrate. Thousands more stood in the street outside, said the *Greenville News*, "waving flags, shooting fireworks, and throwing talcum powder—the stock of confetti having been exhausted." Troops were slowly mustered out, although many remained in Greenville until late summer 1919.

Greenville did not feel many of the same stresses that cities across the nation did in that first postwar year. No race riots here—Jim Crow segregation stomped on any civil rights activity by Black Greenvillians—no violent strikes (unions were considered "Yankee"), and no real problems with prohibition, as Greenville had long been dry. But the community did get caught up in the great baseball scandal of 1919. Greenville native and Chicago White Sox star hitter "Shoeless" Joe Jackson was among those accused of throwing the 1919 World Series. At his 1920 trial, he was found innocent, but Commissioner "Happy" Kennesaw Mountain Landis banned him from baseball for life. That decision, and the fact that he has also been banned from the Baseball Hall of Fame, kept him in the local limelight for a century.

Fire was the biggest news locally. The first destructive conflagration in January destroyed two major North Main Street department stores, doing $100,000 worth of damage. The second, in April, leveled most of the former Chicora College campus, by then the Colonial Theatre and apartments on South Main Street in the West End. It severely damaged the Coca-Cola warehouse across the street, and its sparks leveled a house in the Camperdown Mill Village. Greenville's lack of firefighting equipment, caused by infighting between the City Council and the Fire Commission about what brand of fire engine to purchase, caused much of the destruction. City Council won (although the engine they purchased broke down at its second outing.)

However, there was good news. Newly completed Textile Hall on West Washington Street successfully hosted the second Southern Textile exposition, a huge Upstate automobile and fashion show, and a Southern Baptist meeting to plan a multistate $75-million campaign for Baptist colleges.

And the YWCA was flourishing. The federal government had given the national YWCA responsibility and funds for women—soldiers' wives, mothers, and sweethearts as well as office workers—involved in the war. In June 1917, "Y" leaders came to Greenville, and within three weeks, an eighteen-member board of directors of Greenville's most prestigious ladies was organized, headed by the redoubtable Rhoda Haynsworth. By the end of August, they had an office, hired a director, and adopted a $5,000 budget. Within a few months, the new Greenville YWCA had more than four hundred members, had started gym classes in eleven mill villages, begun a Hostess House at Camp Sevier, and scheduled "teas for strangers" every Thursday afternoon.

Within a year, they had reserved the swimming pool at the Greenville Woman's College for lessons two afternoons a week, had developed two Girl Reserve (Girl Scouts) programs, and arranged their first resident summer camp at Chick Springs. In 1920, the last of the national workers withdrew from Greenville, leaving behind a legacy of superactivity and a gift of $26,000 to renovate a cottage at Dunean Mill as a YWCA headquarters.

During the war, Eugenia Duke had made and sold sandwiches at Camp Sevier. An expert cook, she began making pimento cheese, egg salad, and chicken salad sandwiches: The ingredients were cooked, chopped, ground, mixed with home-made mayonnaise, and spread on sandwiches that were then labeled and wrapped in wax paper in her apartment kitchen and delivered to the base. She priced her sandwiches at a dime each. Mrs. Duke sold a lot of sandwiches, made a small fortune, and started a Greenville tradition.

She delivered a product that tasted like home to the boys from Tennessee and the Carolinas who served in the Old Hickory Division. Her secret ingredient, some said, was the mayonnaise that bound her ingredients. Her recipe, made of oil, eggs, and cider vinegar,

was unsweetened, which was helpful—even necessary—because sugar was rationed. Quick, tasty, and familiar, Duke sandwiches were immensely and immediately popular. Southern tastebuds preferred them to hamburgers and hot dogs, Northern favorites. And they were patriotic: The same people who renamed sauerkraut "liberty cabbage" disapproved of foods—hamburgers (from Hamburg), frankfurters (from Frankfurt) or wienies (from "Wien," the German word for Vienna)—that sounded like the Hun. Sandwiches were all-American.

By early 1918, the Red Cross War Camp Community Club just north of the Ottaray Hotel had become her principal "sandwich stand." It was there, in the spring of 1918, that she sold ten thousand sandwiches in one day. That success confirmed her commitment to an entrepreneurial future: She bought a delivery truck and painted "Duke Sandwich Company" on it in scrawling white letters.

In August 1919, Greenville started planning for the biggest party in its history. The First Divisional Reunion of the Thirtieth—Old Hickory—Division was scheduled for the city beginning on September 28, 1919. About six thousand former soldiers were expected. The program would honor the men who trained at Camp Sevier and showcase Greenville's postwar hospitality and prosperity.

Organizers had to find five thousand beds (local hotels had only three hundred), provide

A festooned downtown Greenville prepares for a reunion of the Thirtieth Division.

six meals for visitors, and arrange transportation and entertainment. The *Greenville News* begged for rooms, featuring a "Bed Pledge" on the top of the front page. Food was prepared at Textile Hall, where six army stoves were installed, and served in shifts there and at First Baptist, First Presbyterian, and St. Mary's

Churches. Festive balls were planned. Main Street, decked in patriotic banners, was illuminated all the way to the Ottaray Hotel. "Aeroplane" exhibitions; a divisional boxing match; and performances by the "Hickory Nuts," a comedy troupe, filled every minute that was not spent listening to speeches recounting the glorious history of the Thirtieth Division. The most honored Greenvillian was battlefield hero Major Heyward Mahon.

On Wednesday, October 1, the entire city must have breathed a collective sigh of relief. They had done it. The reunion had been a rousing success. Testimonials of praise and thanks inundated the organizers, and the biggest news of the day was no longer the need for beds or funds, the intricacies of arrangements, or year-old military exploits. It was the opening of Greenville's Piggly-Wiggly, the town's first supermarket.

Chapter 11

BOOM AND BUST,
1920–40

Greenville boomed in the early twenties. Health care expanded. Main Street modernized. A half dozen new textile mills opened, and a dozen new suburban subdivisions developed. Education dramatically improved. Although Jim Crow limited their lives, conditions for Black residents became slightly more equitable. The "wide-awake" city was thriving.

In November 1920, women—even South Carolina women—voted for the first time. The others elected tall, handsome, and not-very-bright Senator Warren G. Harding of Ohio to replace the ailing Woodrow Wilson. (Greenville remained solidly Democratic.) National prohibition didn't change the Upstate. "Wet" families kept sipping sherry and making "medicinal" use of whiskey. Others, especially college students who enjoyed risks, savored readily available moonshine. Local stills were busy. Even after a five-gallon keg of liquid corn was seized in Greer during Christmas week, the governor was still not convinced that lawmen should be diverted from catching speeders to making prohibition raids.

Locally that December, the big news was the distribution of "hundreds of thousands of dollars" in Christmas bonuses to mill workers, and the city's "gifts" of $5 each to underpaid city workers, including firemen, policemen, and street cleaners. Mayor H. C. Harveley and his Council, concerned about the city's "physical, moral, and hygienic condition," voted to buy thirty-two new garbage cans. Aldermen delayed until the new year discussing the other problems confronting them—sewers, roads, and the new water system.

The 17-story Woodside Building, shown here ca. 1939.
Greenville County Library System.

The biggest news was health care. Thomas
Parker convinced textile executives to contrib-
ute $150,000 to establish a Salvation Army
hospital in West Greenville. The Emma Booth
Memorial Hospital, the only Salvation Army

hospital in the South, opened in January
1921. Army officials borrowed an additional
$290,000 to make it a reality.

In addition, "one of the most modern
institutions in the South for colored people"
opened at the corner of Green Avenue and
Jenkins Avenue. St. Luke's Colored Hospital
would provide, said the *Greenville News*, three
wards, twenty-two private and semiprivate
rooms, and two operating rooms. Its chief
administrator would be Mrs. M. H. Bright, a
registered nurse with twenty-one years of experience at the Tuskegee Institute. It became the
Working Benevolent Society Hospital in 1927.

In the mid-1920s, officials at the Hopewell
Tuberculosis Camp on Rutherford Road began
offering X-ray technology and started raising
money for a truly modern tuberculosis hospital.
It opened on July 27, 1930, with $175,000 in
equipment, a main building with connecting
wings, a service building, and a separate but
identically equipped facility for Black sufferers.

Shriners Hospital for Crippled Children was
conceived in May 1925, when W. W. Burgiss
Charities was established for children's health,
education, and welfare, with assets valued
between $1 million and $1.2 million. A former
textile executive and realtor, Burgiss committed
his first grant to build a $300,000 hospital to
be deeded to the Mystic Order of the Shrine.
In November, Burgiss Charities bought five
acres on Rutherford Road, and J. E. Sirrine &

Co. immediately began constructing a fifty-bed hospital on the site. However, two years later, as the building was being completed, the Burgiss Charities were "financially embarrassed," and the Hejaz Temple had to advance the last $35,000. On September 26, 1927, thousands of Shriners gathered to accept the deed to the hospital. After 1930, the hospital cared for both Black and white children.

Construction changed Main Street during those boom years. Residents celebrated the seventeen-story Woodside Building, the tallest in the state; two elegant new movie houses, the Rivoli and the Carolina; the Poinsett Hotel, on the site of the old Mansion House; and the Chamber of Commerce Building, replacing the county's distinguished but careworn Record Building. The 1824 Robert Mills Courthouse was unpainted and unelectrified, and the Chamber of Commerce, whose offices were there, called it "an embarrassment to the city." After acts of the state legislature and a state supreme court decree, in August 1924, the property was conveyed to the Chamber, which promptly demolished it and had a $250,000, ten-story "skyscraper" erected in its place. The cornerstone for the Chicago-style high-rise was laid in January 1925; in November, members celebrated its grand opening.

By 1926, Chamber membership had grown to more than two thousand. It included a hyperactive Junior Bureau; a Women's Bureau

The Chamber of Commerce Building replaced the Robert Mills-designed Courthouse that once stood on the same site. Architect's rendering. Postcard by E. C. Kropp Co., South Carolina Room Archives, Greenville County Library System.

with nearly three hundred members; and thirteen committees dedicated to improving agriculture, railroad service, social welfare, promotion ("boosterism"), parks, and retailing. Between 1921 and 1926, in addition to the new headquarters, members supported a county fair and a downtown "restroom" for women workers; funded a municipal band; organized a curb market; paid for Main Street Christmas decorations; arranged "Get Acquainted Tours" (to destinations including Havana and Montreal); and promoted Greenville with a monthly magazine, press releases, special license tags, and billboards.

Beginning in 1923, its Women's Bureau sponsored a Better Homes contest that was endorsed by President Coolidge and strongly supported by Secretary of Commerce Herbert Hoover. The contest encouraged communities to build and publicize model homes with modern (electric) conveniences. Because Chamber members had recently toured both Atlanta and Charlotte where they had seen the glories of Druid Hills and Myers Park, they wanted equally splendid housing for their hometown.

With the help of Chamber members, public officials, and educators, Greenville adopted the contest. Ministers of every denomination preached sermons about home life. School children wrote essays. Southern Public Utilities (now Duke Power) sponsored a cooking school using electric appliances. Mayor H. C. Harveley proclaimed June 4–10, 1923, "Better Homes Demonstration Week." Greenville's entry, a "scientifically designed" home on East Prentiss Street, won fourth place in the national contest and was awarded a $50 prize and received a

letter of congratulations from Herbert Hoover, who applauded the community's "virile individualism." In the following years, the Bureau's applications won second place and first place in the contest.

The Chamber also celebrated the new subdivisions that were being developed outside the city's mile-and-a-quarter limits. Several (Buist Circle, Cherokee Park, Overbrook, Cagle Park, Millsdale) had been built before the war, but the paving of Augusta Street to the city limits and the move of the Sans Souci Country Club to Byrd Boulevard led to extensive nearby development. Tindall Park, McDaniel Heights, Alta Vista, and Traxler Park offered elite suburban housing. At the same time, North Main Street, which had stopped at Croft Street because of the deep gullies around branches of Richland Creek to the north, was extended to Rutherford Road by having chain gangs fill in the deep cuts. C. C. Hindman began heavy marketing for his Hillcrest development, and a group that included John Russell, James Gallivan, and Charles Garraux began developing Elizabeth Garraux's former fifty-acre farm and vineyard. Francs Hipp and others developed Arcadia just north of the deepest culvert on North Main Street.

The Chamber also ardently and successfully wooed northern textile executives. The first new mill since 1912, however, was Judson's Silk Mill established to produce DuPont's new rayon fabric. Southern Franklin Processing came next, followed by three mills backed by J. B. Duke: Southern Worsted on Bramlett Road, and Southern Weaving and Southern Bleachery in Taylors. Three years later, Abney Mills opened Renfrew Bleachery north of Travelers Rest, and H. J. Slater began Slater Manufacturing in Marietta. In 1927, boosters proclaimed that Greenville was the only county in the nation where cotton was grown, ginned, spun, woven, dyed, finished, and sewn into garments. The apparel was primarily men's "long johns" sewn at Fred Symmes's Nucassee Manufacturing Co. at the old Huguenot Mill, the largest underwear producer in the nation.

After enabling legislation in 1922, textile executives began the Parker School District. It funded new elementary schools in mill villages and in Brutontown, where many Black workers at American Spinning and Poe Mills lived. The Parker District also began constructing the $150,000 Parker High School for mill village youngsters. By September 1924, its roof was finished, and five hundred students were enrolled, two hundred of them in the seventh grade. In November, hundreds of visitors attended the school's formal opening and admired the seventeen classrooms, spacious laboratories, cafeteria, and study hall. Parker High became a model of progressive vocational education because Pete Hollis, the superintendent, believed in learning by doing. It held the state's first science fair. Its school newspaper and debate club won regional honors. The Parker orchestra, chorus, and glee club performed regularly. Student government began in 1931. It offered both vocational courses and college preparatory ones. *Readers' Digest* called Parker High a "Mill Village Miracle."

Although the innovative Parker District got much of the publicity, Greenville schools also expanded. The high school, formerly confined to the upstairs classrooms of Central School, had been accredited after it added an eleventh grade in 1916; by 1921, officials had constructed a completely new building on Westfield Street. The district built five new elementary schools for whites and three for Black children.

Furman flourished. New construction included a gymnasium and football field for the mighty "Purple Hurricane," which regularly played and beat Clemson College. President McGlothlin and the trustees learned in December 1924 that the university had finally been accredited by the Southern Association after its endowment had climbed to the required $500,000. A day or two later, they received word that, thanks to trustee Bennette Geer, Furman had been included as one of four collegiate beneficiaries of the Duke Endowment together with Davidson College, Trinity College (whose name was changed to Duke University), and Johnson C. Smith University. Furman would annually receive about four percent of the huge endowment's income.

The Greenville Woman's College struggled with accreditation, which required upgrading its faculty, library, and endowment, but it gloried in the construction of an elegant and expensive fine arts center on the college campus that became the site of many community events.

Education for Black children improved, thanks to a fund established by Julius Rosenwald, the head of Sears, Roebuck & Co. Between 1921 and 1931, at least thirty "Rosenwald Schools" were built in Greenville County, thanks to his $20 million fund to improve southern rural schools for African American children. Rosenwald officials accepted segregation as a given and assumed that Blacks would occupy the lowest levels of society, but they wanted to improve schools for African American children and—possibly—shame southern states into spending a few more dollars on their education. The Nashville-based foundation developed architectural plans and insisted on minimum standards for lot size, desks and blackboards, access to water, privies, and play areas. To make every dollar count and to develop a sense of community commitment and ownership, Rosenwald money called for matching funds from Black residents—in Greenville, amounts ranged from $350 to $2,500. They then negotiated an agreement with local school districts (there were eighty in Greenville County) for staffing and maintenance. In 1929, the city school

district purchased private Enoree High School for $2,819, renamed it Sterling High School, constructed a $15,000 Rosenwald-funded vocational building, and finally provided Black students with a public high school.

Black children and adults found new opportunities in the Phillis Wheatley Center. Hattie Logan Duckett, a widowed schoolteacher, began a home for young women in 1919 and, with the help of other Black men and women, raised $3,500 and purchased a modest house on the corner of East McBee Avenue and Heldman Street. It almost immediately became coeducational, because boys as well as girls wanted to attend its story hours and Bible study, but the Black community could not cover the mortgage and operating costs. In October 1923, Mrs. Duckett turned to Thomas Parker for help. Together with a biracial board, they raised $65,000, purchased a lot on East Broad Street, and created a center of Black life in Greenville. The Phillis Wheatley Center was dedicated in December 1924. It offered a full range of services: sewing classes, choral groups, Boy Scouts, a nursery, space for basketball games, meeting rooms for social clubs, and a case worker. With the support of Parker, the first public library for Black people in the state was installed there. Adjacent to the Wheatley Center on the corner of East Broad and Falls Street was the new $50,000 Benevolent Working Society Temple, built by a Black-owned and operated insurance company. It provided meeting rooms (used often for Republican party meetings) and professional offices for Black physicians and dentists as well as offices for insurance executives; St. Luke's Hospital became the Working Benevolent Hospital, and lots on Green Avenue were developed as Washington Heights for Black housing.

Parker was responsible for finally bringing public library services to all of Greenville. In the spring of 1921, with the help of banker J. W. Norwood, the Greenville library opened in a leased basement room on Coffee Street. It had one employee, Miss Annie Porter; five hundred books; and a few locally made pine bookshelves, tables, and chairs. In January 1923, when the city began supporting the library, hours were extended from 9 A.M. to 9 P.M. daily. City funding meant having a professional librarian. Miss Porter, experienced but without any formal legal training, recommended that the Board of Trustees hire Charlotte Templeton, then director of the Georgia State Library Commission.

In February 1923, Parker proposed that a mobile service be started to deliver books to the new Parker District and, with the help of J. W. Norwood, funded it for a two-year experimental period. By October 1923, a small truck had been outfitted with shelves on either side so that, when the shutters that covered them were opened, adults could browse on one side and

Students of the Phyllis Wheatley Center's Harmonica Club, 1929. Elrod Collection, Greenville County Historical Society.

children on the other. The truck made its first visit to Poe Mill village, which enthusiastically responded, as did the other mill communities. Within a year, the Parker District became responsible for funding the mobile library. However, much of Greenville County was still unserved. Once again, Parker and Norwood personally contributed $10,000 to extend the service from Glassy Mountain on the north to Fountain Inn in the south. A three-ton Dodge truck was especially fitted out to carry "Free Reading to Everyone."

By April of 1926, when Parker summed up the accomplishments of five years of Greenville library service, he pointed out that the library had the largest circulation in the Carolinas, had the only "library on wheels" south of Washington, DC, and was the first to serve mill communities on a grand scale.

An equally impressive achievement in the mid-1920s was the creation of Cleveland Park. On December 31, 1924, William Choice Cleveland announced that he had given the city of Greenville one hundred ten acres of land surrounding Richland Creek and the Reedy River. His gift became Cleveland Park, an enduring community legacy. Extending along Richland Creek from Laurens Road to its confluence with the Reedy River and beyond to McDaniel Avenue, and including the old rock quarry, it was the largest land donation in the city's history. The gift was negotiated by John A. McPherson, the J. E. Sirrine & Co. executive who chaired the city's Parks and Trees Commission. The City Council agreed to a $110,000 bond issue for improvements, and the Parks and Trees Commission retained local landscape architect George Schultze to create a design that would include a boulevard (Woodland Way), playgrounds, and eventually a swimming pool. That same bond issue included funds for a park for Black children at the meadow west of Hudson Street.

Two major lawsuits did not slow progress. The first was eventually a triumph for the City Council. A statue of a Confederate soldier had stood at the intersection of College and North Main Street since 1892. By 1922, it had become a traffic hazard. City Council decided to move it to the front of the courthouse. The United Daughters of the Confederacy and the Confederate Veterans Association protested. Acting quickly one September morning, a Council Committee ordered the statue taken down and began moving its pedestal to the new site. When they learned at noon that opponents were seeking a restraining order to keep it in place, they whisked the statue away to a barn on Paris Mountain before the injunction could be served. The case went to the circuit court, which ruled that the city could not relocate it. The City Council appealed to the SC Supreme Court, however, which ruled in its favor. After intense negotiations, the statue was eventually moved from its hiding place and resettled on its pedestal at Springwood Cemetery in June 1924.

The second suit took longer to resolve and was far more expensive. In 1925, little Conestee (population, three hundred) sued giant Greenville (population, twenty-five thousand). The issue was pollution. The Reedy River had powered grist, saw, paper, wool, and cotton mills near the village seven miles southeast of Greenville for a century. Its dam, rebuilt in 1892, had created Lake Conestee, a huge mill pond that had become a major health hazard. Conditions had been bad for a decade, but in the early spring of 1925, they became vile. The Upstate was gripped by the worst drought since 1884. As a result, the Reedy's flow, reduced to a mere trickle, intensified poisonous vapors, odors, and waste.

In May, Conestee Mill President Thomas Charles sued the City of Greenville on behalf of the residents of Conestee. He accused the city of operating an antiquated and inadequate sewer system, pled for immediate relief from the pollution, and asked for $100,000 in damages. The river was delivering (in the descriptive and comprehensive words of the suit) "human fecal matter, kitchen washings and waste from homes, hotels, hospitals, meat and vegetable markets, stores, dye houses, gas plants, laundries, packing houses, garages, undertaking establishments, and slaughter pens" from Greenville to Lake Conestee.

The city's sewer system, completed in 1893, consisted of a network of sewer pipes that emptied waste into the Reedy River and the intersecting Brushy and Richland Creeks without any treatment. The sewage then made its winding way down to the lake at Conestee. In 1891, Greenville had been a town of eight thousand with two small cotton mills, so cavalier treatment of nasty stuff wasn't much of a problem. But times had changed. By 1925, more than thirty cotton mills, two animal crematories, an abattoir, and at least twenty thousand additional people had made the river a health menace.

Greenville residents certainly recognized the problem. Workmen landscaping Cleveland Park complained about the putrid waste in Richland Creek. Golfers at the Greenville Country Club held their noses when they weren't teeing off. Realtors had difficulty selling lots near the river in Traxler Park. Furthermore, County Health Commissioner Baylis Earle and L. M. Fisher, the chief engineer of the State Board of Health, had ordered the city to improve sewer conditions. Two months earlier, a grand jury report condemned Greenville's practice of emptying untreated sewage into the river. In mid-June, the county legislative delegation, responsible for approving any bond issue for remediation, appointed Greenville's first sewer commission. The delegation charged the commission with completing a survey of conditions before the 1926 legislative session but neglected to provide funds for the study.

On July 1, William Sirrine, Conestee's attorney and Thomas Charles's former law partner, began open warfare. He fired off a letter to Mayor Richard Watson, copied to the *Greenville News*, charging that the City Council had not yet discussed the grand jury's assessment of the Reedy and that the legislative delegation was deliberately dragging its feet. Within a week, the newspaper called editorially for immediate action, and the delegation suddenly found $3,000 to fund the sewer survey.

In August, the suit was heard in the Greenville Court of Common Pleas, beginning a torturous six-year judicial journey. First round went to the city: The judge refused to issue an injunction and ruled that the mill president could not file on behalf of the village population. He could, however, refile the complaint with the mill as the single plaintiff. Before the revision could be heard, though, the city objected ("demurred") to the refiling and appealed to the state Supreme Court.

While the case moldered in Columbia, the situation in Greenville changed. In November 1925, the legislative delegation agreed to a $3.3 million bond issue for a sewage treatment facility. The following year, the delegation created the Greater Greenville Sanitary District (later, the Western Carolina Regional Sewer Authority; now ReWa). In the summer of 1926, ground was broken for "the most modern sewage treatment plant in the world," costing about $2 million. It was located four miles south of the city below the intersection of Brushy Creek and the Reedy River, not far from the upper end of Lake Conestee. Planned to serve the community for thirty to forty years, it opened in July 1928. It would be massively expanded just four years later. According to the *Greenville News*, it was the most "progressive and gigantic municipal enterprise" ever undertaken in the South. It

led to the US Health Service's naming the City and County of Greenville the healthiest place in the United States in 1928.

And then, gradually, the boom fizzled. Cotton began the downturn. The boll weevil hit South Carolina in 1917; it attacked Upstate crops in 1923. Worn-out soil, eroded by generations of farming, no longer produced abundantly. Weather—droughts in 1925 and 1926, tornadoes and storms in 1927—lowered farmers' incomes. At the same time, bumper crops on irrigated California land caused cotton prices to drop. With fewer dollars to spend, farmers bought less. Textile mill profits and dividends fell; management responded with money-saving strategies. "Stretch-outs" forced workers to tend more looms at lowered wages. Less productive, often older, operatives were fired; hours were reduced. Rumors of union activity and talk of strikes circulated in West Greenville; downtown merchants worried about the possibility of bank failures and the actuality of falling profits. The Bank of Commerce closed in 1926; Brandon Mill workers walked out for six months in the spring of 1929. The chamber of commerce, dependent on office rents to make payments on their building, had increasing vacancies. The mortgage company foreclosed, and the building was sold to Liberty Life, which was prospering, becoming "the Insurance Building."

In December 1926, Greenville had its first Christmas parade. Merchants were feeling pinched, so the chamber of commerce decided to kick-start the Christmas season. They raised $5,000, purchased garlands of red and green bulbs to string across Main Street, decorated thirty-four trees for downtown corners, and scheduled a parade. Families packed the sidewalks. At 6 P.M., Santa arrived at the Piedmont & Northern train station on Academy Street and then led the parade to the Ottaray Hotel at the top on Main Street, waving cheerfully to the crowds.

As the state was sliding into economic depression, Governor John Reynolds declared in January 1927 that he would make South Carolina the most moral state (if not the most prosperous) in the nation by enforcing all state blue laws passed since 1691. He ordered sheriffs to arrest filling station owners selling gas, drug stores selling soda water (or anything except medicine), and participants in outdoor sports on Sundays. In late February 1927, state constables arrested golfers at the winter colony in Aiken. At a jury trial two weeks later, they were exonerated. The following Sunday, constables arrested four Greenvillians (including attorney and former legislator P. A. Bonham) at the ninth hole of the Greenville Country Club for "desecrating the sabbath." The *Greenville News* compared Reynolds to Mussolini. Although church groups loved Reynolds's "crusade," local people objected so strongly that enforcement stopped by midsummer. However, Sunday baseball and movies remained firmly prohibited in Greenville (as "rock-ribbed as an old-fashioned corset," said *News* sportswriter Scoop Latimer) if they charged admission. Even exhibition games and free movies were questioned.

Then came the 1929 stock market crash. John T. Woodside, who had boasted in 1916 that he was the richest man in Greenville, had purchased sixty-six thousand acres of beach property and built the million-dollar Ocean Forest Hotel near the tiny Horry County village of Myrtle Beach. He went bankrupt in 1931, losing that development, Woodside Cotton Mill, Woodside National Bank, and eventually his Crescent Avenue home. Walter Gassaway—known to local residents as the owner of Isaqueena, a forty-room, twenty-two-thousand-square-foot home off East North Street that was completed in 1924 at a cost of $700,000 (about $12 million today) and the president of three banks and two textile mills—was nearly bankrupt when he died unexpectedly in 1930.

If the elite struggled, the poor despaired. Community services were cut: The library reduced wages. The Red Cross, overwhelmed with needy people, closed its doors. Taxes were reduced, so local government saved money by laying off staff and removing telephones from city offices. (That savings device lasted only a week.) The Seidenberg Cigar Factory closed, throwing two hundred women out of work.

Mills went to one shift; workweeks were cut to three or four days.

Local agencies tried to provide. A citizens' committee ran a Welfare Service, hiring white women to sew and men to chop wood. Black men were employed digging sewers at fifty cents a day, redeemable for groceries at the Phillis Wheatley Center. So many applied that each was limited to two days' work week. The Salvation Army distributed more than five hundred stale loaves of bread each day. Tax revenues fell; teachers and principals, whose salaries averaged $1,080 annually, voted to take a ten percent salary cut to keep schools open for eight months. The Welfare Service reminded the public to turn in their "Penny-A-Meal" boxes and donate canned goods to care for the destitute. President Hoover faced a reeling economy.

Even with economic struggles, there were bright spots. Greenville's first attempt at an art museum began with high hopes in the summer of 1927. The Lions Club decided that, given the success of the library, residents were ready for more culture. The club appointed a board of seven directors (none of them artists) for the Greenville Museum of Art and named Dr. T. W. Sloan, pastor of First Presbyterian Church, the president. The directors began their museum with a display of copies of some of the world's most famous sculpture, ordering copies of the *Venus de Milo*, *Diana of the Chase*, and the *Apollo Belvedere* from a Boston firm

and arranged that the Greenville Library would host museum displays in its auditorium.

On January 23, 1928, the Greenville Museum of Art opened in the library, the auditorium packed with Lions and their spouses. The theme of the evening was that the "statuary" would instill an appreciation of the finer things of life in "young men with good red blood in their veins" and that gazing at Greek gods and goddesses would free their minds, as Furman President W. J. McGlothlin said, of any thought of art as being "sissy." Furthermore, as George Barr, the head of the American Legion and an air ace in the Great War, added, the collection of war relics, which would be "displayed under the same roof with the statuaries . . . would remind boys that war is cruel and thereby bring about a desire for universal peace." They were expecting a lot from three statues and some rusty grenades.

However, in February 1928, the library had its all-time highest number of visitors, and in the first weeks of March, all was well. Then the storm broke. J. D. Gilbert, an insurance agent, rose at a Community Chest board meeting on Tuesday, March 21, to protest the *Apollo Belvedere*. The "so-called art," he said, was offensive. He called for the public to be shielded from its "naked nudity." Both Greenville newspapers carried a complete report of his remarks. The *Greenville News* reported three days later that "a stream of people through the day and into the night mounted the steps to the museum to gaze at the "nude nakedness." Then, a day later, someone unknown (the special delivery package had no return address) sent fragile pale pink and green knickers—ladies' underpants—addressed to "Mr. Apollo" at the Greenville library. Even *Time* magazine carried the story. (Apollo never wore the pants.)

The most anticipated event, though, was the opening of the new Greenville City Airport. It had been a long time coming, but finally, by the late summer of 1928, one hundred thirty-six acres of land near Lowndes Hill Road were ready, and plans were made for a celebratory opening. Lt. George Barr, commander of the American Legion post and a former army pilot, and local barnstormer Errett Williams were in charge. They invited dozens of military units and commercial flyers to participate and organized aerial shows, exhibitions, dinners, and speeches on November 9 as part of the festivities. The first plane to land, on a "leisurely" twenty-minute flight from Spartanburg, which already had an airport, was a giant trimotor Ford capable of holding fourteen passengers. Long-desired airmail service became a reality.

Coca-Cola initiated its handsome new bottling plant on Buncombe Street on November 17, 1930, with a formal celebration followed by a week-long open house with public inspection tours. The elaborate and expensive two-story building with its sanitary and modern bottling equipment, easily viewed through the large plate glass front window, was an optimistic sign (although falsely so) that Greenville's economy might be improving.

The closing of the Salvation Army Hospital in 1931 devastated the mill villagers who had come to depend on it. However, in February 1932, the Franciscan Sisters of the Poor, a German-speaking nursing order from Cincinnati, bought the former West End hospital for $55,000. When the first sisters arrived in May, they scoured, repainted, and renovated the sixty-bed facility before its July opening. By December 1933, St. Francis Hospital had cared for twenty-two hundred patients. In 1934, the Duke Endowment funded a $100,000 addition.

In May 1933, Roger Peace, owner of the *Greenville News*, received approval for a radio station. Broadcasting from the Hotel Imperial, WFBC (the station's name was inherited from First Baptist Church of Knoxville, Tennessee, which had given up its license and offered its equipment to the new Greenville station) had a transmitter on Faris Road. Thanks to extensive free newspaper publicity, improved transmission, more efficient and less expensive receivers (acid from storage batteries no longer dripped on living room rugs), and increasing audiences, WFBC immediately attracted local advertisers.

Greenville voted overwhelmingly for Franklin D. Roosevelt in November 1932 and embraced his New Deal in the years that followed.

The work of the Civilian Conservation Corps in the 1930s was vital to the development of twentieth-century park architecture across the nation, including Table Rock State Park and Paris Mountain State Park. Shown here: the bathhouse at Paris Mountain State Park. Historic American Buildings Survey. Library of Congress Prints and Photographs Division.

And for good reason: Between 1932 and 1938, almost four million dollars in federal funds flowed into local pockets. That aid did not end the Great Depression—it took the surge in textile orders before World War II to do that—but it saved some people from starving and others from losing their homes and jobs, and it made permanent improvements in local life.

The first and probably most popular of the "alphabet agencies" was the Civilian Conservation Corps (CCC). Together with workers from the Works Project Administration (WPA), corpsmen dug a new bed for the Reedy River to increase the water flow and eliminate the stream's still unpleasant odor, improved the

riverbanks, removed undergrowth, and added landscaping. They built two tennis courts, a roller-skating rink, a swimming pool, and a bathhouse. CCC workers worked at Table Rock State Park, fought erosion and forest fires, constructed Camp Buckhead on the site of the former Paris Mountain reservoir, landscaped its drives, and built a bathhouse. In effect, they created Paris Mountain State Park, an Upstate treasure since 1938.

WPA funds paid for a new Greenville High School, Sirrine Stadium, and wings added to both hospitals. The Reconstruction Finance Corporation improved the airport, sewer system, and Boy Scout camp. The National Industrial Recovery Act led the way to a forty-hour week and set the minimum wage for mill workers at $12 a week.

The new high school was a major improvement. It opened on September 5, 1938, cost nearly a half million dollars, most of them federal; and had a capacity of fifteen hundred students. It was, in the words of the *Greenville News*, "the latest in school edifices," modern in every respect with conveniences that students' parents could only have dreamed of. They included indirect lighting, electric fire alarms, a fully equipped domestic science kitchen for girls, and an equally splendid woodworking shop for boys. A gymnasium with folding bleachers and a full-sized basketball court was near the totally modern cafeteria with a hygienic kitchen. The former high school building was converted to Greenville Junior High, with seventh and eighth grades; the senior high school served grades nine through eleven until 1947, when twelfth grade was added.

In 1932, when city officials requested nearly $170,000 from the federal government for a new city hall, the feds said no. Thanks, however, to Senator James Byrnes, Congressman J. J. McSwain, and lobbying by the Chamber of Commerce and City Council, three years later, the government did agree to build a new federal building and post office in Greenville. It would replace the much-loved sprawling 1892 landmark at the corner of Main and Broad Streets. When the postmaster general's office recommended its demolition, however, Greenville officials argued that razing it would cost $5,000 and that citizens were opposed. Furthermore, a better site could be found for the federal building. In a complicated deal, the City Council traded the McBee Street City Hall site to the heirs of the Ware estate in exchange for a large lot at East Washington and Church Streets. City officials then traded that site to post office authorities for a federal building and got in exchange the elaborate 1892 red brick Main Street post office to be the new city hall site. The deal cost the city $75,000; the estimated value of their new building was $200,000. Architects Beacham and LeGrand drew renovation plans, and by September 1938,

when Postmaster General James Farley came to town to dedicate the new federal building (now the Haynsworth Federal Building), Greenville also had one of the most elegant and spacious city halls in the South.

It also had a newly coordinated university. Between 1925 and 1930, Furman and the Greenville Women's College struggled with falling enrollment and economic depression. The South Carolina Baptist Convention, then supporting six colleges, urged them to merge. Bennette Geer, chair of Furman's Board of Trustees, fearful that the Women's College increasing debts would hurt Furman, was vigorously opposed, although the majority of the trustees were in favor. In the spring of 1933, they voted (with Geer dissenting) to coordinate the schools. Just as coordination was about to happen, Furman President Joseph McGlothlin was killed in a car accident, and the trustees, faced with the immediate need for a new president, decided on Geer. Although he remained opposed to coordination and many trustees considered him abrasive and high-handed, he was clearly a leader who loved Furman.

As president, he presided over the coordination of two schools a mile apart that needed cars, buses, and taxis to transport students to their crosstown classrooms. By the end of the first year of the "temporary experiment," as he initially called it, Geer discovered that coordination was working—grades and enrollment were up, finances improved—and he embraced it. He also formed new alliances with the community, supported the arboretum project, developed a nursing program with the city hospital, encouraged the formation of the Greenville Symphony Orchestra, and cooperated with the city to make Sirrine Stadium a reality.

His major focus, however, was on the Greenville County Council for Community Development (GCCCD), which brought $80,000 from the Rockefeller General Education Fund for a five-year program. Housed on campus, it included surveys of conditions in the mill villages and black neighborhoods, offered adult education programs (for whites at Greenville High School and for Blacks at Fountain Inn Negro School), added two new sociologists to the faculty, and improved community health programs. It was remarkably innovative, but many trustees were not happy with the interracial component. Greer opposed athletic scholarships and expenditures; most trustees supported them. They complained that he gave too many scholarships and let the university deficit grow. Also, he supported religion professors whose theological views were considered heretical by the North Greenville Baptist Association. Antagonism between Geer and his trustees came to a head early in 1938, when Herbert Gezork, a highly respected liberal young theologian who later became president of Andover-Newton Theological Seminary, was

charged with heresy. Geer defended him, as he had other members of the religion department, but trustees fired him. Geer resigned, obviously exhausted by the continuing attacks on finances and academic freedom.

Although Geer was a member of a national committee studying wages in cotton mills, at least he didn't have to deal directly with the General Textile Strike, the longest, largest, and most extensive "industrial action" in American history, extending from Maine to Alabama. It hit Greenville on September 5, 1934. In the late 1920s, responding to economic downturns, mill owners reduced dividends, cut wages, and increased workloads. By 1932, the average South Carolina mill worker earned $9.70 a week. The New Deal didn't improve conditions. The United Textile Workers Union launched a strike, with Greenville as their southern headquarters on September 1. On September 5, "flying squadrons" of strikers from Spartanburg arrived determined to shut down local mills, but most workers at Woodside, Brandon, and Monaghan Mills refused to strike. The governor ordered National Guardsmen to set up machine gun emplacements at large mills while soldiers with fixed bayonets guarded factory gates and roofs. Although all four Greer mills had closed the previous day, confrontations at Dunean, Judson, Brandon, Woodside, and Monaghan did not close those mills. On Thursday morning, though, as organizers, deputies, and workers gathered at Dunean, a deputy sheriff challenged a Dunean resident who pulled a knife. The deputy fired, and when the worker ran, the deputy shot him in the back. The General Textile Strike collapsed here on September 7 and across the nation two weeks later. Management won; years of local antiunion sentiment followed.

If textile unions were considered Yankee and dangerous, the coming of the National Association for the Advancement of Colored People (NAACP) in 1938 was viewed by many white Greenvillians as downright perilous. The local chapter, begun by retired schoolteacher James Brier, who had long experience with Republican Party politics, was triggered when the City Council refused to accept a federal grant of $800,000 to build low-rent housing. (Charleston and Columbia had accepted the federal dollars.) Then they refused to fund a park for African Americans on Perry Street in spite of the pleas of J. A. McPherson; Mrs. Rhoda Haynsworth; and Black former postman Elias Holloway, perhaps the most respected Black man in town.

When NAACP members realized that the housing project and park would not become a reality, they also realized that they were powerless because they could not vote. As a result, in the spring of 1939, the NAACP began "an intensive underground movement" to help people register. The state's 1895 Constitution was written to disenfranchise Blacks. It

had instituted the all-white Democratic Party primary, poll taxes, and "literacy" tests (which involved interpreting arcane articles of the Constitution). With the help of union organizers, the GCCCD, and the encouragement of local white attorney John Bolt Culbertson, the only white NAACP member in the state, the chapter held classes in local homes to explain registration procedures, articles of the US Constitution, and the questions that local registration officials were known to ask as part of "literacy tests." Then members began escorting small groups of Blacks—mostly women, primarily teachers—to the courthouse registration office. On July 6, 1939, the *Greenville News* ran a large headline: "57 Negroes Register in a Single Day." They joined several others who had already been approved. "What's Going on in Greenville?" queried the newspaper. Poinsett Klavern head Fred Johnson announced that "the Klan will ride again." And they did. On August 17, white-sheeted men paraded through downtown. On September 30, "Kluxers" rode through Simpsonville and Fountain Inn, beating Blacks whom they encountered.

In November, five cars filled with Klan members parked around Sterling High School to intimidate local residents. A week later, the City Council requested that the police chief, who worked closely with the Klan (according to Culbertson, most policemen were Klan members or sympathizers), ask them "not to parade 'too much' in the Negro districts of the city." Otherwise, police might have to enforce laws. Historian A. V. Huff says that two hundred thirty African Americans registered, and thirty-four brave souls voted.

Finally, there was the US Highway, created when SC Highway 8 became an official part of US Highway 29 in 1926. In the early 1930s, the New Deal allocated large chunks of cash to states for road building. In 1934, federal transportation officials decided to make US Highway 29 between Greenville and Spartanburg the only four-lane highway in the state and the longest (at twenty-eight miles) "dual-lane highway" in the South. On July 7, 1937, the state engineer announced that the first mile of concrete highway had been poured for the "Super-Road." The first section of that expressway, five miles long, was completed in May 1938. Extending about five miles from Stone Avenue to Taylors, it became Greenville's highway to the future.

Chapter 12

WAR AND POSTWAR,
1940–60

On December 11, 1941, just four days after the Japanese attack on Pearl Harbor, the Department of the Army announced that an air base would be established about eight miles south of Greenville. The twenty-six-hundred-acre property would be located among cotton fields and small farms on the Augusta Road near Conestee. Authorities anticipated that one hundred thirty bombers and pursuit planes and forty-five hundred men would eventually be stationed there. The City Council and county commissioners, in a rare show of unanimity, jointly paid for the land, leased to the government for the duration.

Daniel Construction Company of Anderson, which had established a small satellite office in Greenville a year earlier, received the building contract on January 4. A week later,

the company moved its main office to the city and began to clear the site for the anticipated $8 million facility. The first airmen arrived in late March 1942, when it was still under construction; by June, the first planes and four hundred command pilots had arrived at the completed base.

The army converted Municipal Airport to a glider training facility and built a practice bombing range near Caesar's Head. Greenville welcomed the base, its flyers, and their families, and especially welcomed their $250,000 monthly payroll. Recreation centers were established for white airmen at Textile Hall and for Blacks at the Phillis Wheatley Center. The program for Black servicemen was so extensive that Henry Percival, the head bellman at the Hotel Greenville, quit his job to be full-time director at the Center. The YMCA, local churches, and community volunteers provided hospitality and recreation.

Drives for war bonds and stamps, used cooking oil and aluminum, and rationing of sugar, tires, and gas (three gallons a week) that led some drivers to "put their jalopies on stilts for the duration" became a way of life. Nylon stockings were treasured; grocery stores saved Jell-O for favored customers. Air raid wardens and compulsory blackouts hit Greenville in May 1942, although mills kept working through the alarms, and Mauldin, Simpsonville, and Travelers Rest were exempt. From December 8, when the telegram from the War Department informed his parents that Kirk McBee, the great-great grandson of Vardry McBee, had been killed in the attack on Pearl Harbor, families lived in dread of news that husbands, fathers, sons, and boyfriends had perished. The celebration was muted when the town learned that the cargo ship *Greenville Victory* was launched in March 1944.

Perhaps nothing touched the whole community like the news of President Franklin Roosevelt's death in April 1945. More than fifteen thousand Greenvillians waited quietly along the tracks at the Southern Station for the train bearing his body north from Warm Springs, Georgia. Dozens more stood near the crossing on White Horse Road, along the trestle at Queen Street, and at Southern Bleachery

in Taylors to pay their last respects to the only president many had ever known.

V-E Day a week later was celebrated quietly—a few hundred people gathered at Meadowbrook Park to hear speeches—but V-J Day was a "hilarious" event with a day off at local mills and thousands cheering downtown. After V-J Day, Greenvillians assumed that the Army Air Base would close. The Defense Department, however, suddenly faced with a looming Cold War with the Soviet Union, decided instead to maintain the facility as the home of the Sixty-Third Troop Carrier Wing (later the Military Air Transport Command) and to enlarge and expand it. Because the Pentagon planned to spend substantial funds for improvements, they insisted in 1947 that the government have title to the land. Greenville wanted to keep the installation, so the air base commissioners would not agree to transferring the land to the government without a reversionary clause to the city and county if it were to close. The military refused. As a result, the commissioners were subject to intense pressure by county officials and businessmen. Instead of agreeing, they resigned.

A new board of commissioners, headed by James H. Woodside, was appointed. Woodside, with tact and persistence, eventually negotiated a contract with a clause that mandated the return of the Greenville Air Base to local government if it were ever deactivated.

Renamed Donaldson Air Force Base in 1951 to honor Major John O. Donaldson, a World War I air ace from Greenville, the facility soon housed twenty-two hundred men. Starting in 1948, planes from Greenville relieved Berlin, and during the 1950s, they made the city "the Airlift Capital of the World."

When former soldiers returned home in 1945, they found an unchanged town and cotton mill world. No new buildings had been erected on Main Street since 1926. That busy street stretched from the West End, where the old Furman campus was bursting at its seams, across the Reedy River, foaming with multicolored residue from upstream bleacheries, past the Poinsett Hotel, soon to be acquired by the Jack Tar chain, to the 1909 Ottaray Hotel at College Street. The seventeen-story Woodside Building was the town's tallest; City Hall, erected in 1892, its most elaborate. Power wires crisscrossed overhead; cars, buses, and trolleys clogged its streets. All Upstate highways emptied into Main Street.

The first peacetime Christmas was welcomed by the returnees but especially by the sixty-six thousand men who disembarked at Atlantic and Pacific ports on Wednesday, December 19. Trains and buses were standing room only. On Friday the 20th, the *Greenville News* reported that a midwestern snowstorm was drifting eastward. Greenvillians—especially young ones—dreamed of a white Christmas.

By 6 P.M. on Christmas Eve, forecasters' predictions were coming true: Three inches of snow had already fallen, and freezing rain and sleet were predicted for the evening. Greyhound and Eastern Airlines cancelled Greenville service. Trains ran six hours late at the Southern Railroad Station on Washington Street. Early risers awoke on Christmas morning to "a fairy land of Icelandic beauty." And cold houses. Seventy percent of local homes were powerless; thirty-five hundred telephones were out of service. Ice-loaded trees and power lines were down all over the city; roads were blocked. Children, shivering in sweaters and coats, opened their presents before an unlit tree. Fortunate families cooked dinner in front of fireplaces or pot-bellied kitchen stoves. It was an unforgettable holiday.

A real disaster—Greenville's greatest—occurred eleven months later. On November 19, 1946, the Ideal Laundry on Buncombe Street exploded when five thousand gallons of propane gas caught fire. A deliveryman smelling gas alerted the company vice president, who immediately ordered the evacuation of the plant. Then he dashed to a nearby fire station to rouse firemen. While he was there, the laundry exploded, with a huge flash of light and flames darting six hundred feet into the air. Within five minutes, the building was a blazing inferno. The explosion leveled more than a hundred homes and damaged dozens of others. Windows

Mack Library at Bob Jones University, ca. 1950. Mack Library was one of the original set of buildings on Bob Jones University's Greenville campus. Like many other campus buildings, it demonstrates 1950s-era modern architecture. Postcard, Greenville County Library System.

shattered, and chimneys collapsed. Shock waves were felt sixty miles away. Doctors rushed to local hospitals where hundreds lined up to give blood. The explosion left four hundred people homeless, injured one hundred fifty, hospitalized twenty-three, and killed six. Thousands gathered to watch: Some looted, most helped. Although it was a disaster for both Blacks and whites, Black people suffered more. Their homes were destroyed, their jobs were gone, and their nearby community had vanished.

Two major educational decisions in 1947 changed Greenville permanently. The Chamber of Commerce offered Bob Jones College of Cleveland, Tennessee, a fundamentalist Christian school that was searching for a new home, about one hundred eighty acres of land

on the Super Highway. President Bob Jones agreed and dedicated the institution, renamed a university, on Thanksgiving Day 1947.

At the same time, Furman, whose student population had almost doubled since the war, faced overcrowding as well as two decades of deferred maintenance. When trustees considered expanding locally, land prices around the university zoomed upward, so they decided instead to merge the women's campus on College Street and the university campus in the West End and build an entirely new campus in a new location. Beginning in 1947, the board spent two years exploring alternate sites before settling on eleven hundred acres near the new Poinsett Highway.

Postwar business hummed. Early in 1946, the Caine Company announced that it would build Lewis Plaza, an exciting new concept in retailing, on Birnie Hill off Augusta Road. The plaza would consist of a half-dozen single-story connected retail shops surrounding a central building and offer three hundred sixty-eight free and convenient parking spaces, a detail repeated in every press release. As the first shopping plaza in the Carolinas, Lewis Plaza would become a transitional shopping experience between old Main Streets and soon-to-be popular enclosed malls.

In August 1946, Jim Henderson, then twenty-five years old and armed with a degree from Clemson and two years of experience, opened an advertising agency in downtown Greenville. He believed that an agency in a small Southern town could create outstanding national advertising. His trust was rewarded, helped by his relationship with Jack Greer, who had formed a chemical company to manufacture textile products in an old garage in 1945. Together, they made Texize Liquid Cleaner extraordinarily successful. The agency grew to become the largest in the Southeast and among the top 1 percent in the nation. In 1980, *Advertising Age* magazine named Henderson the Agency of the Year, the first time that a company outside of New York and Chicago had been honored. The agency was best known locally for creating Clemson's Tiger Paw logo.

Cotton mills changed hands. In February 1947, J. P. Stevens & Co. of New York bought Monaghan, Dunean, Slater, Piedmont, and a dozen other regional mills. Abney Mills of Greenwood claimed Brandon, Poinsett, and Renfrew; Ely and Walker of Baltimore controlled Poe; Cone of Greensboro owned American Spinning; and Union Bleachery was sold to Aspinook. About a year after the Stevens purchase, realtor Alester G. Furman Jr. asked Robert Stevens, the textile company president, when he was planning to sell his villages. "Never," replied Stevens. "I'll never do that. We'd lose control of our workers."

Control was the central issue. Textile companies feared unionization and absenteeism.

They worried about public relations, about selling community buildings and pastors' houses, and about returning streets to public control. However, they learned that workers with mortgages had more to lose than renters did, and control continued because the mills financed their own mortgages. Within two years, the Furman Company was selling (at three-quarters of their assessed value) all Stevens village homes, with first choice to former renters. Other textile corporations from Delaware southward followed.

Opening up home ownership to workers created citizens with a greater stake in their community. The sales provided corporate funds to invest in new machinery and new, more efficient mills. An era of textile paternalism ended. These sales were the primary reason why Greenville County's rate of home ownership increased from twenty-eight percent in 1940 to sixty-seven percent in 1970.

The brutal lynching of Willie Earle, an unemployed Black laborer, on February 16, 1947, brought international attention to Greenville. In Columbia, Governor Strom Thurmond promised to "exert every force at my command to apprehend all persons engaged in such a flagrant violation." Six law enforcement agencies, including the Federal Bureau of Investigation (FBI), investigated. Within days, they had arrested twenty-eight taxi drivers and three businessmen, all white men. On March 12, the Greenville grand jury indicted all thirty-one of the accused on four counts of murder and conspiracy.

The Greenville Ministerial Association deplored the "lawlessness" of the lynching, but local sympathy was with the defendants. Mason jars were placed in mill village stores to collect money for their defense; "street talk" was that the state would never get a conviction. The controversial trial of thirty-one white men for the lynching was held in the impressive courtroom of the County Courthouse the following May. It was covered by *Life* magazine, the *New Yorker*, the *Christian Science Monitor*, and the Soviet news service (TASS), in addition to the Black press, news services, and every major American newspaper.

Circuit Judge Robert Martin tried the case. When the jury of twelve white men filed into the hot, crowded courtroom on May 12, 1947, they heard defense attorneys argue that the defendants' confessions had been taken under duress, that the "meddler's itch of the FBI" was intolerable, and that Northern interests were trying to dictate local affairs. Prosecutors argued that there was hard evidence that a conspiracy had existed and that the confessions had been obtained legally. "The majesty of the law had been trampled upon," they said; the mob had "spit in the law's face." No defendant testified.

On May 19, both sides concluded. Judge Martin acquitted three defendants for insufficient evidence and reduced the charges on seven others from four to two. Two days later, he delivered a twenty-page charge to the jury, later called "a model of clear, legal language." He instructed the jurors to ignore racial issues, to disregard any acts of Willie Earle as justification for the murder, and not to use the defendants' lack of testimony against them. After deliberating for five hours, the jury returned to the courtroom. The clerk of court read steadily for seven minutes through ninety-six separate verdicts of "not guilty."

Although there was a national outcry about the outcome, some media saw hope in the trial itself. The *Christian Science Monitor* headlined an editorial cartoon showing a southern mansion and an acorn with the words "A seed has been planted in Greenville." Willie Earle was the last man to be lynched in South Carolina. When President Harry S. Truman set up the US Civil Rights Commission the following November, he referred to the lynching as one of the outrages that had to stop. The anger in the Black community led to the first attempts by both Black and white citizens to make facilities, if not justice, equal for all.

In 1948, three Black women leaders asked the YWCA for a "Negro Branch." Their timing was significant. Progressive businessmen, eager for economic development, blanched at the black mark that the Earle lynching had placed on the city's carefully groomed reputation.

Relationships between Blacks and whites were tense. YWCA leadership delayed an answer to their request while City Council moved to defuse tensions by considering urban improvement programs and actually installing traffic blinkers at "colored" schools. Then a biracial community study made Greenville's "Big Idea"—a thorough analysis of the way Black people lived—a reality.

The Greenville Community Council hired the Southern Regional Council in Atlanta to help with questionnaires. The Council also appointed community volunteer Mrs. C. C. Withington and J. E. Beck, the principal of Sterling High School, as chair and co-chair of the one hundred fifty or so volunteers who gathered data and made recommendations. The facts were grim. None of the four Black doctors in the county could practice at Greenville General Hospital, where four Black nurses served fifty "Negro beds," all in wards; the only toilet available to Black women was in a utility room. St. Francis Hospital and the Greenville Maternity Shelter were for whites only, so almost all Black babies were delivered by midwives. Three Black dentists cared for seventeen thousand Black patients; no white dentist saw Black patients.

Law enforcement was biased. No public park in the county was open to Black residents. Schools were overcrowded—all Black students were on double sessions. Dropout rates were eye opening: Of the nineteen hundred thirty-nine Black children who had entered first grade in 1933, only one hundred forty-seven completed the eleventh grade, then the terminal grade for high school, in 1944. Of those, only seventy-nine went on to college. The report did not challenge segregation—in the 1950s, such a challenge was unthinkable in the South—but inequalities in funding and provision for basic needs are revealed on every page.

That inequality was certainly clear to Governor James Byrnes. His 1951 inaugural speech asked for a $75 million bond issue to "equalize" Black and white schools. Byrnes realized that the US Supreme Court could very well integrate Southern schools because segregation was based on the *Plessy v. Ferguson* doctrine of "separate but equal." Perhaps, he argued, if South Carolina showed attempts to equalize, the ongoing separation of the races might be preserved. State Supreme Court Judge Waites Waring had already ruled against the state's closed primaries. Waring was a member of the federal district court hearing *Briggs v. Elliot*, which originated in Clarenden County, where officials spent $166 per capita on white children and $44 on Black children and provided neither school buses nor a high school for Black youngsters. Byrnes's proposed bond issue, backed by a 3-cent sales tax, was meant to equalize Black and white facilities, improve rural schools, and provide school buses for all students. Because poor counties couldn't afford to buy buses, South Carolina became—and it still is—the only state to provide them.

The General Assembly also empowered new countywide school boards, appointed by the governor, to consolidate school districts when equalization could not be achieved within a single district. In Greenville, an educational consultant, a master planner, and a citizens' committee had all recommended consolidating rural and urban districts and merging the city and Parker District schools, attended by two-thirds of the county's children. The problem was that the county had eighty other school districts, many with one- and two-room schools, and district funding that varied from four to thirty-eight mills.

In the summer of 1950, county residents, fearing the "dictatorship" of a countywide board and superintendent, twice defeated consolidation proposals. A year later, despite the referenda, the legislative delegation charged ahead, appointing a school board responsible for creating a single unified system. Greenville's Era of Equalization began on August 23, 1951, with A. D. Asbury as chairman and W. F. Loggins as the new unitary district superintendent. Within a year, all children had free textbooks, the salaries of Black and white teachers with comparable credentials were equalized, thirty-eight one- and two-room schoolhouses for Black children had closed, and fifteen new schools were on the drawing board. By the

time the program ended in 1960, Greenville had closed one hundred two schools and built twenty-four new ones, including Washington and Lincoln High Schools for Black teenagers.

Since 1869, Greenville's boundaries had extended only a mile and a quarter from Court Square. Annexation votes in 1927 and 1931 were easily defeated, but in 1947, Augusta Road and Northgate "suburbs" wanted city services and voted for annexation. Greenville was moving outward. In 1948, Sears & Roebuck erected a three-story building (with escalators!) on Stone Avenue at the end of the Super Highway. Lewis Plaza on Augusta Road opened about the same time. Then, in 1956, Camperdown Mill closed, a victim of low-cost imports and the value of its real estate. A new bank, buildings for IBM, the Wyche law firm, and school district offices were located on the former Camperdown site, and Camperdown Way bridged the Reedy River, covering its falls. By 1959, the only physical trace of textiles remaining downtown was the old Huguenot Mill, then an apparel factory.

Residents embraced the suburban way of life. In the 1950s and 1960s, Parkins Mill, Botany Woods, Gower Estates, Sherwood Forest, and a half dozen subdivisions offered "country living" split-level homes to whites, and New Washington Heights and Pleasant Valley lured Black veterans with GI Bill housing loans. Liberty Life moved from the old Chamber

Building to a "modernistic" headquarters on Wade Hampton Boulevard, leaving a hole in South Main Street. The house that gained the most publicity, however, was a home designed by Frank Lloyd Wright on West Avondale Street in the North Main neighborhood, completed in 1957, one of two houses designed by the master architect in the state.

In 1958, the new Church Street viaduct opened, extending Church Street from two blocks to two miles. The $859,000 viaduct was the largest and most important step in redesigning Greenville's road grid. The newly created corner of Church and East North Streets became the site for Memorial Auditorium, which opened on December 1, 1958, with a basketball game between Furman and the University of West Virginia.

Basketball had been a local passion since the 1920s, when the Southern Textile Basketball tournament was first scheduled in Textile Hall. By 1939, the Textile Hall tournament attracted seventy-three teams and eight hundred players from across the South. World War II temporarily ended it, but afterward it boomed, thanks in part to Pelzer standout Earle Wooten and Dunean coach Ward Williams. The last Southern Textile Basketball Tournament game was played in March 1996. In 1954, Furman gained national publicity when Frank Selvy scored one hundred points in a game against Newberry College.

The city and county were still buckles on the South Carolina Bible Belt, but in October 1959, eight daring movie theatre owners challenged the law forbidding movies on Sundays, opening both popular drive-ins and Main Street movie palaces. Owners argued that enforcement was inconsistent and arbitrary and the laws antiquated. They lost their case, but their protest had reverberations. Mandated Sunday closings ended in the seventies, although it would take thousands of brown bags toted into hundreds of restaurants before Greenville became "wet."

Politically, Greenville was shifting from its long-time allegiance to the Democratic Party, even though, after a brief flirtation with Strom Thurmond's Dixiecrat ticket in 1948, South Carolina had returned to the Democratic fold. Because the county was whiter and more conservative than the rest of the state, it had liked Ike in 1952 and in 1960 embraced Richard Nixon. Locally, however, Democrats—male Democrats— still totally controlled the City Council. In 1959, those Democrats did the unthinkable: They nominated a woman, Mrs. J. Alden Simpson, for alderman. (No man ran.) And she won. Her victory was not, however, indicative of real change: It would be another fourteen years before Republican Pat Haskell-Robinson established a place for women in local politics.

Both the zoo and the farmers' market found new and better sites. The superactive Jaycees and their president, Doug Smith, pressed for a new zoo. City Council provided eight acres of land at Cleveland Park but no money. After the Jaycees raised $3,200, construction began in 1958. The wholesale farmers' market moved from Court Street to Rutherford Road near the former site of Camp Sevier in 1948. Two years later, the retail facility settled into a two-story brick building on newly created Beattie Place.

In 1956, *Life*, the nation's most popular photographic magazine, sent a team to Greenville to investigate local Black life. The article, with photographs by Margaret Bourke-White, was a part of the magazine's series on Black life, focused on big-city Nashville, rural Southern Mississippi, and mill town Greenville. The Greenville segment began with an interview with Mayor Kenneth Cass, who pointed out the $33,000 skating rink; $35,000 swimming pool; and $3,400 children's playground for Black children that resulted from the Big Idea study. In addition, the article mentioned new elementary schools, a recreation hall, street paving, and new code enforcement on rental housing. The white population, said *Life*, "enthusiastically supported all these measures"— and the idea of "equalization."

But the journalists went beyond the mayor's rosy view of race relations. The *Life* team also interviewed unnamed Black leaders who explained that many of their race had become apathetic to civic improvements because they tended to entrench segregation. They preferred, one said, "to go for broke: desegregation or nothing."

Chapter 13

DESEGREGATION AND THE DECLINE OF MAIN STREET, 1960–70

In late October 1959, Brooklyn Dodgers baseball star Jackie Robinson addressed an audience of seventeen hundred at an NAACP-sponsored rally at Memorial Auditorium. Afterward, while he awaited his flight back to Manhattan from Municipal Airport, he was arrested for refusing to leave the "whites-only" waiting room, kicking off what a local columnist called "another round of badwill stories" in the national press. "Why," asked the *Greenville Piedmont* writer, "could we not have done the easy thing and let him alone for ten minutes? Instead, we gave him a club to clobber us with." He went on to say, that "We can't expect to get anywhere with our racial

difficulties by being blindly stubborn," and pleaded with his readers to expend their energy on improving the economic lot of both races.

Although Richard Henry, a Black man, had been ordered out of the waiting room two months earlier, it was the racially charged insult to Robinson that led to Greenville's first major protest. On January 1, 1960, about two hundred fifty African Americans gathered at Springfield Baptist Church for a march to the airport. On a chilly and drizzling New Year's Day, many drove to the intersection of Laurens Road and Pleasantburg Drive and then walked to the airport's entrance. Police and members of the state's Human Relations Committee, who had been informed, protected the road. About two months later, the Fourth Circuit Court of Appeals ruled in Henry's case that segregated waiting rooms were unconstitutional.

The second incident in Greenville's struggle for equity occurred just three months later. In March 1960, the Greenville city library was located in a fifty-six-year-old columned former elementary school on North Main Street adjacent to Springwood Cemetery, whereas the "colored" branch library was located on East McBee Avenue not far from Springfield Baptist Church. In 1952, it had replaced the single room in the Phillis Wheatley Center that had served the Black population since 1924. The main branch had 55,508 books. The "Negro" one had 11,644 (chosen, librarians said, to include those "of most interest to Negro readers"), although officials noted that readers could request any book in the system and have it delivered to their school or branch library.

Late in the afternoon of March 1, 1960, about twenty neatly dressed Black students entered the Main Street branch. Some of the students sat at tables and began reading; others browsed the shelves. Within a few minutes, though, the head librarian, Charles Stowe, called them into his office and told them that they had to use the McBee Avenue branch. He also announced that the library was closing. The students left without protest. According to Margaree Seawright Crosby, a participant, in an interview taped by the Upstate History Museum, when the Rev. Hall of Springfield Church asked them what had happened, they explained that Librarian Stowe had said that they would be arrested if they stayed, so they left. The minister explained that the point was to be arrested, to call attention to the segregated facilities. There seems to be little question that the Rev. Hall sparked this first tentative "study-in," but it also seems clear from Dr. Crosby's comments that little planning was involved.

Library and city officials were rattled. Library Trustee Chair Romayne Barnes, lawyer Dean Rainey, four police officials, and the city attorney immediately gathered to discuss the challenge to separate public facilities. They had more to discuss two weeks later, when seven brave teenagers returned to the building. Five girls and two boys attempted to use the library. This time, they refused Charles Stowe's request to leave. The librarian, acting on instructions from Mayor Kenneth Cass, called the police. Four officers came to arrest the seven Sterling students. They took the youngsters to the Greenville jail, booked them on charges of disorderly behavior, and placed them in cells, where the students began singing patriotic songs. Within half an hour, lawyer Donald Sampson, the Rev. Hall, bail bondsman Tony Shelton, and several reporters gathered. Shelton paid their $20 bail fees, and the students were released.

Sampson announced that he would request a jury trial.

The *Greenville News* immediately published the names and home addresses of the arrested students and editorially attacked their "unseemly behavior." It treated city officials and library trustees as victims who might be forced to close both libraries to ensure segregation and stated that, if that happened, it would be the students' fault. When the case came to the Municipal Court two weeks later, the hearing was postponed. And it continued to be postponed. Four months later, on July 15, eight students arrived and stayed. They too were arrested, imprisoned briefly, and quickly bailed out. Identified as college students, the group included "Jeff Jackson," a name later corrected to Jesse Jackson. NAACP lawyers said that a federal suit, asking for a permanent injunction against racial segregation at the library, would be filed.

Defendants were city and county officials, city and county libraries, library trustees, and Charles Stowe. The *Greenville News* called for a biracial committee to tamp down the "extremists," and Mayor Cass referred to the "fanatical fringes." A federal court hearing was scheduled. Before it took place, at 6 P.M. on September 2, the library trustees, at the request of city government, closed both the Main Avenue and McBee Avenue branches. The public responded angrily. Citizens called the closing "arbitrary," "deplorable," and "high-handed." Dr. Donald

Kilgore compared it to amputating a leg to cure a blister. Furman Professor Al Reid pled eloquently for its reopening. Others suggested that taxes used for library support should be rebated. The *Greenville Piedmont* warned against "an influx of mixed races."

At the September 14 trial, city lawyers argued that the injunction was moot because the library did not exist. Federal Judge C. C. Wyche agreed, but noted that if the library reopened, it could again be sued. The city won a pyrrhic victory, but the community wanted the library reopened, and on September 19 at 9 A.M., it was—to everyone "with a legitimate need." Charges against all students were dismissed. To avoid "racial mixing," tables were initially labeled "male" and "female," but the library was so crowded that the signs vanished within a week. Local editorialists called the decision wise. Others saw a first small step toward a more integrated society.

That summer protests continued. For three weeks in July and August 1960, Sterling High School students and graduates participated in sit-ins at segregated lunch counters at Woolworth's, H. T. Grant's, and S. S. Kress & Co., all Main Street variety stores. Six sit-ins, a picketing incident, some violence, and a curfew resulted. It culminated on August 9, the first time that arrests were made. Eighteen students took seats at the Kress store counter, and the manager called the police. Police told the students they

Statue commemorating the activism of Sterling High School students who protested against racial segregation. Wikimedia Commons.

were trespassing and asked them to leave. The students refused. They were arrested and jailed for about three hours. Weeks later, at a trial in Recorder's Court, they were convicted of trespassing and fined $100 or thirty days in jail. Their NAACP lawyers appealed to the SC Supreme Court, which upheld the verdict. Again,

it was appealed, and in May 1963, the US Supreme Court, which had combined it with other Southern sit-in cases, reversed the decision in *Peterson v. City of Greenville* and began, in effect, to establish equality in accommodations.

In the following winter of 1961, eight young Black men and women attempting to use the skating rink at Cleveland Park were arrested and jailed. In June, the NAACP filed suit, including both the park's skating rink and its swimming pool in the complaint. In October 1962, the federal court ruled that segregated park facilities were clearly unconstitutional. Neither the skating rink nor the swimming pool reopened in 1963. That fall, City Council decided to convert the pool into a "Marineland" with three black sea lions.

In July 1961, Charles Daniel of Greenville, the premier industrialist in the state and longtime champion of economic development, spoke at the Hampton Watermelon Festival. He pointed out that, unless South Carolina integrated its workforce, the federal government would integrate it. "Enlightened self-interest" suggested hiring Black men and women workers for cotton mills and changing the laws that mandated Jim Crow segregation in every aspect of South Carolina life. It was not a rabble-rousing speech, but it signaled that those who ran South Carolina's businesses were about to change direction in the face of political reality.

The time was ripe. In response to Pete Hollis's urging and Daniel's speech, in November 1962, Arthur McGill, head of the Her Majesty apparel company in Mauldin, invited one hundred of his (white) friends to meet at the factory to discuss integration. The group feared that racial violence would slow economic progress, but although those present generally agreed with Daniel's assessment, they took no action, and no further session was planned, although Dunean Mill hired a Black loom fixer that summer. Hollis called another meeting about two months later, this one at the Phillis Wheatley Center and with Black leaders present (fewer whites attended). They suggested that a joint biracial committee be formed to smooth Greenville integration.

In the meantime, local civil rights tension grew. After the Supreme Court ruling in *Peterson*, the City Council rescinded all Greenville segregation ordinances, most of which had been in place since 1912. The change had been expected, but it did not mean that local hotels, hospitals, restaurants, or theatres were immediately desegregated. The Chamber had appointed a biracial committee that provided some help in accommodation issues. Until 1963, members met for lunch at the only restaurant in Greenville that served biracial guests—the YWCA—but immediately afterward, they met in small biracial groups at downtown restaurants, cafes, and lunch counters to ensure acceptance. Members also met privately with hotel and motel management to ensure that Black guests would be received without incident when the Omega Psi Phi fraternity scheduled an alumni reunion in the city.

However, schools remained segregated. South Carolina responded to the 1954 decision in *Brown* with "massive resistance." The NAACP chose what its legal defense office considered less resistant states for the first efforts at desegregation. At Little Rock Central High School in Arkansas, the result was mob violence and hesitant federal response. In South Carolina, the Gressette Committee called for resistance to all attempts at integration by ending state support for desegregated schools, annual hiring of all teachers, eliminating school attendance laws, and prohibiting "forced busing" for integration.

Integration "with all deliberate speed," mandated by the court in 1955, was interpreted as meaning as slowly as possible by most white Southerners. Most southern states erupted with violence in the face of court orders, but South Carolina's segregated schools were not challenged. However, when former NAACP chapter president A. J. Whittenburg visited all-white Anderson Street School in Greenville for a Democratic precinct meeting in 1962, he observed piles of new textbooks ready for students. He remembered the ragged textbooks, cast off from white schools, that his eleven-year-old daughter, Elaine, used.

When she was assigned to Gower Street School for fall 1963, he requested that she be allowed to attend the far closer Anderson Street School. Within two weeks, five other parents, including Black attorney Donald Sampson, also requested transfers into white schools for their children. It was the first challenge to South Carolina's segregated system. The school district said no, so the parents sued. Sampson, attorney Willie Smith, and the NAACP Legal Defense Fund attorneys filed a motion in federal court in September 1963. In February 1964, the district again denied Whittenburg's request and did not acknowledge the others. In March, Federal District Judge Robert Martin gave the district a month to decide about the school placement of all five children. In April 1964, school district officials yielded, announcing that that the children would be admitted to previously white schools. Then Judge Martin ordered the school district to accept all other Black students who applied for the fall. He also ruled that this freedom-of-choice plan be given prominent publicity. NAACP attorneys immediately filed briefs arguing that "freedom of choice" was not integration. In September 1964, forty-nine Black students entered fifteen all-white schools. By 1968, four hundred sixty Black students were enrolled in white Greenville schools, but only two teachers were placed in opposite-race schools, and the dual system remained unchanged.

But then, in May 1968, the US Supreme Court ruled in *Green v. New Kent County* that most freedom-of-choice plans were inadequate, and Greenville schools were again in the news. The school board proposed a full integration plan in the summer of 1969. Judge Robert Martin agreed to the school board plan to integrate students, faculty, and buses in September 1970, but on October 29, in a case from Mississippi, the Supreme Court ruled that integration should occur "at once." Less than two weeks later, Black parents in Greenville and their lawyers, together with the NAACP Legal Fund, appealed Martin's September deadline to the Fourth Circuit Court of Appeals. Attorneys asked the Circuit Court to order immediate desegregation of the Darlington and Greenville Districts based on the US Supreme Court ruling that "at once" means "right now."

On January 19, the circuit court reversed Martin's September deadline and ordered the Darlington and Greenville Districts to desegregate by February 9. It would be difficult even though Judge Martin extended the deadline to February 17. With less than a month to make arrangements, the Greenville School District, with fifty-eight thousand students and two thousand three hundred eighty-four teachers, arranged to have a ratio of eighty percent white to twenty percent Black students and teachers (with a ten percent leeway) in each school. The plan created clusters, with grades one through five in white schools and grade six in Black schools. It made Beck, a Black high school, into a school for seventh and eighth grades, with most of its students transferred to J. L. Mann and Wade Hampton High Schools.

On January 20, the Chamber of Commerce Human Relations Committee pleaded for volunteers. Response was immediate: Seven hundred volunteers, including members of the Junior League, League of Women Voters, American Association of University Women, and Parent–Teacher Association councils, began working nine-hour stints at four newly installed school district telephones answering questions about the desegregation order. Opposition was intense. Nearly three thousand people attended a meeting of the Citizens for Freedom of Choice at Parker High School, launching an effort to get one hundred thousand signatures on a petition opposing integration. On January 25, local politician Carroll Campbell led about eight hundred cars in a motorcade to Columbia to ask Governor Robert McNair to stop Greenville "forced busing" for integration. Because busing was a service, not required, "forced busing" was a non-issue.

Greenville's recently completed US Courthouse will be named for Campbell. He may be the only nonlawyer or judge in the nation to be so honored. He will certainly be the only person so honored who requested that a governor not comply with a Supreme Court decision.

On January 30, school trustees appointed a 30-member biracial Citizens Committee, headed by Furman Professor Ernie Harrill, to coordinate volunteers. Eventually, more than three thousand Greenvillians responded. The Business and Industry Council raised $3,000 from local companies that allowed Publicity Committee Chair Doug Smith of WFBC to organize speeches, radio, television, school poster contests, and buttons supporting schools and proclaiming that "Education is the Important Thing." On Friday, February 13, Mayor Cooper White invited every minister in Greenville County to lunch and asked them to preach Sunday about obeying the law. School ended at 1 P.M. on the day of the move. Over the weekend, one hundred three schools prepared for integration; hundreds of books, desks, and supplies were shifted; bus routes (the district had purchased twenty new buses) were finalized; and plans for greeting new students and teachers were confirmed.

On Tuesday morning, February 17, Greenville desegregated its schools. While a few mothers picketed at Armstrong and Arrington Elementary Schools, and buses ran a bit late, the move, thanks to community involvement, was remarkably smooth. On CBS that night, Walter Cronkite, quoting Professor Harrill, announced that Greenville had integrated "with grace and style."

The following November, however, grace and style vanished. Three days of intermittent fighting between Black and white students at local high schools and shots fired at security guards led to the calling up (but not deploying) of the National Guard. More than three hundred fifty students, most of them Black, were suspended. Those students complained about playing "Dixie" at football games; the lack of Black studies classes; and concerns about Black student participation in activities, including sports. Local media blamed "outside agitators," and *U. S. News & World Report* commented that "Greenville has "lost its luster," but the school district's new superintendent, Floyd Hall, responded positively to the problems. No students were expelled, although some were moved to new schools. Hall appointed Black and white "ombudsmen" for schools to help settle students and douse rumors. Substantial funds were made available for Black history and art materials and Black visiting artists, thanks to a $369,000 federal grant to support integration efforts. In May 1971, an article in the *Christian Science Monitor* was headlined "Greenville Regains its Luster."

The city made the national media twice more in the decade. The first time was positive—the 1964 announcement that native son Charles Hard Townes, a Furman alumnus, class of 1935, who had earned his PhD from the California Institute of Technology, had won the Nobel Prize in Physics for his invention of the principle behind the maser and the laser while he was teaching at MIT.

The second time, negatively, came in 1969 when President Richard Nixon nominated Clement Furman Haynsworth Jr., chief judge of the Fourth Circuit Court of Appeals, to the US Supreme Court. Haynsworth (1912–89) graduated summa cum laude from Furman in 1933 and from Harvard Law School in 1936. He was the senior partner at Haynsworth, Perry, Bryant, Marion, and Johnstone when President Eisenhower appointed him to the appellate court; in 1964, he became chief judge. The American Bar Association rated Haynsworth "highly qualified." His nomination was challenged on his rulings on integration, his attitude toward unions, and possible questions about a stock transaction. The national (but not the local) NAACP lobbied against him, as did the AFL-CIO for his decision involving a controversial mill closing. Complicating the issue was the Democratic antipathy toward President Nixon. The Senate Judiciary Committee voted ten to seven in his favor, but the full senate voted fifty-five to forty-five against him. He was the first Supreme Court nominee to be defeated since 1930.

In the ten years between the first protests and the desegregation of schools in 1970,

Greenville changed in other ways. Furman's male students moved to the Poinsett Highway campus in 1958; in 1961, women from across town joined them. After the university gained legal clearance to sell the women's campus, it was purchased by the City of Greenville with the initial idea of creating a "civic center" there. Instead, it became the city's cultural center (named Heritage Green in 1974) with fundraising immediately underway in the winter of 1964 to build a little theatre on the site of the college's Fine Arts Center. The West End, without students, grew seedy.

New roads, planned to divert cars from "bumper to bumper" Main Street traffic, did so. Church Street had already been extended to Mills Avenue, cutting through the closed Camperdown Mill village, the Furman campus, and the Black Haynie-Sirrine neighborhood. Academy Street went through the old Women's campus, curved through McPherson Park, and took a chunk of the cemetery (those with Black graves) before it met East North Street. The interstate system brought Greenville closer to Atlanta and Charlotte as well as to Anderson and Spartanburg; Interstate 385 (I-385), its access road, passed through fields of cotton that would soon be converted into highway malls.

New shopping centers opened. In 1968, McAlister Square was the first entirely enclosed, air-conditioned mall in the state. Its anchor tenants were Ivey's and Myers-Arnold,

which closed their Main Street stores. Wade Hampton Mall began serving the Bob Jones University community, while Bell Tower Mall tried unsuccessfully to lure shoppers to the West End. Greenville now called itself the Textile Capital of the World, a title underlined by the 1964 opening of New Textile Hall off Pleasantburg Drive. The new exposition hall (the downtown original was abandoned), boasted that visitors would spend over $750,000 in the four days of the twenty-third exposition. The president of the American Textile Institute assured members that the textile outlook had never been brighter: Wages had never been higher; companies were making huge investments in machinery; and the one hundred thirty thousand South Carolinians employed by mills were, slowly, tentatively, entering the middle class.

Greenville Technical College was helping. The county's technical education center, begun in 1962, was the first in the state. Textiles was one of its seven divisions. The city gave the new school seven acres of land, a former dump, on Pleasantburg Drive in 1961; five years later, it had expanded to a campus of one hundred twenty-eight acres with fourteen thousand students enrolled. Although it was still closely linked to Greenville schools (it offered "thirteenth and fourteenth grades," according to counselors), a two-year college transfer program had just been initiated by Clemson University.

The new "Jetport" also boosted textile prosperity. At its opening in November 1962, nearly one hundred thousand people admired its two thousand landscaped acres, art-lined concourse, and fountain pool. "The Jetport," now Greenville–Spartanburg International (GSP), was the first real collaboration between the two competitive cities in history. In the 1950s, Charles Daniel and Alester Furman Jr., working together on regional development, realized that firms looking south wanted better and bigger airline service. They convinced Roger Milliken, head of Deering-Milliken, to head the project. In 1958, they found a site straddling the Greenville-Spartanburg County line; hired Skidmore, Owings & Merrill of New York as architects; and Innocenti & Webel of Long Island, New York, to do the landscaping.

And then Donaldson Air Base closed. The move of the Military Air Transport Command to Savannah initially devastated Greenville. The loss meant the elimination of $20 million from the local economy and a substantial drop in federal school impact funds. Gloomy predictions of economic depression mounted. But in the spring of 1963, the Donaldson Air Base reversionary clause was enforced. On August 19, the base, with its roads, barracks, and huge airstrip, was sold back to the city and county governments, which borrowed $421,000 from local banks for the purpose. The federal government estimated that its investment was

$20 million. The mayor and the County Delegation immediately agreed to sell one hundred acres to Union Carbide. The newly appointed Donaldson Management Committee then sold the base's electrical distribution system to Duke Power and its railroad equipment to Southern Railroad. Those sales covered its entire cost. Initially, its loss caused a slump; eventually, Donaldson Center became the county's industrial powerhouse.

Improved air connections, water resources, and a non-union environment led to the April 1967 announcement by General Electric (GE) that it would build a $50 million gas turbine plant in Greenville at I-85 and East Woodruff Road. The world's fourth largest manufacturing corporation, GE planned to build a three-hundred-thousand-square-foot plant on six hundred seventeen acres of Greenville land. The company's local manager, John Bauer, announced that the factory would employ five hundred people, many of them trained at Greenville Tech, when it opened.

GE's decision came at a critical time in Greenville's industrial history. Its longtime textile industry was beginning to struggle against more cheaply made foreign competition, and mills were beginning to lay off workers. According to GE officials, the Greenville site was chosen because land and water were reasonably priced, technical education programs were superior, and leadership was strongly supportive.

It was so successful that in December 1970, Bauer announced that the company would invest $60 million in expansion and hire six hundred additional workers to increase employment to fifteen hundred people.

Although GE was good news, the other changes—the roads that diverted Main Street traffic, the call of the suburbs, and the closing of Donaldson as well as aging downtown buildings—contributed to the decline of Main Street. One organization that fought that decline was the Carolina Foothills Garden Club, which decided to make the banks of the Reedy River into a park and greenway in 1968. Members began raising funds by sponsoring bazaars and creating handcrafts, but mostly they weeded, hoed, shoveled, and planted. Furman University ceded six riverbank acres for the park, and the city workmen helped by eliminating the "hobo jungle" on the north bank and removing the most obvious litter. The ladies removed (with the help of a billy goat, the Boy Scouts, and Parks and Recreation staff) truckloads of kudzu, honeysuckle, and privet to clear what the *Greenville News* referred to editorially as the "stinking mess" below Bell Tower Mall. The park was dedicated in 1972.

But Main Street remained a problem. As early as 1957, in a speech to the Downtown Greenville Association, Charles Daniel pointed out that it was "unclean and neither attractive nor competitive with comparable progressive cities." When

The Daniel Building rises high over Greenville's North Main Street. Greenville County Library System.

Charlie Daniel spoke, civic leadership responded. City government instituted a clean-up campaign; merchants slipcovered old buildings with sparkling aluminum siding. In 1962, the Board of Directors of the Hotel Company, which owned the Ottaray Hotel, leased the land to the Downtowner Hotel chain. During the following year, the aggressively modern (and extraordinarily ugly) Downtowner Motor Inn replaced it at the top of Main Street.

Dissatisfied by the rate of change, however, Daniel decided to make a personal contribution to Greenville modernization. The story—it may be apocryphal, but it has the ring of Greenville truth—is that Daniel and Roger Peace decided that Main Street needed a boost and agreed that if Daniel would build at the north end of the street, Peace would anchor the south with a new building for the *Greenville News-Piedmont*. On June 29, 1964, in one of his last public acts before his death, he broke ground for the twenty-five-story Daniel Building at 301 North Main Street: "The Business Address of Distinction."

In 1966, the Chamber of Commerce launched a "Total Development Campaign" headed by Alester Furman Jr., who had agreed to chair the committee if Buck Mickel, Charlie Daniel's successor at Daniel Construction

Company, would agree to be vice chair. With five other business leaders, including attorney Tommy Wyche, they hired economic consultants and planners and began to envision a new downtown. They considered making Main Street a seven-block-long "pedestrian strollway"; they dreamed, first of a civic center on College Street, and then, when that idea was rejected, of two ten-story twin buildings, one a new city hall, the other an office building near Broad Street. More successfully, they lobbied for a smoother connection between Spring and Falls Streets and a link between Richardson and River Streets. They also encouraged South Carolina National Bank to raze the Woodside Building and build a new headquarters, and North Carolina National Bank to build a six-story building on the new pedestrian Coffee Street Mall, but none of their ideas seemed to help.

It would take more money, wiser decisions, and a new streetscape to revitalize downtown.

Chapter 14

REINVENTING GREENVILLE
1970–95

South Carolina celebrated its tercentenary in 1970. It was not a success. Lieutenant Governor John West called it a "fiasco"; others labeled it a "flop," "boondoggle," and a "foul-up." The three hundredth anniversary of the state's settlement was over budget, poorly planned, and used untried and structurally inadequate geodesic domes (the one in Columbia collapsed). With three sites—Charleston, Columbia, and Greenville—the result of political jockeying in the state legislature, the Upstate "Piedmont Panorama" was sold to Greenville as a site for a future textile museum. That idea was ditched, however, when the fragile dome design was chosen. Then its opening was delayed for a week, and at an opening night gala, its roof leaked. But its site on Roper Mountain at I-385 was convenient, and fifteen years later, after a remarkably successful fundraising campaign, it became the school district's Science Center with a pioneer farm, observatory, and summer workshops.

Revitalizing Main Street took longer. It also took leaders with courage, imagination, the right timing, and a bunch of cash. With the strong support of Mayor Max Heller, in 1975, the Total Development Committee began a major and risky, private–public partnership. To get the necessary startup funds, they set up a foundation (the Greenville Community Corporation) and sought investors for fifty thousand shares of stock at $100 apiece to be used to help finance property acquisition and construction of a convention hotel, office building,

Portrait of Max Heller, who came to Greenville as a Holocaust refugee and became a successful businessman and politician, serving as the city's mayor, 1971–79. Furman University Special Collections and Archives.

and retail space. Attorney Tommy Wyche, Daniel Construction President Buck Mickel, and realtor Alester Furman Jr. were among the arm twisters who invited twenty-seven potential investors to a meeting in July 1976.

The group pledged $5 million and hired internationally known landscape architect Lawrence Halprin to conduct public input sessions and design a plan for Main Street renewal. That

December, Halprin's San Francisco firm submitted a plan. Thanks to an additional $1.85 million federal grant, street renovations began in August 1977 and included narrowing traffic to two lanes with diagonal parking and adding trees, landscaped corner plots, street furniture, new lighting, and signage.

Meanwhile, however, teenagers claimed Main Street on weekend nights. They "dragged downtown," driving slowly around and around Main Street "because there is nothing else to do." Except avoid construction. West Coffee Street from Buncombe Street to Main Street was pedestrianized to create the "Coffee Street Mall" in front of the new sixteen-story Bankers Trust Building. The Woodside Building was replaced by the six-story, $6 million South Carolina National Bank building. The city demolished the 1910 Masonic Building and replaced it with a ten-story "shimmering brown" City Hall.

Leadership made the difference. Alester Furman Jr. (1895–1980), who had chaired the Total Development Committee for a decade, was Charles Daniel's contemporary and about two decades older than the emerging leaders. Max Heller (1919–2011) came to Greenville when he was eighteen years old, an Austrian Jew fleeing the Nazi takeover of his homeland. In the summer of 1937, he had met and danced with a young Greenville girl on a European tour. He wrote her, asking for help. Mary Mills went to Shepard Saltzman, owner of the

Piedmont Shirt Company, who agreed to provide a job for the refugee. Heller arrived in July
1938 and went to work sweeping floors at $10
a week. Within a few years, he was managing
the company and then went on to start his own
highly successful Maxon Shirt Company.

Retired and active in the Chamber of
Commerce, the Community Chest, and the
Greenville Symphony Guild as well as Congregation Beth Israel, Heller ran successfully for
mayor in 1971. He negotiated federal support
for a convention center as part of a project to
bring an upscale Regency Hyatt Hotel to town
and urged the beautification and narrowing
of Main Street. He encouraged economic development, lured Metropolitan Life Insurance
to the county, and ran a balanced city budget.
When he was defeated for Congress in 1978,
Governor Dick Riley appointed him head
of the State Development Board. His statue
stands, appropriately, on Main Street across
from the Hyatt.

Corporate executive Buck Mickel (1925–
98) succeeded Charles Daniel as president of
Daniel Construction Company. He, too, was
an advocate for downtown, whose support, encouragement, and cash helped create a vibrant
Main Street. A native of Elberton, Georgia,
he embraced Greenville when he was hired by
Daniel after graduating from Georgia Tech. He
was in charge when the company went public
in 1969 and when it was purchased by the

Fluor Corporation in 1977. He was named vice
chairman of Fluor in 1984, a position he held
until he retired in 1987. His "amiable power"
made a difference in the development of Heritage Green, creating the (complex) financing
plan for the Regency Hyatt, helping raise money for the Peace Center, and backing the Governor's School for the Arts and Humanities.
At the time of his death, he was celebrating the
construction of the Bi-Lo Center after years of
struggle and negative votes.

C. Thomas Wyche (1926–2015), a partner in the long-established Wyche, Burgess,
Freeman, and Parham law firm, was the third of
the trio. A graduate of Greenville High School,
Yale University, and the University of Virginia
law school, he may have been the most versatile
of the three. His family connections helped
bring the Hyatt to Greenville; his passion for
conservation led to the Naturaland Trust and
preserved the "Blue Wall" of the area's mountain wilderness. A talented photographer,
pianist, and state champion tennis player,
Tommy Wyche was the decisive force behind
downtown redevelopment.

New construction and streetscape helped
revitalization, but there were losses. In January 1972, the century-old Springfield Baptist
Church on East McBee Avenue burned to the
ground. It was the heart of Greenville's Black
community and a center of early 1960s civil
rights protests. The flames did $650,000 worth

of damage; only the church bell survived. In December 1976, the Rev. John Corbitt dedicated Springfield's modern new sanctuary at the intersection of McDaniel and East McBee Avenues.

In May 1973, after three years, dozens of vituperative City Council meetings, six professional studies, and hundreds of letters to the editor of the *News*, old City Hall was demolished. Demolition cost about $15,000. It was replaced by an "international plaza" and nineteen underground parking spaces.

Then First Baptist Church abandoned downtown. Nearly a century and a half after it had been established in downtown Greenville, and after years of agonizing indecision, most of the congregation moved to Cleveland Street in the spring of 1974. The issues were parking and expansion of both the sanctuary and the Sunday School wing. Construction of their major new building, reportedly the largest church in the state, began in 1972. Those opposed to the move continued worshiping in the old church, named "Downtown Baptist," now Grace Church.

The other "first churches"—Buncombe Street Methodist, Christ Episcopal, and First Presbyterian—stayed and expanded. They were a significant source of downtown stability during the period as were the "second churches"— St. Mary's Catholic, Trinity Lutheran, and the handsome new St. George's Greek Orthodox,

as well as the Black churches—John Wesley Methodist, Mattoon Presbyterian, and Allen Temple AME.

But the churches couldn't do much to stop crime. In 1971, the city ranked fifth nationally in the ratio of homicides to population; by 1973, it was third in the country. There were thirteen homicides during the first two weeks of January 1975. Whether Greenville's location on the I-85 corridor from Atlanta to New York was responsible for the drugs and crime that flooded the county, as many suggested, or whether the homicides were all "crimes of passion," as some officials insisted, it was also a fact that the sheriff's department was riddled with corruption. In 1976, after a mud-slinging campaign that included forged documents, Johnny Mack Brown was elected sheriff. (He became the longest serving sheriff in county history.) Two months before he took office, several deputies quit, and in November, six were indicted for "misconduct in office." Anxiety about crime may have led to more cooperation between the sheriff's office and the city's Chief of Police Harold Jennings, and certainly to the funding of the $9 million City County Law Enforcement Center on East North Street, completed in 1976.

For the first time in South Carolina history, Greenville gained statewide political power, led by reform-minded progressive Democrat

Richard Riley testifying before Congress while serving as secretary of education. CQ Roll Call Photograph Collection, Library of Congress, Prints and Photographs Division.

Richard Wilson Riley. A graduate of Furman, where he had been senior class president, and the University of South Carolina Law School, where he was head of the student body, he was elected to the General Assembly in 1963. With other younger legislators, including Greenville representatives Rex Carter, Nick Theodore, and Harry Chapman (called the "Young Turks," although Nick Theodore's family was proudly Greek), he rewrote eight articles of the State Constitution, leading eventually to home rule for counties, elimination of the county supervisor position, and judicial reform. Although he unsuccessfully challenged Pug Ravenel for the Democratic gubernatorial nomination in 1976, in 1978, Riley was elected governor, the first Greenvillian to serve since 1911, and Theodore was elected lieutenant governor. Carter was already (since 1973) speaker of the house. Riley focused on improving education, passing a one-cent tax dedicated to it. In 1992, President Bill

Clinton asked him to manage his transition team and afterward named him secretary of education after offering him a place on the Supreme Court. *Time* magazine named him one of top ten cabinet officials of the twentieth century.

In 1987, Republican Carroll Campbell, a savvy and popular politician, began serving the first of two terms in the state house. Campbell recruited industry and helped modernize and overhaul state government, abolishing many agencies' governing boards and, over the objections of some legislators, bringing more power to the governor's office. He began his career in Greenville as the owner of parking lots. He later served in the South Carolina Senate (1977–78) and as a US congressman (1979–87) before being elected governor (1987–95).

Black people exerted new public influence. Theo Mitchell was the first African American elected to the legislature from Greenville since Reconstruction. Elections to City Council of

Theo Mitchell (D-Greenville), along with Earl Middleton (D-Orangeburg) and Kay Patterson (D-Richland), speak at a 1979 press conference objecting to the participation of the University of South Carolina golf team in a match held at the Orangeburg Country Club, which excluded Blacks from membership. Mitchell was the first African American to represent Greenville in the state legislature since Reconstruction. The *State* Newspaper Archive, Richland County Public Library.

the Rev. Rayfield Metcalf in 1977; J. D. Mathis in 1979; and, with far longer lasting impact, Lillian Brock Flemming, first elected in 1981, were landmarks politically. Ralph Anderson, a City Council member from 1983 to 1991, went on to serve in the state senate from 1997 to 2013. Attorney and former professional football player Merl Code, a native of Seneca, set up a legal practice here in 1977; in 1982, he was named a municipal judge; and in 1984, the SC Bar named him the most outstanding young attorney in the state. He went on to chair the Chamber of Commerce and the

Urban League. Family Court Judge Robert Jenkins, appointed in 1996, had previously headed Legal Services of the Upstate.

Greenville native Jesse Jackson announced that he would be a candidate for the Democratic nomination for the presidency on November 4, 1983, in a press conference that included endorsements from his "Rainbow Coalition." The civil rights leader was the first Greenvillian to seek the U.S. presidency. Jackson, who grew up on Haynie Street, had quarterbacked the Sterling High School football team. At North Carolina A&T, he served as president of the student body and participated in civil rights sit-ins. He then attended Chicago Theological Seminary and was ordained a Baptist minister.

He began working with Martin Luther King's Southern Christian Leadership Conference and became close to the older man. After King's assassination, he established Operation PUSH in Chicago. As a candidate for the Democratic nomination, he did reasonably well, but by midsummer 1984, it was clear that Walter Mondale would be the candidate. Jackson's convention speech, however, electrified delegates, even if it did not convince them. Afterward, the *Greenville News* commented that he was running not for the presidency but "for the leadership of black America."

Local economics changed dramatically between 1970 and 1995. Donaldson Center flourished, but Greenville's longtime textile industry was pressured by falling profits because of cheaper imports. In 1976, J. P. Stevens, the second largest textile company in the nation and owner of five local mills employing forty-eight hundred people, had a net income of $76 million; in 1983, income had fallen to $18.9 million. Furthermore, Stevens, whose manufacturing center was in Greenville and was one of the largest employers in the county, was under heavy attack from the Amalgamated Clothing Textile Workers Union. It had called a national boycott of Stevens fabrics, and the company had been found guilty sixteen times of violating labor laws. Although local workers and management were aggressively anti-union, national publicity was ugly. Through a leveraged buyout in 1988, company executives sold off its remunerative licensed sheet and towel business to West Point Pepperell for $1.2 billion, but most of its Greenville mills became a part of JPS Textiles, although the sale included huge debts that later led to bankruptcy filings.

In the mid-1970s, Textile Crescent mills began laying off workers. By 1978, Brandon, Poe, Piedmont and Mills Mill had closed; Renfrew, even after massive expenditures to alleviate pollution, gave up a decade later; Woodside, in 1984; and American Spinning ceased operations in 1990. Their rusted water towers and massive brick walls marked the city's western borders.

Parker High School, named one of America's one hundred distinguished high schools in

Flyer from Jesse Jackson's 1984 presidential campaign. Jackson finished third in the race for the Democratic nomination that year but won five primaries (South Carolina, Louisiana, Virginia, Mississippi, and the District of Columbia) and approximately 20% of the overall popular vote. Campaign Flyer: Library of Congress Prints and Photographs Division.

the 1950s and 1960s, was built for cotton mill youngsters. It, too, was a victim of the closings, becoming a junior high school in 1985 and finally closing in 2004. The facility is now the home of the successful Legacy Charter School.

Meanwhile, international development came to the Upstate. In 1973, Governor John West announced that Michelin Tire Company would build two plants, one in Anderson and the other in Greenville, with a total initial investment of $200 million. They would be the first foreign manufacturing facilities for the radial tire manufacturer from Clermont-Ferrand, France, and would employ nearly two thousand workers. Michelin broke ground on the Anderson plant in August; the Greenville plant, located on one hundred fifty-eight acres at Donaldson Center, produced its first tire in November 1973.

Michelin chose South Carolina for its site, officials told Chamber executives, because of its conservative labor environment, availability of qualified labor, and location, as well as a five-year tax holiday. The company continued to build in Greenville, completing a North American corporate headquarters on I-85 in 1988. In the late 1990s, they brought their rotund Michelin Man logo into downtown Greenville with a Michelin store, and in 1999, they announced a massive expansion. By 2002, the company had invested more than $2 billion in South Carolina.

The announcement by Bayerische Motoren Worke AG—BMW—in June 1992 that it would build its first plant outside of Germany and Austria not far from the Greenville–Spartanburg Airport changed the Upstate.

(Greenville ignored the fact that its actual location was in rival Spartanburg County.) Governor Carroll Campbell had the pleasure of explaining that the factory, which would be modern in every way, would have about two thousand employees and make sixty-five hundred luxury cars. The *Greenville News* noted that the final choice was between Nebraska and South Carolina, with the deciding factors being access to the port of Charleston, right-to-work laws, and low average wage as well as substantial tax breaks. Its success in the Upstate and its impact led to what economist Bruce Yandle called "a southern manufacturing renaissance" and, with the building of Clemson University International Center for Automobile Research (ICAR), a new direction for Clemson University.

Greenville recognized its growing internationalism when Bergamo, in the foothills of the Alps in northern Italy, became its first sister city in June 1985. It was chosen because of its similarity to Greenville in textile background and population size; art and music exchanges with the Italian city broadened Greenville cultural life. In 1989, a visiting Bergamese architect helped design Piazza Bergamo on Main Street. While the relationship with Bergamo was Greenville's first successful international step outward, two other sister cities—Kortryk in Belgium and the Tanjin Free Trade Zone in China—were later added.

Industry offered dollars, and malls provided opportunities for spending them, but even they had problems. In December 1981, much of McAlister Mall was destroyed by fire—perhaps the most financially disastrous in county history—when a blaze started at World Bazaar spread to three major department stores and did millions of dollars in damage two weeks before Christmas. Bell Tower Mall in the West End was never successful. After its anchor tenant, Woolco, closed in 1982, only a few stores (and acres of empty parking spaces) hung on until 1984. Then, county government decided to bring all county offices together on the site. County Square, with landscaped parking and skillful redesign by architects Craig, Gaulden, and Davis, opened in September 1987. In 2020, County Council agreed to redevelop the forty-acre site with new administrative buildings and new stores and residences. The anchor tenant would be a massive Whole Foods grocery.

After eight years of planning and negotiations, the 585,000 square foot Greenville Mall opened on Woodruff Road in August 1978. With parking spaces for more than three thousand cars, forty small stores, and anchor tenants J. B. White and Montgomery Ward, it immediately excited shoppers, but competition was fierce after Haywood Mall opened, and by the mid-1980s, the larger Haywood Mall was clearly more profitable. The Woodruff Road

mall declined gradually until 1995, when mall management announced a $65-million makeover and upscale shops. It was the beginning of massive retail development (and snarled traffic) along the once-rural highway.

The problem at Haywood Mall, completed in 1980, was finding a place to park. Business boomed; traffic counts and property values soared. By mid-1982, twenty thousand cars a day used Haywood Road. Bumper-to-bumper Christmas shoppers clogged Haywood Road, and wall-to-wall retail spread to Pelham Road and included Congaree Road and the development of a one-hundred-acre office complex for Fluor Daniel International.

Shopping for cars got easier. Dealerships began accumulating along the newly named "Motor Mile," the Laurens Road. By 1983, ten dealerships were located between its intersection with Haywood Road and I-85.

Greenvillians like to shop, but, as officials learned, they also like to be outdoors. Neither rain of monsoon strength nor cold drizzle, sleet, or hail, all of which have attacked runners over the years, have impeded the enthusiastic response to the Reedy River Run begun in 1978 by the Greenville Track Club and South Carolina National Bank. Even in its very first year, more than one thousand runners turned out to race through downtown Greenville; twenty years later, twenty-five hundred athletes participated. According to founder and first race director H. F. (Gally) Gallivan, the ten-thousand-meter (6.2-mile) race, which started at Heritage Green and wound its way through downtown streets, was the first real downtown event other than Christmas parades in the city's history.

The second event was Fall for Greenville. On October 19, 1982, an editorial writer predicted that "in the future, when the rather elusive term 'quality of life' is discussed, Sunday's taste festival will be a landmark." That "festival" lasted for precisely six hours on a Sunday afternoon. No alcohol was served. (Demon rum—not to mention demon beer—arrived several years later when a nonprofit festival permit was obtained for the Greenville Sunday event. It had been at least eighty years since residents had legally imbibed on the Sabbath. Some ministers were appalled.)

Planning for the first restaurant festival, cosponsored by the Downtown Merchants' Association, American Express, and the Greenville Central Area Partnership (GCAP), began in early spring. Bob Bainbridge, the executive director of GCAP, named it Fall for Greenville. The goal was to reintroduce Greenvillians to their newly beautified downtown. Main Street had vacant buildings—lots of them—in 1982, but the streetscape was in place, with spindly young trees along the sidewalks and new benches and landscaping. The festival extended from College to Coffee Streets, with

the main stage located at the Hyatt Plaza (then generally referred to as Greenville Commons). Volunteers ran it, corporate sponsors supported it, and restaurants usually managed to make a (small) profit and generate future business.

And then Greenville discovered historic preservation. (As did the rest of the nation: Congress passed tax credits for renovation and reuse in 1981.) Between 1977 and 1982, the city nominated three local neighborhoods—Hampton-Pinckney, Pettigru Street, and Earle Street—to the National Register of Historic Places. Other districts, including East Park, Heritage (West Park and several blocks of Townes Street), and the West End came later. In 1981, the Junior League sponsored a decorators' "showhouse" in Hampton-Pinckney.

Once a neighborhood of gracious homes, by the 1970s, Pinckney Street was a decaying block of worn-out boarding houses and vacant homes. Fourteen boarders left the sprawling and dilapidated 1907 Rickman house when decorators moved in to transform it in June 1981. Crowds attended its opening night and continued through the entire three weeks that the showhouse was open; the Junior League donated $50,000 to charity from its proceeds. Then in 1984, the League did it again, with a showhouse in an 1880s building that Courtney Shives renovated into seven "Court Square" apartments. The renovation emphasized the joys of downtown living. Shives was also responsible for major renovations to the 1906 Bank of Commerce building at the corner of East Coffee and Main Streets. When the aqua-colored aluminum siding was stripped off, he discovered part of the original entrance and half of a still intact terra cotta wreath over one window that he had replicated for the entire building. It has housed Ristorante Bergamo since 1986.

In the early 1980s, other projects in historic buildings—such as Town House Galleries at the corner of Main and West North Street and the 1924 Chamber Building, then partially occupied by North Greenville College—were partially redone, and Mark Coburn began massive renovations on the 1913 Traxler Building, still adorned with fading signs from the USO that operated there thirty years earlier. Developers discovered that "the Charleston look" was cheaper, thanks to tax credits, than the new multistory office buildings that US Shelter was building on Beattie Place and the offices First Federal was constructing across from Heritage Green.

That cultural center on the campus of the former Women's College took shape in the early 1970s. Its first building was the $800,000 Daniel Little Theatre, where Robert McLane directed the first show, "Camelot," on opening night in April 1967. Vestiges of the old college buildings still remained, however, when the Greenville Library moved to its new home on the corner of Academy and College Streets

in 1972. After more than thirty years housed in a fifty-year-old former elementary school, the new $2.8 million facility was a major step forward, even though its shelves lacked enough books for the growing community. The art museum, a distinguished brutalist building by architects Craig, Gaulden and Davis, completed the complex in March 1974. Funded in part by a $750,000 donation from textile executive Arthur Magill and with major support from both city and county councils, it replaced the old Gassaway Mansion as the site for Greenville's collection and, several years later, Magill's major holdings in the works of Andrew Wyeth.

Yet downtown was still empty at night. The Central Area Partnership promoted downtown living (and built apartments on Townes Street—the first in town in fifty years) encouraged the extension of Broad Street to Westfield Street; managed One Main Place, the former Meyers-Arnold Department store, now the site of Mast General Store; and supported tax increment financing to fund renovations after the city reached its bonding limits.

All this took the next generation of leadership—City Economic Development Director James Greer; consultant Bert Winterbottom from LDR, which provided an action plan; Wyche attorney Larry Estridge; Minor Shaw, Buck Mickel's daughter; bankers Dempsy Hammond and Grady Wyatt; Councilmember

Knox White; and Kent Manufacturing President Mark Coburn, together with Executive Director Bob Bainbridge. The GCAP was also supported by participants in Leadership Greenville, a program begun by the Chamber of Commerce in the fall of 1974. A ten-month leadership training program, meeting for a full day every month and including longer introductory and concluding sessions, bonded participants who represent a broad community spectrum.

Directed at creating a greater awareness of community needs and enhancing the knowledge of Greenville among emerging young leaders, the Chamber's program brought together a variety of professionals to help solve community problems. Among their projects have been the revitalization of Paris Mountain State Park, the Children's Garden at Linky Stone Park, and a computer lab at Nicholtown Community Center.

Two longtime Greenville institutions— Furman University and the Greenville Hospital System (Prisma Health after 2017) changed dramatically. Furman, under the aegis of the South Carolina Baptist Convention since 1826, with all trustees South Carolina Baptists appointed by the Convention, was caught up in the struggle between religious fundamentalists and moderates in the denomination. In 1990, fearful of fundamentalist pressures, university trustees, led by Chair Minor Mickel,

decided to elect their own successors in office, who were not necessarily Baptist or South Carolinian. An alumni task force had researched South Carolina law for more than a year to ensure the legality of the move. As a result, the Convention voted in 1992 to divert its $1.6 million annual yearly contribution (less than four percent of the university's budget) to its other colleges.

A prime beneficiary was the three-hundred-eighty-student North Greenville Junior College. With James Epting as new president and flowing Baptist money, the Tigerville school began adding advanced classes and became a university in 2004. Now enrolling more than twenty-two hundred students, North Greenville University offers both masters and doctoral degrees. Its social conservativism has drawn many students who might once have enrolled at Bob Jones University.

In the summer of 1992, newspaper headlines announced that Homozel Mickel Daniel had willed the largest legacy in history to South Carolina higher education. Mrs. Daniel, who helped her husband, Charlie Daniel, build an extraordinarily successful construction company before his death in 1964, had invested wisely. Her gift of $15 million to Greenville churches and charities, including the Greenville Humane Society, the library, First Baptist, First Presbyterian, and Buncombe Street Methodist Churches, made a major impact.

But the colleges and universities—Furman, Clemson, Converse, Wofford, Erskine, and the Medical University of South Carolina—benefited most from her generosity. The largest beneficiary was Furman. It received about $20 million to fund three professorships and a major scholarship program and to increase the endowment. The gift also included funds to build a long-desired chapel, as well as the ownership of her home, White Oaks, with all its furnishings, which was conveyed to the university to become the home of its president.

The Greenville Hospital System expanded exponentially, building an empire on Grove Road and at the Patewood Medical Campus on the east side. In addition to the eleven-hundred-bed Greenville Memorial Hospital, the others in the Grove Road complex include Marshall I. Pickens Psychiatric Hospital, Roger C. Peace Rehabilitation Center, the Cancer Center, Shriners Children's Hospital, and a medical office building. Dozens of medical practices in every specialty located across Faris Road in Cross Creek Medical Center and along Grove Road together with the Blood Connection. The growth of the huge eastside Patewood Complex with three multimillion buildings and an outpatient surgery hospital made the system the largest in the state, with revenues of $375 million in excess of expenses by 1990. Although the growth of the Greenville Hospital System was phenomenal, St. Francis Downtown, now part

of the Bon Secours Health System, also expanded rapidly both at its site in West Greenville and at Patewood with a medical office building and Women's Hospital.

The Regency Hyatt, with a lobby that was officially a public park, an attached office building, and a city-financed parking garage, opened in January 1982. In addition to providing much-needed convention space, it also triggered the rebirth of North Main Street. Dempsy Hammond developed Hammond Square opposite the hotel, Bistro Europa placed outdoor tables on the Main Street sidewalk, and new office buildings were erected by US Shelter and the Ogletree Law Firm.

In 1985, Wyche attorney David Freeman established a performing arts foundation and began talking with the Peace family, who had just sold the *Greenville News* to the Gannett Company. When family members agreed to donate $10 million to kick off a campaign to raise the funds, he found the support to bring a first-class arts facility to Greenville. Eventually, thanks to support from the county and state governments and the generous donations of hundreds of Greenvillians, ground was broken on September 22, 1988, on the $42 million facility.

Organizers wanted the center to be multifunctional as well as a focus of downtown development, so they chose the corner of Broad and South Main Streets and incorporated historic buildings—the 1857 Coach Factory,

Riverplace, with hotels, restaurants and housing, developed across from the Peace Center. From Carol M. Highsmith's America Project, Library of Congress, Prints and Photographs Division.

its 1904 Paint Shop, and the 1882 Huguenot Mill—into the plan with the eleven-story central concert hall and the smaller Gunter Theatre. The seven building, six-acre complex was completed in 1990; its grand opening, complete with red carpet, was held on December 1. That year, about seventy-five thousand people attended forty-five scheduled events; in 2015, the audience reached two hundred eighty-seven thousand at three hundred eighteen separate events. By 2022, its economic impact was $1.1 billion annually.

The Peace Center was an important step in Main Street revitalization, although the West

End remained a problem. It had become drug and crime ridden; low-rent bars and muggings made it unsafe at night; prostitutes lingered at its street corners. Even handsome buildings like the long-neglected American Bank at the intersection of River and Augusta Streets lost value; Legal Services Director Robert Jenkins bought it for $40,000. A planning study in 1987 recommended infrastructure improvements in the rundown commercial area, including installing new sidewalks and trees and putting new drainage and power lines underground, but those improvements took more than six years to accomplish. Old buildings around the intersection of River, Augusta, and South Main Streets were nominated to the National Register as the West End Commercial District. Caldwell Harper gave the city two 1890s cotton warehouses at the intersection, and in 1994, the city spent $1.7 million to renovate them into a public market. A new police station cut crime dramatically. Mayor Bill Workman prophesied that, within ten years, the West End once more would be a lively arts center. He was wrong about the arts but right about the liveliness; it took more than a decade, but the West End became Greenville's second downtown.

Chapter 15

TWENTY-FIRST CENTURY WONDER,
1995–2023

Greenville's population grew rapidly in the first decades of the twenty-first century. In 2010, the county population was four hundred fifty-one thousand; in 2022, it was approximately five hundred fifty thousand. After peaking at sixty thousand in 1960, the city's census retreated to about fifty-eight thousand and stayed there for the next forty years. Then, quite suddenly, it spurted upward to sixty-nine thousand nine hundred in 2020, and, in 2023, to nearly seventy-six thousand. The city is among the ten fastest growing in the nation. Increasing numbers of Hispanics (ten percent of the county's residents) are making their homes here; most live west of the city limits, many in the Berea area. They mostly include immigrants from Mexico, Guatemala, and Colombia. The county's Black population remains steady at about eighteen percent, although the city, twenty-three percent Black, has become whiter than it was fifty years ago, when it was about thirty percent.

Greenville did not have "white flight" when schools were integrated in 1970 because of its unitary school system, but it did have "family flight" to the suburbs. Close-in residential neighborhoods—Hampton-Pinckney, Pettigru Street (with as much commercial use as residential), Park Avenue, and North Main—struggled before rebounding dramatically in the twenty-first century. Golf-course communities (the county boasts thirty-four courses)—such as Green Valley, Chanticleer, Pebble Creek, Thornblade, Verdae, and the Cliffs communities, now with seven locations—flourished. Gated communities, swimming pool subdivisions, "new urbanist" communities like Hartness, and manmade—or Duke-made—lakes (from Stone to Robinson, and including Jocassee, Keowee, and Hartwell) created their own worlds while new residents invigorated older neighborhoods.

Many, perhaps most, of these subdivisions are pricey; Greenville's per-capita household income in the 2020s climbed to over $70,000. Flourishing private college preparatory schools are one sign of increasing affluence. Christ Church Episcopal School began in 1959 with early elementary grades in two old houses on the church campus. More than eleven hundred students now attend classes from kindergarten to high school on seventy-two handsome acres on Cavalier Drive off the Mauldin Road. St. Joseph's Catholic School, just east of I-85, opened in 1993; it now enrolls more than six hundred students in grades six through twelve.

Apartment rents and condo prices soared. Many blossomed in once unlikely spaces, drawn by the Swamp Rabbit Trail and the high ceilings and exposed bricks of Mills, Brandon, Monaghan, Woodside, and Judson Mills. In the old West End, condos look down on Fluor Field, and Rhett and Markley Street suddenly boasted elegant high-rise apartments. Pendleton Street Baptist Church was demolished to provide space for an apartment complex. New units edged Westfield Street next to the multimillion-dollar Kroc Center

with its swimming pools and tennis center and the adjacent A. J. Wittenburg School of Engineering. It was the first new school in the city in more than fifty years when it opened kindergarten through second grade with a waiting list in 2010. Lots on steep hillsides became fashionable new enclaves.

The conversion of the old Textile Crescent mills to condominiums, apartments, offices, and business startups came after decades when most of the four-story brick giants sat empty, with bricked-up windows, neglected outbuildings, and decaying villages. Union Bleachery and Poe burned, and Renfrew, closed in 1988, almost collapsed before it was rescued in 2005, owing to its proximity to the Swamp Rabbit Trail. Aside from Mills Mill in the 1980s, most of these massive redos, continuing into the 2020s with mixed-use rehabilitation of Judson and American Spinning and a billion-dollar project at Union Bleachery, have been developed by out-of-state companies. Thanks, however, to the Greenville Revitalization Corporation, the Redevelopment Authority, and the Greenville Housing Fund, new and refurbished homes have stabilized mill villages, a source of needed affordable housing, but the only significant marker of Greenville's mill history is a textile memorial at Monaghan.

"West Greenville" prospered, although not everyone agreed where "west" was. (The village of Greenville Courthouse was not laid out with

The Liberty pedestrian bridge at Falls Park on the Reedy River in Greenville, SC. Photographs in Carol M. Highsmith's America Project in the Carol M. Highsmith Archive, Library of Congress, Prints and Photographs Division.

a compass; Main Street basically runs from southwest to northeast.) The Textile Crescent edged the west side of the city from Union Bleachery on Buncombe Road to Mills Mill, not far from Augusta Street. The West End across the river from downtown became a lively center after the city made major investments in its infrastructure in the late 1990s. Thanks to the Liberty Bridge and the Drive Stadium, the area became a second downtown, with pedestrians strolling its streets, clustering around the bridge plaza, and dining in one of its dozens of restaurants and bars.

The Drive is a West End success story. In 2004, the minor league Greenville Braves moved away after years at somewhat down-at-the-heels Municipal Stadium on Mauldin Road. They were replaced by a Red Sox affiliate,

Fluor Field, home to the Greenville Drive and built with the same dimensions as Fenway Park in Boston, including a replica of the "Green Monster" in left field. Photographs in Carol M. Highsmith's America Project in the Carol M. Highsmith Archive, Library of Congress, Prints and Photographs Division.

The Drive, who have, since 2006, played at Fluor Field, built with the same dimensions as Boston's Fenway Park. The city embraced the Sally League team, offering free trolleys from remote parking. The Drive brought crowds to South Main Street and attracted condos, event spaces, and bars. After the stadium opened, Charlestonian Richard Davis, the entrepreneur behind A&E's show "Flip This House," discovered and bought Shoeless Joe Jackson's home, arranged for it to be cut into two pieces, and moved it to a donated location just behind Fluor Field. It has been located at 356 (the great hitter's lifetime batting average, Jackson house curator Arlene Marcley points out) Field Street, where, after substantial renovations, it opened in 2008, commemorating "the greatest ball player never named to the Hall of Fame."

The "Village of West Greenville," further west, is centered around the intersection of Pendleton, Perry, and Lois Streets between Brandon and Woodside Mills. The area was once a town, chartered in 1914, and, until the 1940s, had a mayor and police force. When Brandon Mill was converted to a combination of apartments and studios, art and artists bloomed at the nearby intersection. By 2015, the "Village" was becoming a lively center with restaurants, a bakery, a butcher, and a jewelry store surrounding the home of the weekly *Community Journals*.

Finally, there's the near westside, the streets leading to and around the old Southern Railway Station, long known as "Southernside." For more than a century, it has been a center of Black life, with churches and schools in Newtown and Meadow Bottom. Some vacant lots indicate sites where tenant houses once stood before they were flooded by the Reedy River and condemned by the city, while others were cleared as a part of "urban renewal" when old SC Department of Transportation plans called for a highway to be laid out through much of the area. Now the edges near Unity Park are gentrifying; a longtime site of railroad warehouses has become the nifty "Commons," with bars featuring craft beers, exotic coffee shops, and cafes, while apartments (some with affordable units) are rising along streets near Greenville's newest park.

Other long-neglected communities have seen positive change as a result of millions of dollars in federal funds, caring city officials such as Economic Development Director Nancy Whitworth and Community Development Administrator Ginny Stroud, and partnerships with community groups. Long-dilapidated Viola Street was totally redeveloped in the 1990s by a partnership headed by the Urban League, and in the first decades of the current century, Green Avenue and Haynie-Sirrine have been upgraded, although the need for lower priced apartments and rental homes remains intense in Greenville's supercharged housing market.

New megamansions replace smaller dwellings in established older neighborhoods. Together with town house communities and towering multifamily complexes, they have diminished Greenville's tree canopy. But the clear-cutting of wooded acres did not cause the county's worst environmental disaster. In 1996, a major diesel oil leak polluted twenty-three miles along the southern stretch of the Reedy River, doing immense damage to its waters and wildlife. Colonial Pipeline was assessed $6.7 million for the damage in addition to paying about $700,000 to landowners along the river. Although remediation of the river and its banks came slowly, one of the results of the oil spill was the establishment of a nature center at Lake Conestee, a four-hundred-acre area that developed around the lake created when the Reedy

River was dammed in the nineteenth century. Led by Dave Hargett for fifteen years, Conestee Nature Preserve has become an Audubon Preserve and a teaching tool for science classes.

Other environmental groups who are helping keep the green in Greenville include Trees Greenville, Friends of the Reedy River, Friends of Paris Mountain State Park, Naturaland Trust, Make Greenville Greener, the Greenville Council of Garden Clubs, and Furman's Sustainability Center. Upstate Forever, an especially effective nonprofit conservation organization started in 1998 by Brad Wyche, has signed more than a hundred conservation easements to protect mountain land—"the Blue Wall" of the county—has contributed to the development of the Swamp Rabbit Trail, and has thousands of local supporters. All of these organizations combine commitments to conservation, the environment, and sustainability.

The Swamp Rabbit Trail is perhaps Greenville's most surprising environmental success. Winding its way along the Reedy River along the rail bed of the Greenville & Northern Railroad, the trail, twenty-five miles long and still growing, has been embraced by local bikers, walkers, and joggers. The Greenville & Northern Railroad was known as the "Swamp Rabbit Line," because it rattled over shoddy and uneven tracks along the swampy banks of the Reedy River from downtown to River Falls. Purchased in 1999 by the county Economic Development Corporation, its future was vague: a light rail "tramway" with commuter service to Travelers Rest, perhaps? The *Greenville News* editorially suggested a bike and hiking trail but admitted that it was an "unrealistic dream." Making the dream a reality took hard work by dozens of volunteers, planning by Upstate Forever, and funds from the Prisma Hospital System, but in January 2008, even before it opened officially, people were walking, jogging, and bicycling along its path. The Swamp Rabbit Trail draws apartments and condominiums to its edges, has revitalized Travelers Rest, and is projected to eventually extend north to Slater-Marietta, east to Conestee Nature Park, and on to Mauldin. It has become a model for other communities.

The climate that nineteenth-century writers so often termed "salubrious" continues to draw residents and visitors alike to the city's shaded downtown streets and its nearly constant schedule of outdoor events. Walkers and listeners cluster around NOMA (short for North Main) Square at the Hyatt for concerts and saunter around Court Square, renovated in 2000 with a $2 million facelift in time for the reopening of the Westin Poinsett Hotel.

Its October 2000 opening was a red-carpet event for the city and a major step in the revitalization of South Main Street. Closed since 1986 and serving as a residence for elderly people for the previous decade, the Poinsett had long lost its luster as an elite hotel. Several attempts had been made to renovate it, but none had sufficient funding. Then Steve Dopp, who had redeveloped the Francis Marion Hotel in Charleston, committed nearly $20 million to gut and totally rebuild the Poinsett. In a public–private partnership that characterizes so much of Greenville economic life, the city erected a six-story, nine-hundred-sixty-space parking garage at its rear, and the Hughes brothers developed the twelve-story, $63 million Poinsett Plaza adjacent to the restored Carolina First Bank (now TD Bank) on the corner of McBee and South Main Street.

Appropriately enough, the city's 2001 Christmas parade began with the dedication of a statue of Joel Poinsett seated on a marble bench outside the hotel. A gift of the Bruce family, the $60,000 bronze figure was joined, six months later, by a life-size replica of Vardry McBee, "the father of Greenville," a gift of the county Historical Society. Then came Shoeless Joe Jackson swinging his bat, followed rapidly by commemorations of the Sterling High School student sit-ins at the corner of Washington and Main Streets, and Charles H. Townes in the West End. In addition, Mayor Max Heller, Pete Hollis, General Nathanael Greene, a Cherokee warrior, and Lila May Brock have been memorialized in bronze.

So have mice. The nine whimsical rodents that hide along Main Street were the idea of Christ Church Episcopal School student Jimmy Ryan. The mayor's office supported the idea of "Mice on Main" in 2000, and now there's even a book that features the mini sculptures. Artistically talented teenagers at the SC Governor's School for the Arts and Humanities have also added to Greenville's arts scene. The school, founded by Virginia Uldrick as a five-week summer program in the arts at Furman in 1980, has grown into a two hundred–student, two-year residential program in the West End overlooking the Reedy River.

Greenville and its visitors like art, especially when it is combined with music and food. The Riverplace Festival, started as an arts festival in 1986, ended in 2002 with more festival than art. But Arts in the Park, starting in 1990 at Cleveland Park by Upstate Visual Artists and the city's Parks and Recreation Department, has lasted longer and has been more solidly artistic, although it has also included popular concerts. The festival's location has changed over time, moving to the West End, then, for two years, to the campus of the SC Governor's School for the Arts and, since about 2004, to Falls Park along the Reedy River. Listed in 2010 among the top one hundred arts festivals in the nation, by 2015, it was among the top ten.

Open Studios, organized by the Metropolitan Arts Council in 2001, is another way of showcasing artists at work. With publicized catalogues giving studio locations and directions,

Statue of baseball legend "Shoeless Joe" Jackson outside Fluor Field. Photographs in Carol M. Highsmith's America Project in the Carol M. Highsmith Archive, Library of Congress, Prints and Photographs Division.

it brings potential customers to the widely dispersed studios of local artists in all media. More than one hundred twenty-five artists participate annually. The Village of West Greenville has been especially welcoming to artists and their studios, but artists' studios can be found all over the city. Alan Etheridge, who has longer headed the Metropolitan Arts Council is responsible for much of local interest and publicity.

Although the Greenville Museum of Art no longer has the Magill Collection of Andrew Wyeth oil paintings that brought fame and crowds in the late 1970s, it does have the nation's largest collection of Wyeth watercolors and a splendid collection of southern-slanted American art, including a substantial collection of Jasper Johns's paintings and pottery by Dave Drake, the enslaved Edgefield potter. The Bob

Jones University Art Gallery has a quite extraordinary collection of Renaissance paintings open to the public.

Musical performers have flourished. (Where else can you find a museum of musical instruments? Especially one in a former Coca-Cola manufacturing plant, ca. 1930, where the Sigal Music Museum is located.) The seventy-five-year-old Greenville Symphony has been especially fortunate. On Sunday morning, February 10, 1991, Edvard Tchivzhel, the associate director of the USSR State Symphony, announced that he had defected from the country and, with his wife and son, was taking refuge with a Simpsonville family. The Tchivzhels had arrived in Greenville to begin a concert tour the previous month. With the assistance of Lena Jankowsky, a Russian speaker whom he met when they arrived, he was able to contact Greenville attorney Larry Estridge, who worked out the details of the defection on the basis of the Latvian conductor's need for political asylum and fear of prosecution while the Soviet Symphony was on tour.

After the Immigration Service granted his request in March, he returned to Greenville, where he looked for positions while learning English and settling in to his new country. After a year, he accepted a position with the Fort Wayne Philharmonic and became principal guest conductor of the Aukland Symphony in New Zealand. In 1995, he accepted the position of conductor of Greenville's Heritage Chamber Orchestra while his wife, Lyouba, was a violinist for the Greenville Symphony. In December 1998, Greenville Symphony officials announced that he had been selected as their next conductor, a position he held until June 2023, when he became conductor emeritus.

Furman's music program—one of the most extensive at a liberal arts college—has delighted audiences for years, and its graduates have gone on to major national roles, including Keith Lockhart, the director of the Boston Pops; Robert Blocker, the dean of the Yale School of Music; and Sarah Reese, the Grammy-winning operatic soprano. Bing Vick, director of the Furman Singers between 1970 and 2010 and director of the Greenville Chorale, which performs in the Gunter Theater at the Peace Center as well as at the university, has built a remarkable tradition of choral music. Free summer evening concerts by the Furman Lake have been a Greenville tradition since the 1960s.

"The Well," the nickname for the Bon Secours Wellness Center, the sixteen-thousand-seat arena that opened in 1998 as the Bi-Lo Center, has brought hundreds of popular concerts to Greenville. Carl Scheer made it happen through an innovative combination of already allocated tax dollars, accommodation tax revenues, and the sale of luxury boxes after three countywide referenda denied new funding for the facility. It replaced the inadequate seventy-five-hundred-seat Memorial Auditorium, which closed in 1996 and was imploded the following year. The arena (and its thousands of paying guests) welcomed Willie Nelson, Shaina Twain, Cher, and Brittany Spears in its first years, as well as the Ringling Bros. and Barnum & Bailey Circus, ice hockey, speeches by religious and political leaders, and many high school graduations over the past quarter century.

Drama, too, has played a major role in the local arts scene. Few cities of less than one hundred thousand people have five professional theatres, but Greenville and its many visitors support them all. The oldest is the Greenville (Little) Theatre, the first building to be erected on Heritage Green. Centre Stage is on River Street, and the Warehouse Theatre on Augusta Street also sponsors Shakespeare in the Park. The newest is the South Carolina Children's Theatre. In addition to the professional-level performances, there are major Shakespearean and operatic productions at Bob Jones University's Rodeheaver Auditorium and plays at Furman's intimate theater. Memories of Joanne Woodward as a high school student starring in local productions in the late 1940s still linger.

One of the major and quite extraordinary areas of growth is the Greenville Library System. Beginning in the early 1990s with a controversial plan (and many objections from County Council about using tax dollars for books), eventually it included $20 million in country money, with twelve localities providing a site and additional funds. The first new branch to be completed was in Greer, followed by new facilities from Berea to Fountain Inn, to Augusta Road. Then, in 2000, the Hughes brothers offered a large lot adjacent to the Little Theatre and the naming gift for the $17.8 million Hughes Main Library, opening in 2002 on Heritage Green. The former library became the Greenville Children's Museum. The eight adjacent acres purchased by Alester Furman III, which included the Coca-Cola Building, allowed the expansion of Heritage Green to Buncombe and Atwood Streets and included the land where the Upstate History Museum, now sponsored in part by Furman, opened in 2007.

Other gifts to the community include the massive legacy of John D. Hollingsworth Jr. His entire estate, worth perhaps half a billion dollars, was left to local charities. Furman University, which he had attended for one year in the 1930s, received forty-five percent of the income; the Greenville YMCA got ten percent; and other Greenville charities to be selected annually by the board of the J. D. Hollingsworth Fund divide the remaining forty-five percent.

Hughes Main Library, Greenville County Library System, located on Heritage Green. Carol M. Highsmith's America Project, Library of Congress, Prints and Photographs Division.

Profoundly secretive, Hollinsworth lived alone in a trailer near his factory, shunned publicity, and insisted on remaining anonymous when he made contributions. (*Forbes* magazine, in an article on the four hundred wealthiest Americans in the 1980s had called him "a mean miser.") His holdings included about $400 million in real estate (he "bought big and never sold") as well as the profits from his company, J. D.

Hollingsworth on Wheels. His land holdings included eleven hundred acres along Laurens Road, developed as Verdae, which now includes homes, apartments, and office buildings.

The Hollingsworth name and dollars have become famous, but judicial power attracts little attention. Although Greenville has lost political clout in Columbia, Greenvillians have led the Fourth Circuit Court of appeals since

1986. William (Billy) Wilkins, (chief judge, 1986–2009) was also chair of the Sentencing Guidelines Commission that included the infamous "three strikes and you are out" clause. Wiliam Traxler has been chief since 2009. His Greenville office is in the new federal building across from the courthouse on East North Street.

Locally, politics settled into the old and consistent pattern of conservative county and (relatively) liberal city. The Olympic Torch, which was lit on Mount Olympus, Greece, and planned to run more than sixteen thousand miles through the United States on its way to the Summer Olympics in Atlanta in 1996, was scheduled to be carried through Greenville County on Tuesday and Wednesday, June 25th and 26th. Just a day before it arrived, however, the Atlanta Torch Organizing Committee decided that, although it would run through the city, it would be shrouded in the county because of an antigay resolution passed by the County Council three weeks earlier. The committee reasoned that the resolution, urged by conservative religious leaders and Council Republicans concerned for "family values," opposed the Olympics' values of inclusivity and toleration. When the flame reached the Spartanburg County line, it was shrouded until it arrived at the Greenville City Limits. There, it was greeted loudly by thousands of spectators, where a "rollicking celebration" followed at the Peace Center. The torch was later carried

(attorney Tommy Wyche was one of the carriers) along Main Street, Park Avenue, and Stone Avenue until it was once more shrouded at the city limits on Rutherford Road. Then it was driven to the North Carolina line. The county also lost the Tour DuPont bicycle race and the Special Olympics because of the resolution. It wasn't until 2000 that South Carolina became the last state in the nation to declare the third Monday in January as Martin Luther King Jr. Day. However, despite pleading by Councilmembers Lottie Gibson, Xanthene Norris, and Wade Cleveland, the Greenville County Council voted no. Four times. Finally, on February 1, 2005, the Council, with three new members, agreed to the holiday.

Both county and city, however, agree that food has become a Greenville story. Called "a foodie heaven" by one magazine, the county has emerged in the past two decades as the home of (sometimes briefly, since the life cycle of most restaurants is short) more than a hundred Main Street eateries, and according to one count, eleven hundred in the county. The single person most responsible is probably Carl Sobocinski, a Clemson graduate who founded what has become the Soby 301 Group empire. Soby's on Main Street opened after a thorough restoration in 1996 of a nineteenth-century building turned shoe store ; the group now includes ten other restaurants. With singer Edwin McCain, Sobocinski began a three-day

Southern Exposure food and music festival in 2006 (which has since been renamed Euphoria), with wine and cooking seminars, Michelin-starred chefs cooking dinners, and concerts. VIP tickets cost $1,525 and sell out months in advance; proceeds go to charity.

Events, food, and mild climate bring tourists and a growing number of hotels to serve them. The number of hotel rooms in downtown doubled between 2015 and 2019 and, together with more than a hundred hotels and motels in the county (many along I-85) in 2023, offer more than eleven thousand rooms. Several are located in new downtown complexes such as Camperdown (the former site of the *Greenville News*) and Riverplace, but there's one on almost every block around the Reedy River. The Hyatt's opening sparked much of Main Street's vitality in the 1980s, and the Westin Poinsett completed the resurgence in 2000, the most recent (and most expensive) is the Grand Bohemian Lodge on the north bank of the river, on the site of the former Wyche law firm.

Modern tourism echoes Greenville's resort history, but for many local residents as well as those from such far-flung places as Ohio, New York, and Florida, Greenville is a full-year retirement choice. Rolling Green Village, opened in 1985, was the first. It was followed by Cascades at Verdae and Woodlands at Furman. All three offer continuing care options, including assisted living and memory care, together with

apartments and cottages, restaurant dining, and extensive exercise facilities. A draw for many seniors has been Furman's OLLI (Osher Lifelong Living Institute) program, with four terms of noncredit classes ranging from hiking to cooking, to history, literature, religion, and languages. Now enrolling about twenty-five hundred people, it is the tenth largest Osher program in the nation.

With roots deep in the community, Knox Haynsworth White, mayor since 1995, has been the catalyst for Greenville's quite remarkable achievements. His timing has been impeccable, and certainly his quarter century in office has been a success. One of his finer moments occurred in 2004, when he welcomed residents and visitors back to the Reedy River at the opening of Falls Park and the Liberty Bridge. For nearly forty years, the Camperdown Bridge had covered Greenville's waterfalls and blocked views of its riverbank gardens. It took a courageous vote by the Mayor and City Council to remove that bridge and to commit city funds to build the park and the $4.8 million arched and cantilevered Liberty pedestrian bridge that became its focus.

Since 1969, the Carolina Foothills Garden Club had been involved in restoring and beautifying the riverbanks. Thanks to member Pedrick Lowery, who designed the gardens, and Project Chair Anna Kate Hipp, the club helped raise more than $4 million and established an endowment fund. (Greenville accommodation tax revenues cover maintenance.) The bridge, twelve feet wide, three hundred forty-six feet long, and designed by Boston architect Miguel Rosales, rapidly became a new center of downtown life and the heart of West End revitalization. Visitors lined it to watch Fourth of July fireworks, to cheer their favorite yellow duck at the annual River Duck Derby, and to photograph the rushing river after a rainfall. Couples became engaged on strolls along its length. By giving visitors a bird's eye view of the Reedy River—the heart of downtown—the bridge has become an iconic Greenville symbol and has sparked $100 million in development.

Nearby Riverplace, originally conceived by Tommy Wyche in the 1980s, is a multimillion-dollar development on the west bank of the Reedy at Main Street. It was announced in November 2003 by developer Bob Hughes, who planned an investment of $55 million. It includes condos, office buildings, and a Hampton Inn and Suites to create a new downtown focus. As a public–private partnership, the city government provided a parking garage, walkways, and other municipal infrastructure costing more than $15 million. Riverplace was built on about ten acres of vacant land across from the Peace Center and the Huguenot Mill, but it faced on Main Street and also included properties that the city took through controversial eminent domain proceedings. Landscape

architects Innocenti & Webel of Long Island, New York, designed the setting; construction took more than a decade to complete.

Building cranes and construction workers had become local icons before the pandemic hit, and they certainly didn't cease when COVID-19 struck the Upstate in 2020. The Prisma Hospital System admitted its first COVID-19 patient on March 13; by June, there were more cases in the county than in the states of Vermont, Wyoming, and West Virginia combined. By mid-2022, Greenville County had had more than one hundred eighty-one thousand cases and more than two thousand deaths attributed to the disease. The city was the first in the state to issue a mask mandate for grocery stores, restaurants, and pharmacies; county government did not. Greenvillians— there were few visitors during the following year—became used to Zoom meetings, virtual concerts, closed schools, or reduced classroom hours. The jail population plunged; streets were empty in the evenings; small businesses struggled to survive; and restaurants closed, laid off employees, and began takeout services. In January 2021, Prisma opened a vaccination center in a vacant K-Mart on Mills Avenue. Thousands flocked to it, even while vaccine and mask mandates became political and social issues.

The pandemic was picking up steam and victims in May 2020, when George Floyd, an African American, was killed in Minneapolis by a white police officer. Nationwide protests and civil rights reckoning followed; in Greenville, there was a nearly daylong protest with some tense moments in the West End and protests at the statue of the Confederate soldier at Springwood Cemetery.

Unity Park, on the west side of the city off Hudson Street, was in the planning long before the civil rights protests, but its opening (if not necessarily completion) in the summer of 2022 was, in part, a response to long-smoldering issues of equity. The $60 million park occupies a former swampy meadow where professional baseball teams played at Meadowbrook Park and Black youngsters played at Mayberry Park.

Whether it was Riverplace, the Liberty Bridge, Euphoria, the Drive, the Reedy River, or Main Street's sparkling lights and shaded benches is unclear, but somehow Greenville became a fad. National media discovered it, national television featured it, and glossy magazines drooled over it. Even amid the pandemic, it made the news. Since 2012, there have been five hundred thirty mentions (city officials counted) in media outlets ranging from *Men's Health* to "60 Minutes," from *U.S. News & World Report* to *Colliers National Market Report*, and from *USA Today* to *Southern Living* and *Travel and Leisure*. Some of the "Top Tens" and "Bests" are a tad exotic: "Ten Best Barbecue Cities," "Best Christmas Destinations," "Ten

Cities Virtually Untouched by the Housing Bust," "Best Cities for Summer Internships," "20 Best Beer Towns," "17 Best Running Routes," and "Ten Best Cycling Towns." Others are downright flattering, if occasionally contradictory: "Coolest Main Street in the South," "Ten Most Romantic," "Best Cities for People Under Thirty-Five," "Top Places to Retire," and "America's Friendliest Cities." South Carolinians are used to Charleston being a world class city, but even Mayor Knox White could not have predicted the current celebrity of Greenville.

Greenville's pulsing energy and downtown development is spreading out from Main Street. In the summer of 2023, the community awaits the total renovation of City Hall to include more stories, a new Council Chamber, and a thoroughly reworked facade; the total redevelopment of County Square; and the long-awaited start of the Gateway Project on the site of old Memorial Auditorium. Those seeking new housing alternatives will have the Heritage Green Tower on the reworked College Street "Cultural Boulevard," and Woven, an apartment and mixed-use complex in West Greenville. The "Golden Strip" towns of Mauldin, Simpsonville, and Fountain Inn are all growing rapidly, although the four-hundred-fifty-thousand-square-foot development at Bridgeway Station in Mauldin is, by far, the largest project. Greer, with its location near BMW and the airport and its highly ranked Riverside High School, has had particularly significant growth, expanding from twenty-five thousand people in 2010 to nearly forty thousand in 2023.

In 1826, Robert Mills predicted that Greenville would become a "considerable village" because of its climate, its "rapidly improving" life, and the people who were moving here. In the nearly two hundred years since, the county has more than fulfilled his expectations. It has seen boom times and depression, war and disease. It has been an antebellum resort, a regional and then national textile manufacturer, and now an automotive center and entrepreneurial success story. Greenville in the twenty-first century continues to attract new people and new improvements and has, indeed, become a "considerable" place.

ACKNOWLEDGMENTS

I could not have completed this short history without two keen-eyed readers: my husband, Bob Bainbridge, and our dear friend, Scott Henderson. Bob read every chapter as it emerged from the printer and picked up every copy error, misplaced word, and factual error. Scott, the George Kenan Professor of Education at Furman and a trained and sensitive American historian, read and edited each one. Any errors and all interpretations are mine.

I am also grateful for the assistance of the librarians at the South Carolina Room of the Hughes Branch of the Greenville Library. They answered emails on often exceptionally obscure points with speed, accuracy, and goodwill. In addition, Furman Archivist Dr. Jeffrey Makala and his assistant, Julia Cowart, were absolutely reliable sources for both the county's and the university's history as well as all things Baptist. Having access to the Furman Library database for census information and scholarly publications was consistently helpful.

Digital resources for Greenville at the South Carolina Room of the Hughes Branch as well as those from the University of South Carolina and the South Carolinian Library, including Sanborn Insurance Maps (available for Greenville from 1884 to 1920) were extremely helpful.

From June 1999 to December 2021, I wrote a biweekly column on the history of Greenville for the *Greenville News*, where the editors were consistently helpful. I have drawn extensively upon those columns as well as the more than two hundred "shorties"—one or two paragraphs about local history—that the *News* published in 2014 to celebrate the newspaper's years in downtown Greenville and its move from the corner of Broad and South Main Streets to the Camperdown development. Many paragraphs in this book were originally published in the newspaper.

My primary sources have been newspapers, many of them available through Newspapers.com and others (including the *Greenville Mountaineer*) through scholarly databases.

ANNOTATED BIBLIOGRAPHY OF FURTHER READING

The sources discussed below represent the core of the supporting literature and archives that I used to research this book. They also provide a starting point for readers and future researchers who wish to learn more about Greenville's history. In addition to written sources, conversations with Greenvillians—including Paul Ellis, Russell Stall, Knox White, Lillian Brock Flemming, and Douglas Dent—who remember the past have given me facts and perspectives that I would not otherwise have had.

The definitive Greenville history is A. V. Huff's *Greenville: The History of the City and County in the South Carolina Piedmont* (Columbia: USC Press, 1995). Walter B. Edgar's *South Carolina: A History* (Columbia: USC Press, 1998) is useful for putting Greenville in statewide context.

For other sources of early Greenville history, see the following:

Crittenden, S. S., *The Greenville Century Book: Comprising an Account of the Settlement of the County, and the Founding of the City of Greenville* (Press of the *Greenville News*, 1903; (Facsimile reprint, Forgotten Books, 2015).

Mills, Robert. *Atlas of the State of South Carolina*. Columbia: South Carolina State Legislature, 1825. Reprint, 1994, S. Emmet Lucas, (Charleston: Southern Historical Press).

Roy McBee Smith's *Vardry McBee, 1775–1864: Man of Reason in an Age of Extremes* (Columbia, SC: R. L. Bryan Co., 1992) also includes details that are not available elsewhere.

Materials on public figures are available in the many volumes of the *Biographical Directory of the South Carolina House of Representatives* (Columbia: USC Press, 1984).

In 1871, Benjamin Perry published a series of reminiscences of early Greenville in the *Greenville (SC) Enterprise*, which I accessed through Newspapers.com, as they have not been collected separately. These articles have details about life and people that are not available elsewhere.

Two heavily illustrated county histories written under the aegis of the Chamber of Commerce are especially useful for the business profiles included:

Nancy Vance Ashmore's *Greenville: Woven from the Past: An Illustrated History* (Northridge, CA: Windsor Publications, 1986) and my own *Historic Greenville: The Story of Greenville & Greenville County* (San Antonio, TX: Historical Publishing Network, 2008). An earlier photographic history by Kenneth and Blanche Marsh (providing the photographs and text, respectively) in *The New South: Greenville, South Carolina* (Columbia, SC: R. L. Bryan Co., 1965), is an interesting view from the period.

For the immediate antebellum period, I relied extensively on newspapers, primarily the three Greenville weekly papers—the *Greenville Mountaineer*, the *Southern Patriot*, and the *Greenville Enterprise* (a complete run from 1854 to the twentieth century is available on microfilm)—as well as comments in newspapers from surrounding towns, especially those from Abbeville, Anderson, and Pickens.

For Greenville during Reconstruction: I made extensive use of J. W. De Forest's *A Union Officer in the Reconstruction* (New Haven, CT: Yale University Press, 1948), an extraordinary source for a small South Carolina town because De Forest served as head of Greenville's Freedman's Bureau and published a series of essays in *Harper's Weekly* in the 1860s about his experiences.

The Letter Books of the Post Quarter Master, Greenville, South Carolina, December 10, 1862–April 25, 1865, assembled by E. D. Sloan in 1995 from materials at the South Caroliniana Library, is an essential resource for homefront Greenville. (A typescript copy is available at the Hughes Library in Greenville.)

For Furman history, I relied on A. L. Reid's definitive history, *Furman University: Toward a New Identity, 1925–1975* (Durham, NC: Duke University Press, 1976); even for the early period, it is more useful than Daniel's 1940 *Furman University*. For the Women's College, my own *Academy and College: A History of the Woman's College of Furman University* (Macon, GA: Mercer University Press, 2001) is the only full-length study. In addition, Special Collections at Furman's Duke Library has extensive materials on local Baptists and their churches.

For materials on other churches, I used A. V. Huff's *A History of South Carolina United Methodism* (Columbia: South Carolina Conference of the United Methodist Church, 1984) and Bishop Albert Thomas's *A History of the Protestant Episcopal Church in South Carolina, 1820–1957* (Columbia, SC: R. L. Bryan Co., 1957), as well as extensive research I did many years ago for a monograph, *J. D. McCollough, Building the Walls of Jerusalem,* (Spartanburg, SC: The Reprint Company, 2001). I had access to only one biography (dated and not very good) on Joel Poinsett, titled *Joel Poinsett: Versatile American* (Durham, NC: Duke University Press, 1935), but a publication by the University of Pennsylvania Library, which holds his papers on his correspondence, was helpful.

I have made extensive use over the years of Greenville City Directories, especially those from the nineteenth century (1876, 1883, 1887, and 1896) and early twentieth century, which are available in the SC Room of the Hughes Library in Greenville.

Edward Ayers's *The Promise of the New South* (New York: Oxford University Press, 1992) is helpful for the postbellum period, as are two statewide surveys from the 1880s. *Historical and Descriptive*

Review of the State of South Carolina, Including the Manufacturing and Mercantile Industries of the Cities and Counties of Abbeville, Anderson, Greenville, Newberry, Orangeburg, Spartanburg, Sumter, Union, Camden, and County of Kershaw, and Sketches of their Leading Men and Business Houses: Vol. 3 (Charleston, SC: Empire Publishing, 1884) has sixty pages on Greenville; and John Hammond Moore's book *South Carolina in the 1880s: A Gazetteer* (Orangeburg, SC: Sandlapper Press, 1989) includes a *Charleston News and Courier* article from 1886. Frank Barnes's *The Greenville Story* (self-published, 1956) is great for odd facts (sites of baseball parks, the schedule of the Opera House, etc.) from the turn of the century to about 1915 and has some biographical notes and first-person reminiscences of the time that can be enlightening but not always reliable; unfortunately, the book has no index.

For the early history of cotton mills, I made use of Ray Belcher's *Greenville County, South Carolina: From Cotton Fields to Textile Center of the World* (Charleston, SC: The History Press, 2006), but I relied more on the newspaper research and the materials at the Strom Thurmond Institute at Clemson University that I used when I wrote "poster histories" of every cotton mill in the county for the Greenville County Redevelopment Authority between 1994 and 2005. They were published with twelve-hundred-word histories, maps, and photographs on the back with art on the front. Another helpful resource was *Cotton Magazine*, the Textile Exposition edition (January 1915).

Many years ago, then-City Manager Aubrey Watts gave me a copy of the 1912 Greenville City Ordinances; it has proved remarkably helpful.

James Richardson's *History of Greenville County, South Carolina* (Greenville, SC: A. H. Cawston, 1930; reprinted with a new index, Greenville, SC: Southern Historical Press,1993) is especially helpful for biographical data from the 1920s.

In addition, from 1964 to 2014, the Greenville Historical Society published collections of papers read at its quarterly meetings. Although many writers did not have access to contemporary digital resources, they often had firsthand knowledge of their subject, although the final volume (for papers given between 2006 and 2015) used more recent materials. Commissioned local histories can be helpful, including full-fledged histories such as *Greenville-Spartanburg International Airport: Upstate South Carolina's Gateway to the World: A History*, by Dave Partridge (Spartanburg, SC: The Reprint Company, 2007); *P.D. Gilreath: Biographical Sketch of Perry Duncan Gilreath, July 9, 1836 to January 28, 1912. High Sheriff Greenville County South Carolina 1876-1900*, by John H. Gilreath (Self-published, 1968); *Weaver of Dreams, The Parker District 1922–1951*, by Mary Arial and Nancy J. Smith (Columbia, SC: The R. L. Bryan Co., 1977); and *The First 80 Years: Greenville Hospital System, Its History Through 1992*, by Dave Partridge (Greenville, SC: Southern Historical Press, 1992); as well as those that I was commissioned to write: *Attorneys and Law in Greenville*, for the Greenville Bar Association (Charleston, SC: The History Press, 2015) and *The Furman Co., Community & Commerce, Influence and Leadership Since 1888* (Greenville, SC: The Furman Company, 2008), as well as pamphlet-length histories of the Greenville Chamber of Commerce, the Poinsett Highway, and the First National Bank.

Memoirs can shed light on the world in which the writers lived: for example, Henry B. McKoy's *Greenville, S.C.: Facts and Memories* (Greenville, SC:1989); Doyle Porter's *Wildflowers Among the Cotton Seeds* (Chapel Hill, NC: Chapel Hill Press, 2006) for mill village life between 1941 and1959); *The Mountaineer of Cleveland, South Carolina* by Melvin Jarrard (Cleveland, SC: Author, 1995) for life in the upper part of the county is useful, among other resources.

INDEX